# Taboos in German Literature

# TABOOS IN GERMAN LITERATURE

*Edited by*
**David Jackson**

*Berghahn Books*
Providence • Oxford

Published in 1996 by

**Berghahn Books**
Editorial offices:
165 Taber Avenue, Providence, RI 02906, USA
Bush House, Merewood Avenue, Oxford, OX3 8EF, UK

**Library of Congress Cataloging-in-Publication Data**
Taboos in German literature / edited by David Jackson.
    p.   cm.
Includes bibliographical references.
ISBN 1-57181-881-2 (alk. paper)
    1. German literature--History and criticism. 2. Literature and society-
-Germany--History. 3. Taboo in literature. 4. Sex in literature. 5. Homo-
sexuality in literature. 6. Politics in literature. I. Jackson, David.
PT111.T3  1996
830.9'353--dc20                              95-52174
                                                  CIP

**British Library Cataloguing in Publication Data**
A CIP catalogue record for this book is available from
the British Library.

Printed in the United States on acid-free paper

# CONTENTS

—❧—

1911'

# ACKNOWLEDGEMENTS

This book originated in the seminars on 'Taboos in German Literature' organised by the School of European Studies in 1993/94. My thanks are due to colleagues here and at other universities who – in these stressful times – gave so generously of their time and energy. An appreciative audience of staff and students had ample opportunity to appreciate the human as well as the academic face of scholarship! David Hanley provided much more than the necessary financial support. Karen Owen and Amanda Attwood supplied invaluable secretarial help. Finally I would like to thank Marion Berghahn for again being prepared to back one of my projects.

University of Wales Cardiff                                    David Jackson

# INTRODUCTION

―――~∾∾~―――

## David Jackson

Those of us who have spent most of our academic lives studying German literature will, I suspect, have asked ourselves at
one stage or another why certain topics have received saturation
treatment over the last two centuries while others have been either
ignored entirely or at best grossly neglected. Part of the story is, of
course, that our vision of literature has been mediated by literary
historians who have been highly selective both in compiling the
literary canon and in interpreting it. For example, hardy critical
perennials in the 1950s and 1960s such as fate and necessity, the
artist, *Innerlichkeit*, the uncanny, and the demonic, when linked to
the *textimmanent* approach, blocked off questions about literature's relation to state and society and isolated nineteenth-century
German literature from its French and British counterparts. Elevated notions both of what literature is about and how one must
discuss it have combined with sexual and political taboos to mar-
ginalise or even banish certain topics. Conditioned in this way,
even as readers who pride ourselves on our critical vigilance, we
can easily read over or unconsciously edit out anything which
does not fit into such frameworks.

However, the filtered literary stock and the restricted perspectives are not the whole problem. One can try to get beyond that
barrier, and perhaps as commentators standing outside the German national-cultural tradition UK critics are well placed to do so.
For us German literary forms and registers of language are systems
whose workings we are trained to study from a distance. It is true,
of course, that our own unrecognised Anglo-Saxon prejudices can
queer the pitch. Further, in many areas and over long historical
periods, our perspectives will be close to German ones in as much
as we are all heirs to the same Christian-Enlightenment tradition
and have been moulded by similar experiences as our states and
societies have moved via different democratic and constitutional

arrangements to similar forms of capitalist organisation. Because we both belong to a historical and cultural continuum marked by Eurocentricity, whiteness and patriarchy, we may be guilty of not even registering glaring omissions or of accepting as 'normal' and 'natural' presentations of problems which are in fact ideological constructs.

However, all these caveats having been made, states, societies and norms have in the interim themselves changed sufficiently for us to be almost forced to recognise the vast discrepancy between past literary portrayals of 'life' and 'reality' and the picture of those eras which emerges from historical research into contemporary data and documents. One is often struck by the gap between the lives and experiences of writers when viewed from our present-day vantage points and the interpretations they themselves put on them in their works, diaries or letters. Those of us who employ the biographical approach are frequently conscious of a significant gap between writers' private preoccupations and sentiments and the issues and positions one encounters in their works. One asks why there should be this disparity and how writers who claimed to be seekers after truth should now be seen to have blotted out whole areas of contemporary life and, in other instances, to have promoted views of it that today smack of propaganda or wilful make-believe.

This volume is not an investigation into the origins and nature of taboos.[1] None of the contributors is an anthropologist. Nor does it attempt the Promethean task of providing a systematic overview of sexually taboo topics. Sex will certainly loom large, but only as one commonly tabooed area among others. Our concerns are those of literary historians as distinct from purely social ones. What is important for us are the forms which taboos have taken in literature, and also the literary strategies and artistic devices employed by writers to breach or at least broach them. The general definition of taboos within which most contributors work is straightforward. On the one hand there are those persons, things, qualities and activities deemed so sacred or privileged as to be beyond all debate and discussion. At most they can be addressed in reverential terms. On the other – and they will often be mirror-reflections of the latter – there are the entities considered so dangerous, unfit and unclean that they cannot be touched upon at all. In the case of some writers dissent may amount to attempting to turn negative poles into positive ones or vice versa. But that is only one possibility. The more interesting cases are less clear-cut.

In his paper David Constantine argues that in Hölderlin's case personal disappointment together with disillusionment with the French Revolution bred a constant tension between, on the one hand, the need to believe that the poetic imagination could incarnate and in so doing bring about the divine ideal that had once been achieved in Greece and, on the other, deep scepticism about the validity of the whole poetic enterprise and harrowing doubts about the realisability of ideals in his lifetime. Certain things could not be said; utterance and revelation could be a crime. My own paper on Poetic Realism considers the intellectual turmoil and heart-searching of writers in Bismarck's Germany when compelled to question hallowed beliefs elaborated in the 1850s and 1860s.

Taboos thrive at times when old regimes are being forcibly restored, as after 1815; in the aftermath of revolutions, whether unsuccessful, as in 1848/49, or partly successful, as in 1918/19; after victories/defeats and brutal transitions to new forms of government, as in the period 1864–71, in 1918, 1945 and after 1989. Individual and collective pasts have to be obscured, suitably adjusted or even created to build new traditions, destroy others, and justify the new 'realities'. Helmut Peitsch offers a fascinating, detailed study of how from the late 1950s onwards West German writers, critics, journalists, and academics began to question the hitherto dominant memory of the Nazi past. In speaking out about the previously unspeakable, they went beyond the institutionalised *Vergangenheitsbewältigung*, or mastering of the past, and called for a break with specific German traditions.

Taboos also flourish at times of acute political and socio-economic tension when competing definitions of goals, norms and traditions vie with each other – for example in the *Vormärz* after 1840, in the Weimar Republic, or in the two rival post-war German states. They also tend to proliferate at junctures when dissent is bursting apart a dominant ideology and/or artistic creed, as in the case of the Storm and Stress movement around 1770 or the advent of Naturalism around 1880. Frequently the ideal promoted is too brashly confident and/or too fragile and insecure for its champions to subject it to close scrutiny: instead it has to be elevated beyond all discussion and debate. On the other hand, its negative pole can be treated in a number of ways. Either one strenuously ignores it on the assumption that the safest policy is not to attract any attention to it – the policy long favoured towards homosexuality and, in many quarters, towards the holocaust; or one noisily consigns it to oblivion – as in many liberal-radical

attacks on the Catholic Church, especially the Jesuits, or in conser-
vative-orthodox diatribes against free-thinkers, socialists and communists; or, finally, the anti-ideal can be devalued and destroyed
by its opponents turning it into something evil, inhuman, ugly
or ridiculous. Depictions of Prussian militarists and capitalist
exploiters, of middle-class philistines, emancipated women, for-
eigners and ethnic minorities often fall into this category. However, taboos also flourish in ages when the dominant group's sway
seems so absolute and its confidence about enjoying a monopoly
of truth is so secure that it maintains a strictly regulated system:
subjects, in literature as in life, if deemed fit to be presented at all,
must be introduced in ways and with emphases which mirror and
consolidate the socio-political hierarchy. Fortunately even the
most tyrannical system cannot permanently impose a cemetery-
like stillness and immobility on state and society; mature civilisa-
tions become senescent; party programmes, religious faiths, moral
systems, and cultural movements unravel; doubts are thrown up
from within; contrary tendencies emerge outside. Sacred cows
become offal; Napoleon's generals turn Cologne cathedral into
stables – but only temporarily. The stricter the taboos, the more
likely they are to generate satire, parody, and ridicule. Such presentations are perceived as the most effective means of stripping
them of their sacrosanct aura and dragging them into the arena of
'common sense', criticism, and scepticism. Heine's *Deutschland.
Ein Wintermärchen*, which destroys the awe surrounding both tem-
poral and heavenly majesties, is a perfect example of this. However, such an option may not be open to writers in other cases.
They may have to evolve more devious, indirect approaches, to
employ masks and camouflage.

Taboos have nothing to do with the 'goodness' or 'badness' of
a cause: they are spawned by any orthodoxies and programmes.
They serve needs and ends. Thus the 'liberal', 'enlightened' standards in which most of us believe, may, for example, have little to
do with 'objective', verifiable entities and everything to do with a
need to believe that they are achievable goals within a coherent
system. We prefer to blot out unpalatable, unthinkable alternatives. In short: we taboo. The distinction between critique and dis-
passionate analysis on the one hand, and faith and propaganda
on the other, is more shadowy than we often care to admit. In
looking at taboos, the sacred cows of the liberal-enlightened tradition like the red, red-and-green, or pink sepulchres of the 1990s
have to be scrutinised as closely as the villains of the conservative,

nationalistic, racist past – if only for their own chances of survival. The alternative is humbug.

Taboos are proteus-like sphinxes. Old ones believed dead are suddenly resurrected; new ones emerge from them or spring out of nothing. Present in virtually all areas, they are constantly shifting. In addition, they are often so relative, so 'group-specific' that at any given time certain topics which are taboo for particular groups are meat and drink for others. In contrast, discussions of taboo topics in books on censorship sometimes suggest that it is a simple case of an authoritarian, oppressive state suppressing just, rational demands for liberal/democratic freedoms and human rights.[2] It is worth remembering Macauley's view in the mid-nineteenth century that although the freedom of the British press had been constantly growing for a hundred and sixty years, 'the restraint imposed on writers by the general feeling of readers has been constantly becoming more and more strict'.[3] As everything here revolves round specific administrative measures or court decisions designed to enforce particular statutes, studies of taboos from the angle of censorship also tend to present writers as people with clear goals, pitted against authorities determined to resist such challenges. The reader's sympathies are enlisted for the writer in his/her struggle with tyrannical and/or stupid authorities. While writers – one thinks of Grillparzer – were often caught up in this administrative net without ever having consciously intended to break taboos or challenge the authorities, so many of the writers who did actually set out to question taboos took great pains to avoid being pilloried. Notoriety and social martyrdom are not to everyone's taste. Challenging taboos can also be fraught with inner tensions and conflicts. One's own identity may be at risk. Above all, once a writer voices dissent, a whole range of external pressures and constraints come into play both in the narrower personal, private sphere of relatives, friends and local community and also in the wider public domain. Being very public revelations, open to all kinds of prying, preying eyes, literary works can easily turn into highly destructive public self-exposures. If writers do not enjoy the support of a like-minded coterie, of influential patrons and supporters, of a congenial sub-culture, or even the sense of being backed by the invisible hosts/humanity/the *Idee*, the prospect of having to endure the glare of public scrutiny can prove unnerving.

In periods of pronounced social antagonisms in particular, where class identities are acutely sensitive issues, writers' consciousness of their place in the social nexus often made them acutely aware of the limits they had to respect if they wanted to treat subjects which their personal circle or their editors and readers would not have tolerated in certain guises. They knew, too, that they could only hope to weaken the hold of taboos over readers in their thrall if they succeeded in walking the delicate tightrope between subtly steering readers towards new positions and alienating and antagonising them. As social beings conditioned by society, caught up to a greater or lesser extent in dominant social, cultural and literary traditions and trapped in a web of social pressures, writers themselves have often had ambivalent attitudes to taboo topics. The impulse to explore psychological, religious, and political issues without let or hindrances has been counterbalanced by deep-seated inhibitions and apprehensions about possible consequences. For the literary historian what is fascinating is analysing how writers' use of genres, imagery and symbolism mirrors these tensions. Negotiating the potentially fatal reefs of official and/or widespread public opinion was a hazardous business. Certainly Christa Wolf emphasised the baneful effects of self-censorship: 'Der Mechanismus der Selbstzensur, der dem der Zensur folgt, ist gefährlicher als dieser: Er verinnerlicht Forderungen, die das Entstehen von Literatur verhindern können, und verwickelt manchen Autor in ein unfruchtbares und aussichtsloses Gerangel mit einander ausschließenden Geboten...'.[4] On the other hand, inner and external repressions have generated creative tensions and energies which the luxury of slack self-indulgence can destroy. The often implicit assumption that in the liberal or socialist millennium art would inevitably flourish is suspect. The explicitness and tension-less nature of a literature which hymns systems and solutions, paradises and products, enthrones propaganda and the self-congratulatory humbug of official publications. In his wide-ranging consideration of works by Kleist, Goethe, Stifter, and Fontane, Martin Swales reminds us of Lacan's stress on the volatile interplay of substance and lack, of things acknowledged and exorcised, incarnated and banished in language. Revelation alternates with concealment; the literary work is both a safety-valve and a turn-on.

Conscious that the authorities, readers, friends, and acquaintances would not take kindly to certain taboos being broken, writers have in many cases given readers of both sexes, of all ages, and with varying levels of education and literary sophistication the option, not simply to read between the lines and arrive at the 'true' meaning, but also to read the lines and arrive at a coherent, but ultimately superficial or even wrong meaning. Providing such layers of meaning, such varied points of access meant that one could not be pinned down by bigots or hostile critics and labelled seditious, blasphemous, or immoral. One remained in the mainstream, in contact with the broad, educated public and established editors and publishers; one continued to enjoy the resultant financial rewards and was not driven into bohemian or outsider roles – or even silenced altogether. The more pluralist the literary market becomes as publishers and editors cater for specific interests and interest-groups, the greater is the freedom the writer enjoys.

The relationship between socio-political systems and sexual taboos is a complex one. One is acutely conscious of huge gaps in one's knowledge and of straying into areas where anthropologists, social historians, cultural historians and psychologists themselves often work with questionable hypotheses and imperfect data. Generalisations often do not stand up to close scrutiny. Thus it is often assumed that authoritarian regimes are equally strict and prudish in moral and sexual matters and that sexual permissiveness goes hand in hand with political freedoms. The student movement of 1968 with its attack on sexual taboos worked from such premises. Feminists have since pointed out just how sexist and patriarchal that sexual revolution was. It also played into the hands of the very one-dimensional, consumerist, behaviourist conformism it denounced. In his entertaining paper on the GDR Hamish Reid argues with a wealth of informative detail that there, contrary to the myth, political repression was not matched by sexual repressiveness.

As Jim Reed points out later, one has to distinguish between activities which are taboo and those which, even if reference to them is taboo, are rife. Sexual matters have often come into this category. The literary taboo on presenting certain areas of sexuality has little to do with timeless human nature and a lot to do with the socio-economic organisation of state and society, especially the role allotted by men to women and patriarchal definitions of the ideal socio-economic and sexual arrangements. To write about certain forms of sexual behaviour and even to commend them as 'natural' and demand that they should be put on an equal footing with dominant definitions was and continues to be threatening to all sorts of patriarchal structures. Edward McInnes traces how in late eighteenth-century tragedies the concern with exploring psychological problems led writers to conclusions about the relation between fathers and daughters which had no place in their conscious ideal. The 'sub-text' in dramas by Lessing, Lenz and Schiller is subversive.

If the taboos attaching even today to depictions of heterosexual love and sex may reflect older Christian norms, they are also bound up with definitions of love formulated in the eighteenth century in opposition to orthodox Christian teachings. Viewed from one angle, the harmony which the idealist-classical scheme sought to achieve between spirit and senses was a bold critical venture, directed as it was against both the cynical, frivolous libertinism of the aristocracy, the supposed brutishness of the masses, and the austere, ascetic respectability of the middle classes. Yet there was no intention that this union should be anything other than a decorous one consummated and confined within wedlock. Women might be elevated into worshipped sweethearts, guardian angels of male souls, and domestic repositories of *Humanität*, but their practical, social identity continued to be defined in terms of very restricted roles as dutiful daughters, ministering wives and devoted mothers. Virtue, premarital virginity, fidelity, and monogamy continued to uphold the structures of patriarchy. Gender roles and identities were strictly separated. Poems like Schiller's 'Das Lied der Glocke', 'Macht des Weibes', 'Würde der Frauen', which provided the clichés of the nineteenth century, debarred women from the world of politics, business, literature and scholarship. Beauty and grace constituted woman's true identity. Emancipation and independence – not simply from tyrannical fathers but also from demanding male suitors and husbands, from patriarchy in general – were taboo. For male writers the liberation of women from conventional constraints – itself a taboo topic in the eyes of conventional morality – was desirable in terms of enhancing male sexual satisfaction or inspiring males to creative activity, as in the case of Gutzkow's novel *Wally die Zweiflerin*. The focus remained outside women. The restriction of true love to 'romantic' heterosexual, monogamous love further shut off any debate by allotting love the status of a surrogate religion and elevating it into *the* redeeming, sustaining force on which true human happiness and salvation allegedly depended. Calling it into question became blasphemy, heresy, especially as so many liberal, democratic and socialist socio-political aspirations hinged on this definition of human fulfilment. It has to be remembered that much of late nineteenth- and early twentieth-century criticism of contemporary forms of love – whether of aristocratic decadence and depravity, bourgeois hypocrisy or sordid proletarian animality – was inspired by traditional visions of monogamy based on wholesome sex and established gender roles. Socialists have often been singularly prudish in sexual matters.

In studying female sexuality as presented in prose works by Gabriele Reuter, Hedwig Dohm, Helene Böhlau, Lou Andreas-Salomé, and Franziska zu Reventlow, Chris Weedon comes to the conclusion that in the period between 1890 and the outbreak of the First World War the possibilities of realising sexual feelings and desires were still circumscribed by dominant patriarchal social values which denied women the right to be both independent and sexual, inside and outside marriage. Elisabeth Boa focuses on the same period, but from a different angle. In her analysis of Kafka's *Der Proceß* and other stories she examines how, by mixing different levels of representation in modernist fashion, Kafka's depictions of male bodies are sacrilegious. They blur the distinction between a double taboo on the male body: on the one hand, the sacred taboo on the phallus as the symbolic sign of the power accruing to men by virtue of their sex; on the other, the taboo on the penis or more generally the sensuous male body as the site of what is prohibited, unlawful, and unclean. Allying this thesis to attention to gender, class, and racist ideology in the imperialist culture of Kafka's time, she brings new light to bear on key passages in the novel.

The presentation of male homosexuality was long taboo.[5] Critics at best talked of Winckelmann, Platen, and George in terms of the Greek cult of male beauty and male friendship. After a brief period around 1800 when the principles of enlightenment and tolerance were still sufficiently strong for the issue to be discussed sympathetically, if privately, within the narrow circle of the cultured few, homophobic attitudes soon hardened again.[6] In *Das allgemeine Landrecht für die preußischen Staaten* of 1794, sodomy was defined as one of similar unnatural sins 'welche wegen ihrer Abscheulichkeit hier nicht genannt werden können'.[7] Heine's vicious attack on Platen was symptomatic of attitudes in Biedermeier Germany. Homosexuality tended to be reduced to acts of anal penetration and legally was still classified under sodomy. Attempts in the 1860s to give homosexuals a distinct identity and a name – 'urnings' – prompted horrified responses. Engels made disparaging references to pederasts. Homosexuality was banned from fiction to medical, psychiatric studies. Interestingly, while researching for this volume at the State Library in Wiesbaden, I found that such works had once been classed 'gesperrt'. Although that instruction had been over-stamped with 'ungültig', the books were alas still 'ausgelagert' because of reconstruction. Freud's account of homosexuality does not need reiterating here. *Meyers Kleines Konversationslexikon* in 1909 still defined it as a perversion of the sexual urge: 'Die mann-männliche Liebe äußert sich in schwärmender Korrespondenz, Küssen, mutueller Onanie, in höchster Potenz in Knabenschändung (Päderastie)'.[8] In his paper on *Der Tod in Venedig* Jim Reed defends Thomas Mann against the charge that he lacked the courage to 'come out', arguing instead that behind the overt conformity to public morality and taboos there was a covert act of defiance and that confrontation and revelation may not have had the long-term effect which the work's cultural presence and acceptance must have had.

Lesbianism barely surfaced in the eighteenth or nineteenth centuries. Indeed Heinse applied himself to rescuing Sappho from the charge of lesbianism while not caring or daring to be explicit. Instead he spoke of 'verschiedener sonderbarer Ausschweifungen in der Liebe' which would have made her 'die Stifterin der gefährlichsten Rebellionen im Bereiche des Amors'.[9] Reticence and euphemisms are among the frequent by-products of taboos! In Grillparzer's *Sappho* lesbianism disappears entirely. Typically, C. F. Meyer when confronted by the lesbian Helene von Druskowitz attributed her swing from adulation of Nietzsche to bitter denunciations of him to the workings of love,[10] and in the novella *Angela Borgia* the figure of the heroine, a pure, strict virago and amazon who has the seductive eyes torn out of an immoral male for whom she feels an involuntary attraction, may be based on her. The outcome is monogamous maternal bliss. In her study of lesbianism and language in post-war German literature Georgina Paul analyses the shifting social parameters which permitted the lesbian voice gradually to emerge and then concentrates on lesbian writers' attempts to wrest new meaning, new perspectives from pre-existing language.[11]

Despite or rather precisely because the bourgeois regulation of sexuality in the nineteenth century depended on prostitution and the double standard to safeguard the virtue of middle-class daughters and make it possible for males to marry only when their professional future was secure, prostitution, although so frequently studied in government surveys and medical reports and although condemned in published sermons and tracts, rarely figures in literature until late in the century. The positive mirror image which literature was expected to provide of the German male and female, of healthy German *Sittlichkeit* – one thinks, for instance, of Gustav Freytag's *Soll und Haben* – did not include such things. Such moral depravity was left to the French or Slavs, and when naturalism strayed into such areas, its depravity was attributed to baneful French influences. Emile Zola inherited from Eugène Sue the mantle of the corrupting purveyor of filth. Stefan Zweig's retrospective account of moral and sexual relationships in Vienna around 1900 provides a classic account of the taboos under which young people grew up:

> War die Sexualität schon nicht aus der Welt zu schaffen, so sollte sie wenigstens innerhalb ihrer (i.e. jener Zeit) Welt der Sitte nicht sichtbar sein. Es wurde also die stillschweigende Vereinbarung getroffen, den ganzen, ärgerlichen Komplex weder in der Schule, noch in der Familie, noch in der Öffentlichkeit zu erörtern und alles zu unterdrücken, was an sein Vorhandensein erinnern könnte. [12]

Masturbation, onanism or *Selbstbefleckung*, while a subject obsessing pedagogues at the end of the eighteenth century, had become strictly taboo. Wedekind's *Frühlings Erwachen* has to be seen against the best-selling *Wir jungen Männer! Das sexuelle Problem des gebildeten jungen Mannes vor der Ehe* where masturbation, if no longer the cause of all sorts of fearful mental derangements and physical illnesses, can still cause irreparable damage. It is still a man's sacred duty towards himself, his parents, and his future family to remain strong and rigid in the fight against it! [13]

In view of its prevalence and the welter of medical studies and surveys on it, it is remarkable that venereal disease should have been so taboo in the nineteenth century. But then studying it as a doctor was a professional, clinical matter; treating it as a writer, in contrast, could be construed as evidence either of personal experience or prurience. Attitudes to victims were markedly punitive, and attempting to promote a more sympathetic response could easily be equated with violating all the taboos painfully erected by conventional morality. Büchner's *Dantons Tod* is a rare example of a presentation of the ravages of syphilis. Whereas one might have expected writers like Gottfried Keller to commend it for conveying the bankruptcy of materialist, sensualist aristocratic hedonism, horror at Büchner's presentation of such an 'unpoetic' subject predominated. [14]

Much attention has focused on distinguishing between 'true' literature and mere pornography. [15] The distinctions made tend to be quite subjective. Certainly printed material, drawings and photographs which make no claim to do anything but arouse sexual desire have always led a lusty under-the-counter, tobacco-kiosk existence just as sex and variety theatres have co-existed with their 'respectable' counterparts. Whereas 'legal' literature had to cater for mixed and family audiences, so-called *Schmutz- und Schundliteratur* catered for private male fantasies. However, while the illegal producers of porn had few limits restraining them, their counterparts had no such freedom, and it is particularly rewarding for the literary historian to study how self-censorship operated. In his diary Wilhelm Heinse (1746–1803) wrote:

> Die allerstärksten Veränderungen aber giebt das Gefühl; je fester der Körper ist, worin es herrscht, desto entzückender werden sie. Ein harter vollgedrängter Schwanz in einer jungen wollüstheißen Fotze auf und ab in süßer Feuchtigkeit mit gierigen und heftigen Zügen und Stößen, Haar in gekräuseltem wohlgenährtem Haare, zarter Bauch an zartem Bauche, rauches Herz auf elastischen derben glatten Brüsten gewiegt, feuchte Lippen in schnalzenden Küssen, wüthige Zungen in jubelndem Girren und jauchzendem Schrey des Uebermaßes von Liebesjucken in allen Nerven, daß die Flammen aus den Augen schlagen; dieß sind die Momente, weßwegen die Schöpfung enstand.[16]

Yet, while having felt impelled to evoke something which in his view was a supreme human experience, he did not attempt to incorporate such elements into a fictional evocation of love making. His novels may have scandalised contemporaries by recommending free love and depicting sexual orgies, but in *Ardinghello und die glückseeligen Inseln* (1787) he retreated to the safer ground of an exotic, historical setting. Detailed description of specific physical details yielded to language and imagery – often hackneyed and inflated – compatible with aesthetic conventions at least. A recent commentator has suggested that Heinse was a repressed homosexual who even in his diaries and letters was only prepared to enounce an ideal of bisexuality.[17] Several of the essays in this volume seek to probe this process of self-censorship and to illuminate writers' attempts to find solutions which reconciled their own will to analyse and uncover on the one hand, and their need to mask and cloak on the other.

Goethe's fortunes with erotic themes strikingly illustrate this problem of self-censorship. Lessing dismissed the *Anthologia Graeca* and the *Carmina Priapea* as 'filthy follies', and in general Greek and Latin erotic poetry was felt to be beyond the pale for decent, educated readers. Although Goethe demurred, his commentary on the latter was couched in Latin and intended solely for the Duke of Weimar, Karl August. He excluded his own priapic poems from the *Römische Elegien* (which were originally to be entitled *Erotica Romana*) and sought a legitimating tradition in the triumvirate of Catullus, Tibullus and Propertius. Even then, on the advice of Karl August and Herder, he sat on the elegies for several years. Schiller privately found them 'salacious and not very proper', and in order not to offend too much against decency, the 'coarsest' two – no. III with its naked lovers on the creaking bed and no. XVII with its reference to venereal disease – were omitted from the version published in *Die Horen*.[18] The subsequent fate of the work in editions of Goethe's works is itself a testimony to the power of taboos. The chequered history of the poem 'Das Tagebuch', itself a prime example of self-censorship, also illustrates the refusal of the German critical, academic establishment to see beyond a limp or erect phallus to the real thrust of the poem: the 'erotic-moral' insight that Eros is the most reliable basis for marriage. The UK critical establishment, with the rare exception of David Luke, tended to connive with such prudishness.[19] Significantly, the first English verse rendering of the poem appeared in *Playboy* in 1968.

To conclude, a few words on one of the prime causes of so many of the taboos which have haunted modern German literature, namely the legacy of the classical-idealist definition of art. The clearest testimony to the strength of its hold is the fact that so many writers have subsequently felt bound to ironise and parody both its language, its concepts, and – perhaps even more importantly – the uses to which they have been put. In his review of Bürger's *Gedichte*,[20] Schiller stipulated that literature must provide a purifying, ennobling mirror reflection of contemporary civilisation. Writing was and should remain the preserve of the 'mature' and 'educated', and an educated man (!) was justified in demanding that the writer should share his own intellectual and moral *niveau* since in hours of enjoyment he would not wish to sink beneath that level. Any writer wishing to appeal to the common herd, should not pander to them and thereby impair the dignity of art. He should go down towards the masses but only in order to draw them up to his own standards, to boost their moral impulses and to purify their passions:

> Als der aufgeklärte, verfeinerte *Wortführer des Volksgefühles* würde er dem hervorströmenden, Sprache suchenden Affekt der Liebe,

der Freude, der Andacht, der Traurigkeit, der Hoffnung u.a.m. einen reinern und geistreichern Text unterlegen; er würde, indem er ihnen den Ausdruck lieh, sich zum Herrn dieser Affekte machen und ihren rohen, gestaltlosen, oft tierischen Ausbruch noch auf den Lippen des Volks veredeln.[21]

A century later Kaiser Wilhelm II pronounced:

Kunst soll mithelfen, erzieherisch auf das Volk einzuwirken, sie soll auch den unteren Ständen nach harter Mühe und Arbeit die Möglichkeit geben, sich an den Idealen wieder aufzurichten... sich an dem Schönen zu erheben und sich aus ihren sonstigen Gedankenkreisen heraus- und emporzuarbeiten...Die Kunst soll uns nicht hinabziehen in den Schmutz der Gemeinheit, in den Sumpf des Häßlichen, sondern sie soll uns erheben in die Höhen des Idealen, in den reinen Äther des Schönen.[22]

The taboo is dead. Long live the taboo!

## NOTES

1. The old classics on taboos include: E. Durkheim, *Les formes élémentaires de la vie religieuse*, Paris, 1912; J.G. Frazer, *The Golden Bough*, 2 vols, London, 1907–15, esp. vol. 2, *Taboo and the Perils of the Soul*, and also his article in the *Encyclopaedia Britannica*, vol. XIII, 9th edn, London, 1888; S. Freud, *Totem und Tabu*, Leipzig and Vienna, 1913.
2. Books on censorship include: H.H. Houben, *Verbotene Literatur von der klassischen Zeit bis zur Gegenwart*, 2 vols, 2nd edn, Dessau, 1925, reprinted Gerstenberg, Hildesheim, 1965; idem, *Der gefesselte Biedermeier*, Leipzig, 1924, reprinted by Gerstenberg, Hildesheim, 1973 ; H.P. Reisner, *Literatur unter der Zensur. Die politische Lyrik des Vormärz*, Stuttgart, 1975; M. Kienzle and D. Mende eds, *Zensur in der Bundesrepublik. Fakten und Analysen*, Munich, 1980; D. Breuer, *Geschichte der literarischen Zensur in Deutschland*, Heidelberg, 1982; B. Dankert and L. Zechlin eds, *Literatur vor dem Richter*, Baden, 1988; B. Ogan ed., *Literaturzensur in Deutschland*, Stuttgart, 1988; R.J. Goldstein, *Political Censorship of the Arts and the Press in Nineteenth-Century Europe*, London, 1989.
3. See D. Thomas, *A Long Time Burning. The History of Literary Censorship in England*, London, 1969, 6.
4. Quoted in *Die Zeit*, 25.5.79. See Kienzle/Mende, *Zensur in der BRD*, 43.
5. See H. Mayer, *Außenseiter*, Frankfurt a.M., 1975; G. Bleibtreu-Ehrenberg, *Tabu Homosexualität. Die Geschichte eines Vorurteils*, Frankfurt a.M., 1978; J. Campe ed., *Andere Lieben. Homosexualität in der deutschsprachigen Literatur. Ein Lesebuch*, Frankfurt a.M., 1988; P.Derks, *Die Schande der heiligen Päderastie. Homosexualität und Öffentlichkeit in der deutschen Literatur 1750–1850*, Berlin, 1990; G.

Härle *et al.* eds, *Erkenntniswunsch und Diskretion. Erotik in biographischer und autobiographischer Literatur*, Berlin, 1992.

6. See Derks, *Die Schande der heiligen Päderastie*, 11f.
7. Ibid., 144ff., and F. Kuhn, 'Tabus', *Sprache und Literatur*, 18 (1987): 25.
8. *Meyers Kleines Konversationslexikon*, vol. 6, Leipzig, Vienna, 1909, 127.
9. See Derks, *Die Schande der heiligen Päderastie*, 39.
10. See A. Langmesser, ed., *Louise von François und Conrad Ferdinand Meyer. Ein Briefwechsel*, 2nd edn, Berlin, 1920, 235 and H. Gronewold, '"Die geistige Amazone".* Autobiographische Mitteilungen in den literaturwissenschaftlichen und philosophiekritischen Texten von Helene von Druskowitz', in *Erkenntniswunsch und Diskretion*, Härle *et al.*, 137–148.
11. For recent publications see W. Peters ed., *Bibliographie deutschsprachiger Veröffentlichungen zur weiblichen Homosexualität 1968–1989*, Siegen, n.d.
12. Stefan Zweig, *Die Welt von gestern* (1944), Frankfurt a.M., 1962, 71.
13. H. Wegener, *Wir jungen Männer! Das sexuelle Problem des gebildeten jungen Mannes vor der Ehe*, Königstein, Leipzig, n.d., 158. See also L. Lütkehaus, ' " O Wollust, o Hölle" – in der Onanie-Literatur', in *Literatur und Sexualität*, ed. J. Cremerius *et al.*, Würzburg, 1991, 173–199.
14. G. Keller to P. Heyse, 29.3.1880 ('nicht zu reden von dem nun vollständig erschienenen "Danton", der von Unmöglichkeiten strotzt.'), in *Paul Heyse und Gottfried Keller im Briefwechsel*, ed. M. Kalbeck, Brunswick, 1919, 178.
15. See L. Marcuse, *Obszön. Geschichte einer Entrüstung*, Munich, 1962.
16. W. Heinse, *Sämtliche Werke*, edtrs. C. Schüddekopf, Leipzig, 1903ff., vol. 8/2, 211.
17. See W. v. Wangenheim, ' Man wird dabey zum Tantalus. Zum Erotischen in W. Heinses Schriften', in Härle *et al.*, *Erkenntniswunsch und Diskretion*, 293–305.
18. See Derks, *Die Schande der heiligen Päderastie*, 111–128, 267–271, and N. Boyle, *Goethe. The Poet and the Age*, vol. 1: *The Poetry of Desire*, Oxford, 1992, 571ff, 633ff.
19. See J.W.v. Goethe, *Roman Elegies and The Diary*, trans. F.D. Luke, introd. H.-R. Vaget, London, 1988.
20. See F. Schiller, *Sämtliche Werke* (Säkularausgabe), vol. 16, Stuttgart and Berlin, n.d., 226–250.
21. Ibid., 231.
22. See G. Schulz, 'Naturalismus und Zensur', in *Naturalismus. Bürgerliche Dichtung und soziales Engagement*, ed. H. Scheuer, Stuttgart, 1974, 108. R. Pascal, *From Naturalism to Expressionism. German Literature and Society 1880–1918*, London, 1973, continues to be a mine of information about this period.

# 1

## TEXT AND SUB-TEXT: REFLECTIONS ON THE LITERARY EXPLORATION OF TABOO EXPERIENCE

*Martin Swales*

From Sigmund Freud to René Girard commentators on the cultural placement of the taboo ('cultural' understood in senses that embrace the mythological, the ritualistic and the literary) have drawn attention to all-important mechanisms of exchange and displacement.[1] There can be no taboo without a threshold; a site of complex psychic placements and negotiations which house (without simply domesticating) and which contain (without ultimately earthing) powerful currents and cross-currents within the human psyche. At the level of ritual, of sacrificial enactment, a person or experience or place is taboo by virtue of being at one and the same time holy and defiled, sacred and foul, sublime and debasing. Transfiguration and transgression are, then, closely linked. The commerce of psychic energies invested in the sacrificial victim is one of both overlapping (the taboo self stands for us) and separation (it is, precisely, not us; it replaces and displaces us). Hence, we both acknowledge and disavow it, moving constantly between perceptions of otherness, radical alterity (on the one hand) and complicity, empathy, identity on the other. Our confrontation with the taboo realm is one that is charged both positively and negatively; and, as so often, there is a current that conjoins positive and negative poles.

The dizzying economy of psychic ambivalence finds eloquent expression in language – one thinks of Lacan's stress on the volatile interplay of substance and lack, of things acknowledged and exorcised, incarnated and banished in language.[2] Lacan's view of language is particularly suggestive if one applies it to the language of the literary text, with its dialectic of revelation and concealment. One thinks, perhaps, of Morris Zapp's lecture, in David Lodge's *Small World*, on the literary text as striptease. The spoof is splendid, of course; but the issues behind it are weighty and complex, and they have to do with the ontology of the literary text, with its ability to straddle the realms of both licit and illicit experience. The literary work can function both as a safety valve and as a turn-on – often it is both things simultaneously. As Girard constantly suggests, there is an overlap between the imitative, replicatory function of sacrificial and taboo processes and the mimetic, representative aspiration of the work of art. In this sense, the work of art is complicit in the socio-psychological displacements which it so often explores.[3]

—*ʘʘʘ*—

At the risk of displaying my own repressed condition, I should say that I find literary works eloquent precisely in the dialectic which they sustain – at both psychological and aesthetic levels – between text and sub-text. I believe that our task as critics and interpreters is to respect both the surface text and the sub-text – and the traffic between them. We should not be vulgarians indulging in a kind of disreputably reductive decoding of the 'nudge-nudge, wink-wink' kind. Nor should we go in for the willed simplicities of counting surface textual features. We should, in other words, neither take the text at face value nor should we deface it. The dialectical interplay of the permissible and impermissible, of the licit and illicit remains, I suspect, perennially constitutive of our social and psychological lives and of the art which derives from and speaks to those lives. The friction at the frontiers is perennial; the definition and placement of the frontiers varies from one age and culture to the next.

Oddly enough, where the dialectic does not operate, a complex and intensely felt dimension of our experience is missing – as is the case with the tedium of pornography or with the (in my experience) curious insubstantiality of a film such as *Empire of the Senses*. That film is more explicit in terms of sexual organs and physical functions than anything I have ever seen. One would therefore assume that precisely such a film would be about as carnally substantial as one can get. Yet I did not feel it to be such – because naked bodies without the contextualising framework of the clothed and the unclothed seem curiously inexpressive. It was (for me, at any rate) a film bereft of text and sub-text; one had no frame of reference by which to know the licit from the illicit. Conversely, where one can detect such a frame of reference, literature from the past or from another culture can offer the enormous pleasure of discovery, discovery of frontiers, thresholds, dividing lines – precisely because we cannot take their placement for granted. We notice the modalities of repression and taboo because they are constitutive of the rhetoric of the work before us. We perceive where the frontiers are because they are not second nature to us; but we know why there are frontiers – and how they function.

I want now to comment briefly on a number of key texts from German literature of the period (roughly) between the late eighteenth century and the late nineteenth century. Three concerns are central:

1. The issue of a demonstrated, situated frontier between acceptable and unacceptable experience.
2. The sense in which so many of the texts are unstable in that they both conceal and disclose, both acknowledge and repudiate the taboo realm. And this is a property of both the psychology of the characters and of the aesthetic artefacts in which they figure.
3. There are many possibilities and modalities of taboo experience; but in the examples that will concern me, the central – and recurrent – issue is that of sexuality, of carnal emotions and imaginings. The omnipresence of this theme may have much to do with the particular repressed character of the bourgeois psyche – although (as I have already indicated) I confess to the sneaking suspicion that, because such themes also haunt fairy tales, Greek tragedy, and medieval literature, the term 'bourgeois' may cover a set of responses that is well-nigh ineradicable from the socialised human psyche as such.

—◈—

To begin with a generalisation: German Romanticism constantly delights in bringing into friction the illumined world and the night-side of experience. In Ludwig Tieck's masterly tale *Der blonde Eckbert* the process works in and through conflicting narrative registers. The text establishes two kinds of narrative mode – the traditional fairy or folk tale on the one hand and the modern psychological case study on the other. Structurally it embeds one in the other, only then to dissolve the membrane that seems to separate them. Indeed, it is the act of narration that unleashes one set of registers upon the other. As the story moves to its grisly close and the supernatural apparitions come thick and fast, we, like the protagonist, ask what kind of text we have entered, what kind of life is being unfolded. Self-consciousness is not the solution to the problem; it is part of the problem. Meta-narrativity does not stabilise the narrative. It defines a frontier, only then to blur it.

Let me come to Kleist's *Die Marquise von O*. The tale begins with an inexplicable pregnancy. We gradually, as the narrative unfolds, unravel the crucial event sequence. The Marquise was rescued from marauding soldiers by a man who raped her when she was unconscious. That event is not reported; rather, it is reduced to a passage of such laconicism that the unmentionable takes place in and as a gap – a lacuna, a dash. Much of the rest of the story has to do with the attempt, by both the characters and the narrator, to account for that moment, to make the dash, the gap, the discontinuity in experiential modes speak. In all kinds of ways, then, the text would seem both to describe and also to partake of the repressed mentality of the characters. Yet the story can also be very articulate about the experiential slither that is sexuality – particularly within the domain of the strait-laced family. The Marquise is thrown out by her father for whorishness. When the father is persuaded of his daughter's innocence, he takes her back in a scene which is alive with sexual intensity – an intensity that is spelt out in a remarkable mini-drama that steadfastly acknowledges every possibility of salacious farcicality. The mother is forced into the role of voyeur at an erotic assignation:

> Sie vernahm, da sie mit sanft an die Tür gelegtem Ohr horchte, ein leises, eben verhallendes Gelispel, das, wie ihr schien, von der Marquise kam; und, wie sie durchs Schlüsselloch bemerkte, saß sie auf des Commendanten Schoß, was er sonst in seinem Leben nicht zugegeben hätte. Drauf endlich öffnete sie die Tür, und sah nun – und das Herz quoll ihr vor Freuden empor: die Tochter still, mit zurückgebeugtem Nacken, die Augen fest geschlossen, in des Vaters Armen liegen; indessen dieser, auf dem Lehnstuhl sitzend, lange, heiße und lechzende Küsse, das große Auge voll glänzender Tränen, auf ihren Mund drückte: gerade wie ein Verliebter! Die Tochter sprach nicht, er sprach nicht; mit über sie gebeugtem Antlitz saß er, wie über das Mädchen seiner ersten Liebe, und legte ihr den Mund zurecht, und küßte sie. Die Mutter fühlte sich, wie eine Selige; ungesehen, wie sie hinter seinem Stuhle stand, säumte sie, die Lust der himmelfrohen Versöhnung, die ihrem Hause wieder geworden war, zu stören. Sie nahte sich dem Vater endlich, und

sah ihn, da er eben wieder mit Fingern und Lippen in unsäglicher Lust über den Mund seiner Tochter beschäftigt war, sich um den Stuhl herumbeugend, von der Seite an. Der Commendant schlug, bei ihrem Anblick, das Gesicht schon wieder ganz kraus nieder, und wollte etwas sagen; doch sie rief: o was für ein Gesicht ist das! küßte es jetzt auch ihrerseits in Ordnung, und machte der Rührung durch Scherzen ein Ende.[4]

This passage strikes me remarkable for its interplay of erotic explicitness and willed ignorance; and to this interplay of psychological text and sub-text both the characters and the narrator are party.

I come now to Goethe, who seems to me inexhaustibly fascinating in the context of this present inquiry. I think particularly of *Die Wahlverwandtschaften*, a text in which four characters play with fire, with the energies of human passion, in the fond belief that they, like chemists presiding over some kind of experiment, can stay in control. But they cannot. Behind all the repressions of their consciousness the sub-text of desire swirls, coming to a head in the scene of spiritual adultery in which, remarkably for this utterly reticent narration, the text makes explicit the amazing cognitive implications of human sexual response:

Charlotte war eine von den Frauen, die, von Natur mäßig, im Ehestande ohne Vorsatz und Anstrengung die Art und Weise der Liebhaberinnen fortführen. Niemals reizte sie den Mann, ja seinem Verlangen kam sie kaum entgegen; aber ohne Kälte und abstoßende Strenge glich sie immer einer liebevollen Braut, die selbst vor dem Erlaubten noch innige Scheu trägt. Und so fand sie Eduard diesen Abend in doppeltem Sinne. Wie sehnlich wünschte sie den Gatten weg: denn die Luftgestalt des Freundes schien ihr Vorwürfe zu machen. Aber das, was Eduarden hätte entfernen sollen, zog ihn nur mehr an. Eine gewisse Bewegung war an ihr sichtbar. Sie hatte geweint, und wenn weiche Personen dadurch meist an Anmut verlieren, so gewinnen diejenigen dadurch unendlich, die wir gewöhnlich als stark und gefaßt kennen. Eduard war so liebenswürdig, so freundlich, so dringend; er bat sie, bei ihr bleiben zu dürfen, er forderte nicht, bald ernst bald scherzhaft suchte er sie zu bereden, er dachte nicht daran, daß er Rechte habe und löschte zuletzt mutwillig die Kerze aus.

In der Lampendämmerung sogleich behauptete die innere Neigung, behauptete die Einbildungskraft ihre Rechte über das Wirkliche. Eduard hielt nur Ottilien in seinen Armen; Charlotten schwebte der Hauptmann näher oder ferner vor der Seele, und so verwebten, wundersam genug, sich Abwesendes und Gegenwärtiges reizend und wonnevoll durcheinander.

> Und doch läßt sich die Gegenwart ihr ungeheures Recht nicht rauben. Sie brachten einen Teil der Nacht unter allerlei Gesprächen und Scherzen zu, die um so freier waren, als das Herz leider keinen Teil daran nahm. Aber als Eduard des andern Morgens an dem Busen seiner Frau erwachte, schien ihm der Tag ahnungsvoll hereinzublicken, die Sonne schien ihm ein Verbrechen zu beleuchten; er schlich sich leise von ihrer Seite, und sie fand sich, seltsam genug, allein, als sie erwachte.[5]

This is a breathtaking passage, I think. Breathtaking in its acknowledgment of the interplay of passion and inhibition in human sexuality – and above all for its comprehension of the complex tangle of the licit and the illicit. The narrator speaks of 'das Erlaubte', of multiple, both intersecting and diverging, 'Rechte', the rights of two bodies in physical proximity, the conjugal rights of the husband, the rights of the imagination, of 'innere Neigung', and the rights and wrongs – 'Vorwürfe', 'leider', 'Verbrechen' – of moral scruple.

Or one could think of the figure of Ottilie in this novel. At one level, she is the dependent orphan who pushes fulfilment and happiness away from her in a set of renunciations that enact and symbolise her social destiny. At another level she can be seen as a saintly figure who wills herself into extinction in order to escape the tangle of passion and guilt that is omnipresent on the estate. But at still another level she is a creature more profoundly threatened than Esther Summerson in Dickens's *Bleak House*, that paradigm of Victorian housewifeliness deconstructed by a number of sceptical critics[6] into a near-hysterical victim of the domestic ideal. Under this aspect one can hear behind Ottilie's great moment of moral clarity – 'Ich bin aus meiner Bahn geschritten'[7] – the desperate sub-text of self-loathing, of anorexia. The mind legislates against its own indwelling in bodiliness, compulsively underwriting the taboo of adultery in a fiercely manichean act of self-immolation.

Or one could think of Goethe's *Novelle*, a perceptive tale which is centrally about regressive imaginings in socialised men and women, imaginings that surface because of the scrupulously maintained foreground of decorous, restrained social living. The characters inhabit that register of 'Unbehagen in der Kultur' which informs every line of the narrator's own unmistakably repressed discourse.

I pass now to Adalbert Stifter who is unforgettable in his understanding of the mechanisms by which men and women seek to legislate for the good life; in consequence, he has a great deal to

say about the repressions that bespeak in equal measure both sub-
limity and sublimation. In *Das alte Siegel* Hugo loses Cöleste
because of the emotional fixity bred into him by his father. The one
and only moment of emotional release that briefly unites them is
held at bay – both by his own consciousness and by the narrative
mode that fully respects the taboos of Hugo's psyche:

> Sie war wieder sehr schön gewesen, und in dem schlanken zarten
> dunkelgrünen seidenen Kleide, das die kleinen Fältchen auf dem
> Busen hatte, sehr edel. Es war ihm, wie ein Rätsel, daß sich die
> Pracht dieser Glieder aus der unheimlichen Kleiderwolke gelöset
> habe, und daß sie vielleicht sein werden könne.[8]

On her naked body neither the narrative nor the character's mind
dwells. That physicality is both uncanny ('Rätsel', 'unheimlich')
and unreal (hence the subjunctive mode of 'habe' and 'könne').
But, after Cöleste's flight from her rented house, many sentences
are devoted to the empty rooms she leaves behind her. That bare-
ness can be registered and said – but not the naked body. Similarly, in *Brigitta* there are few, but telling acknowledgments of
passion. Or one thinks of *Kalkstein*, where the austere, unlovely
landscape parallels the unyielding rectitude of the priest's way of
life. The sartorial sub-text of the white linen worn guiltily next to
the body, the memory of the girl, the flashback with its central
emblematic nexus of the delicate peach and the cheeks flushed
with sexually fuelled guilt – all the key resonances of the text
conspire to articulate the taboo realm, endlessly repressed, endlessly acknowledged. And in *Der Nachsommer* multiple frames of
high-mindedness and decency enclose, but do not ultimately
blunt, the desperate novella of emotional catastrophe. The great
emblem of the novel is Risach's 'Rosenhaus', at one level a temple
erected to the good (that is: repressed) life, at another a site of
endless haemorrhage.

No discussion of German literature's ability to explore the
workings of the socialised consciousness would be complete without reference to the work of Theodor Fontane. At the end of the
great scene between Innstetten and Wüllersdorf in *Effi Briest* both
men agree that personal happiness has to be sacrificed to the
'graven image' that is society. Wüllersdorf says: 'Die Dinge ver-
laufen nicht, wie wir wollen, sondern wie die *andern* wollen.'[9] But,
as Fontane's incomparable artistry makes clear, this distinction
between 'us' and 'them' is too simple – and too comforting. 'The
others' are not (as it were) 'over there' – they are inside Innstetten

and Wüllersdorf. Both men are society to their own selfhood. In this sense, one which cuts more insidiously deep than Innstetten knows, 'es gibt keine Verschwiegenheit'.[10] Social conditioning generates the taboo realm that expresses itself most spectacularly in the ghostly figure of the Chinaman, in the uncanny site of the 'Schloon', but more unemphatically, if all-pervasively, in countless tiny gestures, both verbal and physical. The most resonant verbal hint in the first thirty pages or so of the novel is the 'so was', that indeterminate gesture towards the taboo realm of sex. Take the following moments: Effi speaks of Innstetten's despair when his love is thwarted: 'Nein, das Leben hat er sich nicht genommen, aber ein bißchen war es doch so was.'[11] Effi and her schoolgirl friends talk of the Eastern custom of drowning unfaithful women: 'Nein, nicht hier ... hier kommt so was nicht vor.' 'So was vergißt man doch wieder.' 'Ich nicht. Ich behalte so was.'[12] Or take the father's reference to a sexual indiscretion on the estate: 'Wir haben hier, während ihr fort wart, auch so was gehabt: unser Inspektor Pink und die Gärtnersfrau.'[13] The deliberately vague gesture towards 'that sort of thing', in its repetitiousness, is both the enactment and the marginalisation of the not-quite-sayable, the not-quite-knowable.[14] Thereby it captures the all-pervasive ambivalence of the taboo realm.

Thus far I have been concerned to illuminate those moments in literary texts where the verbal and physical behaviour of the characters is part echoed by, part interrogated by, the stylistic mode of the narrative voice; thematic repression is both replicated by and deconstructed by narratological expression. I want now to draw attention to one particular expression of the repressed realm which is shared by both characters and narrators – and that is the symbol. In the work of literature, the symbol, by virtue of the dialectic which it enacts of revelation and concealment, disclosure and enclosure, is ideally placed to express both the regimentation and the release of human feeling. Symbols are supremely the nexus at which text and sub-text meet, where objects, events, situations are invested by the repressed inner life with weightier value than their simple thereness. In respect of the symbols which the characters themselves create and employ, from Kleist and Goethe to Stifter and Fontane, it is crucial that we note the interplay of knowingness and ignorance, of seeing and not seeing. Sometimes the characters know what they are doing or saying and why; at other times they are enacting patterns whose force is entirely subliminal. Over and over again, the life of socialised men and women is revealed to be one anchored in psychic dramas of surrogacy and displacement – and to those dramas the discourse of both the characters and the narrator bears witness. Of these processes a text such as *Die Wahlverwandtschaften*, with its claustrophobic density of symbolic statement, speaks at every turn.

This brings me to the final issue I wish to highlight, and it has to do with what one might call the thematised symbol or metaphor. Let me draw attention to a key moment from Kleist's *Penthesilea*. The play explores with matchless subtlety and power an interplay of military and sexual discourses. Common to both are (metaphorical and literal) notions of domination and subservience, of authority and acquiescence. When Penthesilea succumbs to the fierce psychological tension between her needs both to subjugate and be subjugated by Achilles (militarily and sexually), she physically tears him to pieces. At this point the similes and metaphors of the play that have linked human beings to animals become palpable fact. At the eerie climax Penthesilea reflects that the words 'Küsse' and 'Bisse' rhyme.[15] Their linguistic kinship seems to her crazed mind to legitimate – perhaps even to necessitate – the telescoping into physical interchangeability of two related activities of the human mouth. If people can be devoured by love, perhaps they can also, with a certain (psycho-)logic, devour for love. Yet Penthesilea's consciousness of (and self-consciousness about) the phonic overlap that unites 'Küsse' and 'Bisse' neither clarifies nor stabilises nor redeems the desperate act which she has performed. Symbolic sub-text becomes literal, enacted mutilation. The displacement and surrogacy of metaphor collapses into literalness.

All of which brings me back to an issue with which I began – to René Girard's work on the sacred displacement, by strategies of ritual and taboo, of violent emotions and imaginings. As we have seen, the notion of surrogacy whereby one entity symbolically stands for another is crucial. We are, of course, all familiar with the argument that suggests that precisely the ability to displace, to replace, to sublimate is central to civilized life. In a complex interplay of texts and sub-texts, then, violence is enacted and repressed, is vented and checked in the emblematics of sophisticated social living. In his great drama *Iphigenie auf Tauris* Goethe explores this disturbing phenomenon with marvellous sensitivity and intelligence. In one sense, the play is a hymn in praise of the possibility of decorous, controlled, humane living. In another sense it also knows of the dark deities that will never allow themselves quite to be banished, that continue as potent metaphors to haunt the modern secular consciousness. In ways that have too long gone unrecognised, Goethe's *Iphigenie* does know of the heart of darkness, the 'lord of the flies' that modern humanity carries round with it. Perhaps the taboo is the place where those deities can be held at bay (if only just) by being both acknowledged and appeased by art and ritual.

Yet notions of appeasement vibrate with an unsettling political resonance in our century, which has managed at times to reify the metaphors, displacements and complex negotiations of our sociocultural life into the terrible simplicities of totalitarian brutality, of politically underwritten holism. The appeasing of dark gods can take terrible forms, but then the taboo always has entailed playing with fire ...

## NOTES

1. S. Freud, *Totem and Taboo*, London, 1950; R. Girard, *Violence and the Sacred*, Baltimore, 1977.
2. See M. Bowie, *Freud, Proust, and Lacan: Theory as Fiction*, Cambridge, 1987.
3. R. Girard, *'To Double Business Bound': Essays on Literature, Mimesis, and Anthropology*, Baltimore, 1978.
4. H. v. Kleist, *Werke* (Deutscher Klassiker Verlag), vol. 3, *Erzählungen, Anekdoten, Gedichte, Schriften*, ed. K. Müller-Salget, Frankfurt a.M., 1990, 181.
5. J.W. v. Goethe, *Werke* (Hamburger Ausgabe), vol. 6, *Romane und Novellen I*, ed. E. Trunz and B.v. Wiese, 9th edn, Munich, 1977, 321.
6. See especially W. Axton, 'The trouble with Esther', *Modern Languages Quarterly*, 26 (1965), 545–57. See also Q.D. Leavis's fine discussion of the novel in Chapter 3 of F.R. and Q.D. Leavis, *Dickens the Novelist*, London, 1970.
7. Goethe, *Romane und Novellen I*, 462.
8. A. Stifter, *Werke* (Winkler Ausgabe), *Studien*, ed. F. Krökel, Munich, 1966, 709.
9. T. Fontane, *Sämtliche Werke* (Hanser Ausgabe), *Romane, Erzählungen, Gedichte*, vol. 4, ed. W. Keitel, Munich, 1963, 237.
10. Ibid., 237.
11. Ibid., 13.
12. Ibid., 15.
13. Ibid., 25.
14. See E. Swales, 'Private mythologies and public unease: on Fontane's *Effi Briest*', *Modern Language Review*, 75 (1980): 114–23.

# 2

## 'VERLORENE TÖCHTER': RETICENCE AND AMBIGUITY IN GERMAN DOMESTIC DRAMA IN THE LATE EIGHTEENTH CENTURY

*Edward McInnes*

The emergence of domestic tragedy around the middle of the eighteenth century in England, France and Germany marks a transforming development in the history of European drama. The commitment of influential playwrights to this new realistic, psychological mode brought with it a powerful impetus to innovate and experiment, a will to engage new concerns and explore new dramatic forms which renewed the drama and opened it to the tensions of contemporary experience. In this paper I would like to suggest that the attempts of the leading exponents of domestic drama in Germany to grasp the possibilities of this new mode carried them further than they were themselves aware: that their quest for radical kinds of psychological realism repeatedly forced them to contradict their explicit dramatic aims and to subvert some of their deepest moral and artistic convictions. Over and over again the impetus of their creative preoccupations drew them to probe, covertly and obliquely, areas of experience they were unwilling or unable to confront and to touch levels of awareness beyond the reach of their rational understanding.

The development of domestic tragedy as a serious, critically acknowledged form reflected, as its advocates repeatedly claimed, the individual's deepest emotional and moral experience.[1] Despite the fact that the new genre was called *tragédie bourgeoise* in France and *das bürgerliche Trauerspiel* in Germany its supporters in both countries – most notably Diderot and Marmontel in France and Lessing in Germany – consistently pointed out that this was not a mode which represented the outlook or aims of a particular social group. On the contrary, they declared, its concern was with that world of essentially unchanging, inward awareness which all human beings had in common.[2] It should really be called 'Privat-Tragödie' Wieland insisted, taking over Lillo's description of his *A London Merchant* as a 'tale of private woe'.[3] Similarly, Christian Schmid suggested that more specific terms like 'häusliche Tragödie' or 'tragisches Familiengemälde' would indicate more clearly the shaping preoccupations of the new form.[4] It was above all this intensifying of imaginative focus which the advocates of the domestic drama in the late 1750s and 1760s saw as a historically significant breakthrough. This preoccupation with the private, familial sphere marked, they believed, the freeing of the genre from its traditional concern with the wider impersonal world of history.[5] The drama was now free to explore that realm of inward feeling and aspiration in which human beings grasp the deepest impulses of their selfhood and assert their transcendence over circumstance. Most of these critics also recognised that the emergence of this intimate, probing form had brought about far-reaching attempts to regenerate the received conventions of the drama and develop new, more subtle, psychologically sensitive conceptions of language and characterisation.[6]

However, despite the fact that many critics in Germany were keen to claim that domestic drama significantly extended the artistic limits of the genre, it was Lessing alone who, as far as I can see, made a critically concerted, rigorous attempt to grasp the historical importance of these developments.[7] In the *Hamburgische Dramaturgie* he confronted the realisation that the drama in the late eighteenth century was bound by scientific notions of causal coherence and accountability which restricted the creative freedom of the playwright in ways which his contemporaries had failed fully to acknowledge. We can see the radical drive of this concern most clearly perhaps in his tenacious, questioning examination of the tragedies of Corneille (L5, 133–48). He argues here that the drama cannot hope to derive genuine imaginative authority from the fact that it re-enacts actual historical events. Its power to possess the mind of the reader or spectator must stem rather from the unanswerable logic of its *inner* development: from its capacity to articulate the impulses of the dramatic action as an integrated process of causation which is open to investigation and verification at every stage. The playwright – Lessing is insisting – cannot take for granted the ready assent of the recipient but must actively seek to win it by the relentless clarity of his diagnostic presentation. He must motivate the smallest actions and counter-actions of the dramatic characters with such 'algebraic' precision, 'daß wir überall nichts als den natürlichsten, ordentlichsten Verlauf wahrnehmen; daß wir bei jedem Schritte, den er seine Personen tun läßt, bekennen müssen, wir würden ihn, in dem nämlichen Grade der Leidenschaft, bei der nämlichen Lage der Sachen, selbst getan haben' (L5, 146). Here, as in other parts of the *Hamburgische Dramaturgie*, Lessing seems to be envisaging a mode of realistic drama which is disconcertingly narrow in its imaginative scope and in the rigour of its analytical structure. The thrust of his polemic, it seems, is to define a pragmatic, intellectualised kind of drama which, in its accommodation to the increasingly empirical outlook of the late eighteenth century, breaks fundamentally with the inherited formal categories of heroic tragedy.

The most original practitioners in the field of domestic tragedy in Germany – Lessing, Lenz and Schiller – all attempted to develop modes of realistic drama which, as we can see looking back, were in keeping with the conception of a modern analytical form set out in the *Hamburgische Dramaturgie*. This was for all them, however, a more far-reaching and treacherous enterprise than they were able to acknowledge. For these playwrights were, in their different ways, all intent on upholding a strong theoretical view of the tragic protagonist as a seeing, articulate, self-responsible agent, while presenting the figures in their plays in a relativising empirical perspective which emphasised their inner divisions and confusions with a force which called in question their ability to understand and control their behaviour. Lessing, Lenz and Schiller all recognised intuitively this tension at the heart of the realistic, psychological mode and sought (as I shall try to show) to exploit the ambiguous exploratory possibilities it opened up.

I would like to concentrate on three historically important and influential works: Lessing's *Miß Sara Sampson* (1755), generally acknowledged to be the first domestic tragedy in the German language; *Der Hofmeister* (1774) by Lenz, the first and most subversive domestic drama of the *Sturm und Drang*; and *Kabale und Liebe* (1784), the last significant attempt in the eighteenth century to extend and regenerate the tradition of family tragedy. There are striking thematic similarities between these works. All three enact – each in its own distinctive way – a fundamental crisis in the patriarchal family, a crisis in the relationship between father and daughter. This relationship, as social and literary historians have repeatedly pointed out, was the focus of vital moral and emotional concern throughout the late eighteenth century. The tie between father and daughter was widely hailed as the most sensitive, tender bond within the family unit, but also at the same time as the most exposed, the most vulnerable to insidious pressures of misunderstanding and mutual estrangement.[8]

In *Miß Sara Sampson* the dramatist seems at pains throughout to assert the essential goodness of father and daughter, the two main protagonists.[9] Lessing portrays Samson as the model of a benevolent patriarchal father, wise, authoritative yet understanding and generous in his devotion to Sara, his only child. Even though at times he sees himself as partly to blame for Sara's plight, such self-reproach, as Lessing makes clear, only reveals the depths of his kindness and humility.[10] His Christ-like goodness is stressed in the way he comes (like the father in the parable of the Prodigal Son) not to judge but to forgive, and to offer his child a new beginning (L1, 262f.). Samson, as even Mellefont, Sara's seducer, is drawn to acknowledge, is a 'göttlicher Mann', who radiates in his every action the undying love of the heavenly Father.

The unfolding action of the tragedy similarly serves to vindicate the goodness of Sara, 'die verlorene Tochter'. Whatever her reputation in the eyes of society, her spiritual self, her capacity for love and trust, remain intact. In her readiness to forgive Marwood, her treacherous killer, and to embrace her death as part of God's redemptive purpose, Sara (as the dramatist makes clear) re-enacts the Passion of Christ.[11] On her death-bed she recognises that the will of Providence is fulfilled through the hand of the murderess: that God takes her to Himself to spare her temptations of the flesh she would not be able to resist, thus ensuring her eternal salvation (L1, 299f.). In the triumphant faith of the heroine divine grace prevails over contingency, spiritual certitude overcomes sensual nature.

Yet despite Lessing's concern to assert the ultimate metaphysical significance of the tragic process he is driven constantly to probe the behaviour of the characters from a searching psychological point of view. At the same time as he asserts their status as responsible moral agents he exposes their dependence on subconscious forces which undermine their capacity for self-understanding and ethical choice. This tense, divided way of seeing informs Lessing's portrayal of Samson in the crucial expository scenes at the beginning of the play. Lessing is concerned to present Sir William (as we have seen) as an exemplary Christian father, but he also sounds the weakness of the ageing, lonely man stricken by the sudden, unexpected loss of his daughter. In showing the intensity of the father's love Lessing also contrives, despite himself it seems, to suggest the depths of his need and his fear that he may have lost his daughter for good. As the dramatist affirms Sampson's quest for reconciliation, he also suggests that the father is asserting an inexorable claim upon Sara's love. When Sir William speaks, for instance, of Sara as the crutch of his old age, the vessel of sweetness in his declining years (L1, 227f., 254f.), he is betraying, Lessing seems to imply, a sense of his *right* to possess and use his daughter which is quite alien to his conscious sentiments. Is Lessing then obliquely suggesting that Samson is a man divided, a man who deceives himself in his gestures of selfless, forgiving Christian love? Does the dramatist sense at some profound imaginative level that Sampson is using the accepted rhetoric of religious piety as a mask behind which he remorselessly asserts the paternal power he claims to have renounced?

A similarly unsettling ambiguity also pervades Lessing's presentation of the experience of the heroine. Here he is explicitly concerned to lay bare the contradictions in Sara's experience of sexual love, but his analysis seems to drive him much further than he can consciously acknowledge. He shows that in her love for Mellefont Sara does mature greatly as a woman and achieve a new, releasing awareness of her passionate nature. However, at the same time he makes clear that this awareness involves a recognition of the full depths of her attachment to her father. In the lonely, guilt-ridden weeks following her elopement she is forced to realise anew her inescapable responsibility to him and at moments of extreme remorse senses that she may have abandoned him to a grief which will destroy him (L1, 257). The experience of her father's forgiveness, far from releasing her from this sense of obligation, serves – Lessing shows – to heighten her awareness of indebtedness. Soon after she receives her father's letter of forgiveness she is able to explain to Mellefont her newly found certainty that her father's love is the sustaining force at the very heart of her emotional existence: it is this love which has made her what she is, enabled her to become the passionate woman capable of loving Mellefont with such self-forgetting intensity. Sara is acknowledging here that her powers of sexual devotion are rooted in assurance of Sampson's love and are thus finally dependent upon it (L1, 269f.). Her confession here is precipitated by the realisation that her father has forgiven her and accepted Mellefont as his son and heir. Yet even at this moment of joyful triumph Lessing enables us to sense what Sara herself cannot see – that this emotional dependence on her father's love is a constraint, a bondage even, from which she can never be free. Very soon afterwards Sara herself, however, is drawn to acknowledge this tragic entrapment. Somehow she is overtaken by the terrible realisation that Mellefont, despite all his ardent assurances to the contrary, may not be willing to marry her and that thus once again her love for him would be in conflict with her father's will (L1, 299f.). But this is not all. In this horrifying recognition there lies another even more terrible and destructive one: that even if Mellefont does refuse to marry her she would still be held captive by her desperate sexual need for him. Sara's recognition of her utter inward vulnerability undermines, as far as I can see, the dramatist's overt view of the tragic denouement. Lessing's creative imagination is reaching out here beyond his perception of the martyr-heroine which governs his intellectual concern and allows us to see a helpless victimised girl in the grip of compulsions in her own self which are beyond her understanding or control. The ready acquiescence of Sara in her death at Marwood's hand appears in this perspective not as a triumph of religious faith but as a despairing surrender, a helpless recoiling from relentless contradictions in her own nature which she dare not even contemplate. Sara appears here as a passive, broken being trapped between a sensuality she cannot resist and an emotional dependence on her father she cannot question. This is a heroine denied that transcendent assurance on which Lessing's overt view of the tragic ending depends, a heroine racked by a disabling hopelessness without meaning and thus devoid of all reconciliatory power.

In the early 1770s the domestic drama entered a quite new phase of development. At this time a group of abrasive, disaffected young playwrights, most notably Lenz, Wagner, and Klinger, took over the forms and preoccupations of the by now established and highly topical form and attempted to regenerate these by the force of their radical socially critical concerns. These dramatists were intent above all on discrediting what they saw as the evasive, moralistic view of family life shaping the *bürgerliches Trauerspiel* in the previous decades by asserting in their different ways a vision of the family as a world torn and disfigured by the contradictions ravaging the life of society as a whole.[12]

Lenz was by far the most innovative and ambitious exponent of this new critical, iconoclastic family drama. His work is shaped by a strong instinctive sense of a seemingly insuperable gulf between parent and child, and of the helplessness of both before the treacherous force of impersonal social pressures at work in this seemingly private relationship. This impelling awareness of the peculiar exposure of the individual within the world of the family pervades the conception of this Lenz's most startlingly original play *Der Hofmeister*.[13] Here the dramatist makes no attempt to disguise his concern to portray the relationship between Major von Berg and his daughter, Gustchen, as a belittling parody of that between Sampson and his daughter in Lessing's celebrated play. Even so, Berg, however much he aspires to the serene authority of Sir William, is in fact a man haunted by a sense of eroded power and social standing. He is aware of being ridiculed by his progressive intellectual brother, scorned by his striving, unfaithful wife and ground down by the realisation of the seemingly inevitable economic decline of his family. Gripped by this draining sense of inadequacy the Major finds solace only in his love for Gustschen. In his devotion to her he is able to suppress the feelings of impotence and futility which threaten to unhinge him (WB, 18f., 44, 49f.). The Major loves his daughter but, as Lenz makes clear, he also uses this love to create an imaginary world subservient to his wishes. Involuntarily, it seems, he sees his daughter as a saving angel who through her magnificent marriage restores the ravaged fortunes of his family (WB, 19). The dramatist shows, however, that the more the Major yields to this fantasy, the more he loses touch with the vulnerable adolescent who desperately seeks from him direction and support. However this, Lenz suggests, may not be all.

Is it possible (he seems to ask) that the father's vision of Gustchen's grandiose marriage in the future may spring less from a longing for social advantage than from an unrecognised desire to tighten his hold over her, here and now? For since he is so painfully conscious of the impoverishment and remoteness of his estate, must he not know in his heart of hearts that the great romantic encounter of which he dreams will never take place? And if this is so, is the Major not using this fantasy subconsciously as a means of warding off those young men who show an interest in his daughter in the present? When the Major declares with apparent bravado that if the King himself came for Gustchen he would send him packing, is Lenz revealing more about his real feelings than Berg himself knows (WB, 19)?

Lenz also makes his literary-satirical intentions quite plain in his presentation of Gustchen. In comparison with Sara she seems strikingly bereft of passionate commitment and moral longing and appears rather as immature, weak and infinitely suggestible. Even her seduction (if seduction it is) arises out of inner confusion rather than overmastering desire. At the crucial moment Gustchen is drawn to her hapless and initially reluctant tutor solely (it seems) by the fact of his physical presence, his availability (WB, 40f.). Her thoughts are with her distant cousin Fritz with whom she believes she is deeply in love. However, even this attachment, it soon transpires, is equivocal. Lenz shows that it is not simply Fritz who excites her love but a subversive fantasy of Romeo, Shakespeare's tragically despairing hero, which she projects on to the decent, steadfast but essentially everyday youth she claims to adore. At the moment of surrender she sees not the face of Läuffer, her seducer, but of Fritz, a Fritz, however, who is transfigured by her vision of Shakespeare's ardent, stricken lover.

Although Lenz's ironic portrayal of Gustchen's seduction denies it all emotional power and tragic dignity, it still marks a decisive turning-point in the dramatic action. As soon as her shameful secret is discovered she flees from home in disintegrating panic. Discovering she is pregnant, she seeks refuge with an old beggar woman in the forest (WB, 64f.). Here, as she awaits the birth of her bastard child, she spends the lonely days and nights worrying, like Sara, about the father she has betrayed. She fears – again like Lessing's heroine – that he may have died grieving for his lost daughter, and after she has seen his dead body in a dream she is driven to kill herself. However, just as she throws herself into the cold waters of the lake, her father who has been looking for her for over a year happens to pass by and drags her to safety (WB, 68f.).

Lenz presents the deepening emotional confusion of Gustchen in a way which forces us to question the nature of her relationship with her father. He suggests that it is the intensity of the Major's love and the immense expectations it brings which drive her to seek escape more and more from her everyday life into the richer, freer world of literature. But Lenz goes further. He suggests that Gustchen's unpredictable responses to the young men around her may also be due in part to the pressure of her father's devotion. Is it even conceivable – he seems to ask – that her attraction to literary heroes is fed by suppressed fantasies of her father's youthful exploits as a strong and fearless officer? This may seem far-fetched, but does Lenz not in fact show such fantasies come true when the dramatically rejuvenated Major dispatches his two 'rivals', shooting Läuffer (though he does not kill him) and exposing the

cowardice of Graf Wermuth himself triumphantly saving Gustchen from certain death?

With Gustchen's rescue, however, Lenz loses all interest in her
emotional problems and also, as soon becomes apparent, with
those of the other two youthful protagonists, Läuffer and Fritz,
who like Gustchen, have been driven to the very edge of despair.
Some three quarters of the way through the play Lenz seems to
realise suddenly that the experience of these helplessly driven
characters is quite devoid of tragic power and pathos and that he
should thus really be presenting these developments as part of a
comic action. He has therefore no choice, he seems to declare with
fatalistic, self-denigrating irony, but to reverse the catastrophic
impetus of events and this means (awful as it is) ruthlessly impos-
ing on the action the crude devices of traditional comic plotting.
For how else is he to get out of this impasse and bring about the
reconciliatory happy ending a comedy requires? Lenz sets about
this task with gleeful effrontery. Gustchen (as we have seen) is
saved by a miracle of split-second timing; Läuffer is saved by an
equally incalculable intervention. Lise, a beautiful peasant girl,
appears out of the blue promising him life-long devotion, quite
undeterred by the fact that he has castrated himself in the belief
that Gustchen has committed suicide. (WB, 81, 93f.). Meanwhile
Fritz, far away in Leipzig, has also been thrust into a state of guilty
depression by the news of Gustchen's death (WB, 84ff.). Before
his health further declines, however, he is enabled to return home
at once by a gigantic win on the lottery (WB, 88f.).

Lenz makes no attempt to hide the fact that all these events are
outrageously improbable and that they, moreover, mark a disabling break with the dramatic crisis which he has motivated with
such painstaking psychological realism. He seems, in fact, intent
on pointing up the arbitrariness of his attempts to move the action
of the play out of the familiar, observed social world into a wishful realm of comic make-believe, in which all conflicts can be
painlessly resolved and the wishes of the characters effortlessly
granted (WB, 100ff.). How else, he asks in mock resignation, is he
to resolve conflicts rooted in the condition of contemporary society, when this society itself is manifestly unchanged and probably
unchangeable? If the suffering of his socially constrained characters is not tragic, as Lenz is making clear, it is equally averse to
comic presentation as this was currently understood. If the gravity
of the socially conditioned predicament shows up the falseness of
the comic resolution, this finale also exposes the intractability of a

crisis which is fated to recur in one form or another on numberless occasions in the future – a future shaped by the unresolved prejudices and injustices of the present.

*Kabale und Liebe*, written a decade after *Der Hofmeister*, is another work which openly declares its roots in the domestic tragedy of the 1760s while seeking in fundamental ways to challenge inherited conceptions of the genre.[14] Schiller seems driven here to confront opposing notions of dramatic form in an incisive experimental attempt to probe new kinds of tragic experience. He is concerned to embrace the social realism of the dramatists of the 1770s and to explore, like them, the victimisation of the individual in a hostile, impersonal society.[15] At the same time, however, he is intent on developing a new intense form of *Seelentragödie* which asserts the centrality of the protagonist as a vessel of sensitive tragic awareness. It is no accident that the play has had two titles. In rechristening it *Kabale und Liebe*, Iffland, the experienced wily man of the theatre, was out to emphasise the dynamics of the powerful external action; *Luise Millerin*, Schiller's original title, stresses by contrast the primary significance of the lonely, divided heroine as the agent of an essentially inward conflict.[16]

Schiller's play, for all its melodramatic energy, is rigorously analytical in conception. When the stage-action begins the characters are already trapped by a contradiction from which there seems no escape. Luise has already met Ferdinand and is aware that she has been irreversibly changed by her love for him. She struggles to explain to her perplexed and anxious father that in her love for Ferdinand she has experienced the creative power of God at work in her own being and recognised the ultimate meaning of her existence (S, 270f.). However, as Luise goes on to declare, she accepts that she can never be united with Ferdinand, the President's son, in her mortal life and that their love can only be fulfilled in the world of eternity. At this point she is sure that her faith is so strong that she can renounce her claim on Ferdinand for this world and await the supreme joy of their union in the blessed life to come (S, 271).

Luise soon discovers that the force of her physical longing for Ferdinand sweeps aside her best resolve. In her very next encounter with him she feels thrust into agonising turmoil (S, 272f.) A wild presumptuous longing, she realises, is driving her to seek a fulfilment she knows can never be, a happiness to which she has no right. The full depths of the inner crisis become apparent in the fourth scene of the third act. Here Ferdinand urges Luise to flee with him abroad so that they can live together in freedom (S, 304ff.). As the scene develops it becomes clear that Luise cannot even envisage this as a possibility; it is for her quite literally inconceivable. As Ferdinand presses her, Luise fights with increasing desperation to grasp the reasons for her refusal. First she claims that they cannot flee as this would leave her father open to the vengeful fury of the President. When Ferdinand assures her that Miller would accompany them, she says that she fears the paternal curse of the President which will bring divine retribution on their heads. Since Ferdinand can only regard his father as a treacherous cynical murderer, Luise is driven to claim simply that she *knows* her desire to marry Ferdinand is wrong and that it is God's will that she renounces this love which offends society and violates the divinely decreed order of the world (S, 305). Ferdinand is at first bewildered, then increasingly enraged by Luise's reaction. He cannot believe that such petty moral scruples could block her love. The girl who had seemed to share his passionate devotion now confronts him as a cold, elusive stranger. And from this sudden, incomprehensible change in Luise he draws what for him is the only possible conclusion: that her appeals to duty are a calculated deception, an attempt to hide the fact that she loves someone else.

Ferdinand's inability to penetrate the mind of Luise is the driving impetus of the tragic development in *Kabale und Liebe*. The intricate intrigue which Wurm precipitates at the President's behest serves merely to exploit the ravaging suspicion of Ferdinand and the jealous rage which lurks within it. We have to notice, however, that Schiller is not just showing the self-destructive blindness of Ferdinand here, but also the inability of Luise to penetrate the determining motives of her own behaviour. Where she believes she is undertaking a willed moral act of renunciation, the dramatist allows us to sense the inexorable forces of constraint which bind her will in ways she cannot see. Schiller is drawing us to recognise that Luise's feelings of obligation to her father, her awe of the President's authority, her unquestioning acceptance of the class-structure – that these are all aspects of a fixed, conditioned understanding of the world and of her place within it, an understanding upheld by a conviction so fundamental, so much part of herself that she cannot put it into words: that the world is as it is because God has made it so, and that any attempt to defy the ordained order of things is an act of blasphemy. However much her love for Ferdinand has changed her, this primary certainty remains untouched and, it seems, untouchable.

Schiller's expository aim throughout most of the dramatic development is to lay bare the pressure of socially enforced constraints
on the behaviour of the protagonists. In the final act, however, he
seems to open up a new and disconcerting perception of the experience of Luise. In the opening scene Miller who has just returned
from a period of detention is pierced by the intuitive certainty that
Luise is dead. In his tortured struggle to make sense of this
unspeakable calamity he is driven to see his daughter's death as
God's judgment on him for loving her with an overweening, idol-
atrous devotion, a devotion due only to his Creator (S, 325).
Almost immediately afterwards he realises that Luise is not dead
and has in fact heard his agonised self-reproach. Before he can
experience relief, however, Luise informs him that she does intend
to take her own life and to die alongside Ferdinand. Miller, over-
whelmed by dread at this revelation repeats the confession he has
just made: that his love for his daughter has been so strong, so
obsessive, that it is hateful in the sight of God: 'Du warst mein
Abgott. Du warst mein Alles' (S, 327).

Throughout the rest of the scene Schiller is intent on probing
the ambiguity of Miller's confession here.[17] He makes it clear that
Miller speaks not just as a distraught and terrified father, but also,
more and more insistently, as a man who seeks to challenge Ferdinand for the right to possess Luise. Miller himself seems to be
obliquely suggesting this when he condemns Luise for her *idola-
trous* devotion to Ferdinand, thus subconsciously equating Luise's
erotic passion with the love he has just declared for her. Schiller
emphasises the opposition of the two men more directly a few
minutes later. Here he shows how Miller tries to lure Luise (just as
Ferdinand had done) to flee with him to an idyllic life, free and
alone together, across the border (S, 329). Here Miller makes clear
(like Ferdinand) the exclusiveness of his claim upon her: she must
choose – he tells her – between the kisses of her Major and the love
of her father.

Throughout this scene Miller presents himself in a way which
undercuts the image of the pious, honourable father concerned
only with the spiritual welfare of his daughter which he had presented earlier in the play. Is he here conceding that his protective
attitude towards his daughter was not impelled by religious concern? That this was just a mask under which he fought to keep
possession of her? Our questions though, do not stop here. This
disconcerting encounter between father and daughter forces us to
look back and re-assess our understanding of earlier developments

in the action. Is it possible – we have to ask – that Luise's refusal to flee with Ferdinand is determined less by moral-social inhibitions (as Schiller seemed to be suggesting) than by a compulsive emotional attachment to her father which she herself is unable to acknowledge? When Wurm remarks that Luise loves her father 'bis zur Leidenschaft' (S, 299), is he implying that this is a love strong enough to thwart her full inner commitment to Ferdinand, the man she claims to adore? And if we accept that some abnormal sexual pressures are present in Luise's relationship with her father, how do these interact with the working of social determinants to which Schiller had seemed to attach compelling importance?

These are questions to which we find no answers. Schiller exposes these different kinds or layers of impulse but he does not seek to integrate them in a coherent, accountable process of motivation. He presents both Miller and Luise as victims of forces which they cannot grasp, but he does not show the extent of this failure of self-understanding or explore how deeply it impinges on their actual behaviour. It soon becomes apparent, however, that such questions are largely irrelevant to Schiller's presentation of the tragic catastrophe. Here the dramatist's concern is to show Luise, who has fallen victim to the terrible avenging jealousy of Ferdinand, rise above a death which seems unjust and meaningless. Under her redeeming influence Ferdinand is able, as he too faces death, to forgive the father who has remorselessly abused his son, and who now in his turn is moved to hand himself over to the forces of justice (S, 339ff.). In these final scenes Schiller seeks to portray the outreaching moral power of the stricken Luise as a force which transforms the horrifying cycle of treachery and violence which now culminates in the death of the lovers. As far as I can see, however, this quest for tragic reconciliation ascribes to the protagonists a capacity for ethical choice, for inner transcendence, which the probing empirical presentation of their behaviour throughout the earlier parts of the dramatic development had seemed to preclude.

At the centre of interest in these domestic dramas is the figure of the daughter in the patriarchal family, a figure divided against herself and helplessly entrapped. The three playwrights see their heroine as caught between a strong inner drive to sexual self-realisation and a constraining attachment to her father which is itself (the dramatist implies) driven in some degree by sexual energies which remain beyond the scope of her conscious awareness. Although all three dramatists in their different ways seem to sense the intractable force of this predicament none of them acknowledges it as tragic. Certainly, they all certainly seem concerned throughout most of the action to probe the possibilities of a new kind of radically deterministic, psychological tragedy in which the heroine appears overwhelmingly as the vehicle of emotional compulsions beyond her understanding and control. None of these playwrights pursue this empirical impetus to its logical conclusion; rather all three attempt to realise a more conventional and, for their contemporaries, more acceptable kind of resolution. In *Miß Sara Sampson* and *Kabale und Liebe* both dramatists, as we have seen, elevate the heroine at the moment of catastrophe to a position of overriding authority from which she asserts a vision of religious certitude, a vision so powerful in its spiritual intensity that it renews the other protagonists and brings the action to a climax of triumphant reconciliation. In so doing, however, both dramatists (I have suggested) effectively detach the tragic ending from the psychological-social tensions which they have laid bare in the exposition. Lenz, by contrast, clearly shows the victimisation of his heroine as leading to her moral collapse. From this he draws the (for him) irresistible conclusion that since Gustchen lacks the inner power and dignity of a tragic heroine, she must therefore be a 'comic' figure. At a stroke he transposes the seemingly calamitous crises of his characters into the vulgar, escapist world of popular comedy, a world freed from the pressures of social causality and open to the capricious, wishful manipulations of the dramatist.

The conception of these three plays is informed by a profound imaginative ambivalence, an ambivalence which, as I have tried to show, is most strikingly apparent in the dramatist's starkly divided view of the suffering of the heroine. Both Lessing and Schiller are intent on portraying their female protagonists as moral agents who understand the nature of their actions and are prepared to answer for them before their Creator. Both playwrights, however, portray the unfolding experience of the heroine with a sceptical analytical force that increasingly undermines this view of her inner autonomy and calls in question her capacity for the act of free, self-transcending love which is presented in both works as the source of the tragic reconciliation.

This two-fold mode of apprehension shapes, albeit in a very different form, the presentation of the dramatic action in *Der Hofmeister*. Lenz, as we have seen, emphasises throughout that the suffering of Gustchen is blind and impotent and as such empty of tragic grandeur. He enacts this inadequacy symbolically by 'demoting' his heroine to the lower contingent world of comedy, in which all her despairing anguish can be negated by an arbitrarily imposed and vacuous happy ending. Despite this ironic concern to denigrate the experience of his heroine Lenz is drawn repeatedly to explore it from within. In Gustchen's awareness of failure and break-down he continues to evoke a remorseless force of calamity, of utter dereliction, which is instinct with the final, irreconcilable force of tragedy.

In this discussion I have tried to show the disruptive force of the tensions at the heart of these three works which reveal in each case (I have claimed) a fundamental dichotomy between the dramatist's moral-artistic intentions and the shaping energies of his creative imagination. Lessing, Lenz and Schiller were all in their different ways committed to theoretical conceptions of tragedy as a transcendent metaphysical form; as practising playwrights, however, they are drawn intuitively to probe visions of human violation and failure which denied all possibility of reconciliation, all yearning for ultimate transforming meaning.

## NOTES

**Abbreviations**

L1, etc. = *Lessings Werke*, ed. J. Petersen and W. v. Olshausen, Berlin, 1925.
WB = J.M.R. Lenz, *Werke und Briefe*, ed. B. Titel and H. Haug, Stuttgart, 1966, vol.1.
S = F. Schiller, *Werke in drei Bänden*, ed. G. Fricke and H. Göpfert, Munich, 1966, vol. 1.

1. Several authoritative studies of the development and structure of the patriarchal family have appeared in recent years. I have found the following particularly relevant to my present discussion: O. Brunner, W. Conze and R. Koselleck, *Geschichtliche Grundbegriffe*, vol. 2, Stuttgart, 1975, 253–301; G. Saße, *Die aufgeklärte Familie*, Tübingen, 1988; P. Borscheid and H.J. Teuteberg, *Ehe, Liebe, Tod*, Münster, 1983. For a feminist perspective see I. Weber-Kellermann, *Die deutsche Familie. Versuch einer Sozialgeschichte der Familie*, Frankfurt a. M., 1974. There are also some interesting critical examinations of the presentation of the family in eighteenth-century German drama. The following seem to me particularly important: B.A. Sørensen, *Herrschaft und Zärtlichkeit. Der Patriarchalismus und das Drama im 18. Jahrhundert*, Munich, 1984; J. Greis, *Drama Liebe. Zur Entwicklungsgeschichte der modernen Liebe im Drama des 18. Jahrhunderts*, Stuttgart, 1991; C.F. Good, *Domination and Despair. Father-Daughter Relationships in Grillparzer, Hebbel and Hauptmann*, Berne, 1993; I. Walsøe-Engel, *Fathers*

*and Daughters. Patterns of seduction*, Columbia, 1993; H. Scheuer, 'Väter und Töchter'. Konfliktmodelle im Familiendrama des 18. und 19. Jahrhunderts', *Der Deutschunterricht*, 46 (1994): 18–31; P.-A. Alt, *Tragödie der Aufklärung*, Tübingen, 1994. Two outstanding feminist studies on this subject have appeared in the past few years: C. Lehmann, *Das Modell Clarissa. Liebe, Verführung, Sexualität und Tod*, Stuttgart, 1991; E. Liebes, *Mütter-Töchter-Frauen. Weiblichkeitsbilder in der Literatur*, Stuttgart, 1993

2. A. Wierlacher, *Das bürgerliche Drama*, Münich, 1968, 64ff.; D. Kafitz, *Grundzüge einer Geschichte des deutschen Dramas von Lessing bis zum Naturalismus*, Königstein, 1982, 49ff.; Alt, *Tragödie*, 162ff.

3. G. Lillo, *A London Merchant*, ed. W. McBurney, Lincoln, Nebraska, 1965, 8. See K.S. Guthke, *Das deutsche Trauerspiel*, 3rd edn, Stuttgart, 1980, 13f.

4. C. Schmid, 'Litteratur des bürgerlichen Trauerspiels', *Deutsche Monatsschrift*, December 1798, 284ff.

5. See E. McInnes, 'Lessing's *Hamburgische Dramaturgie* and the Theory of the Drama in the Nineteenth Century', *Orbis Litterarum*, 28 (1973): 293ff.; Kafitz, *Grundzüge*, 54ff.

6. See Scheuer, 'Väter und Töchter', 20ff.

7. See H.-J. Schrimpf, *Lessing und Brecht*, Pfullingen, 1965; Alt, *Tragödie*, 239ff.

8. See Sørensen, *Herrschaft*, 34ff.; Walsøe-Engel, *Fathers and Daughter*, 57ff.

9. I have found the following discussions of *Miß Sara Sampson* especially helpful: K. Eibl, *Miß Sara Sampson*, Frankfurt a. M., 1971, 138ff.; Sørensen, *Herrschaft*, 73ff.; F.J. Lamport, *German Classical Drama*, Cambridge, 1990, 16ff.; Walsøe-Engel, *Fathers and Daughters*, 59ff; Alt, *Tragödie*, 191ff.

10. Sørensen, *Herrschaft*, 12ff.

11. This aspect of Lessings's conception is emphasised by Eibl, *Miß Sarah Sampson*, 158f.

12. See E. McInnes, '*Ein ungeheures Theater*'. *The Drama of the Sturm und Drang*, Frankfurt a. M., 1987, 75ff.; A. Huyssen, *Drama des Sturm und Drang*, Munich, 1980, 157ff.

13. For a detailed review of recent studies of *Der Hofmeister* see K. Wurst ed., *Lenz als Alternative?*, Cologne, 1992, 229ff.

14. See Huyssen, *Drama*, 202ff.

15. See Lamport, *German Classical Drama*, 61f.

16. See Alt, *Tragödie*, 279ff.

17. For a searching exploration of this aspect of Schiller's conception of Miller see I. Graham, 'Passions and Possessions in *Kabale und Liebe*', *German Life and Letters*, 6 (1952/3):12ff. See also Alt, *Tragödie*, 270ff. Alt also gives a wide critical survey of recent discussions of the play.

# 3

# SAYING AND NOT-SAYING IN
# HÖLDERLIN'S WORK

―――୬୬―――

## David Constantine

Man's life is thought,
And he, despite his terror, cannot cease
Ravening through century after century,
Ravening, raging, and uprooting that he may come
Into the desolation of reality.

Yeats, 'Meru'

A couple of Latin words to begin with. They are the adjective *nefandus* and the noun *nefas*. *Nefandus* means 'unspeakable', 'unutterable'; it can be used to describe a subject about which it is not permissible to speak. *Nefas* has the larger meaning of 'something unlawful, a thing it is not permissible to do'; but the two words are closely related and come from *ne...fari*: 'not...say'.

Hölderlin's Empedokles utters 'Unauszusprechendes',[1] and in doing so commits a sin which he seeks to expiate by his suicide. It is a 'Wortschuld' which is understood as a fateful *act*.

King Oedipus' crimes, inexorably brought to light in Sophocles' play, are such that it feels like a sin even to utter them. They are, says the Chorus, αρρητ᾽ ἀρρήτων – of unspeakable things the most unspeakable'. 'Unsäglichstes' is Hölderlin's translation (V, 143).

My subject is 'Saying and Not-Saying in Hölderlin's work'. The penultimate strophe of 'Germanien' will serve as a point of departure and orientation:

> O trinke Morgenlüfte
> Biß daß du offen bist,
> Und nenne, was vor Augen dir ist,
> Nicht länger darf Geheimniß mehr

Das Ungesprochene bleiben,
Nachdem es lange verhüllt ist;
Denn Sterblichen geziemet die Schaam,
Und so zu reden die meiste Zeit
Ist weise auch von Göttern.
Wo aber überflüssiger, denn lautere Quellen
Das Gold und ernst geworden ist der Zorn an dem Himmel,
Muß zwischen Tag und Nacht
Einsmals ein Wahres erscheinen.
Dreifach umschreibe du es,
Doch ungesprochen auch, wie es da ist,
Unschuldige, muß es bleiben.

It is enough for the moment to note how contradictory and inhibited these lines are; and to stress the close connection they establish between 'saying' ('nennen', 'reden', 'sprechen') and 'appearing' ('erscheinen').

———◈———

The premise of Hölderlin's mature poetry is absence. Really, every poem has that as its situation: the absence of the things that would constitute what Brecht (in *Der Gute Mensch*) calls 'ein menschenwürdiges Dasein'. Absence, and in it: disappointment. After the summer of 1800, when he parted from Susette Gontard, Hölderlin seems to have given up all hope of any private and domestic happiness. She died two years later, as his own drift towards the edge accelerated. By then the Revolution, in which he, like many of his best contemporaries, had invested a colossal hope, had passed through terror into dictatorship, and what the French armies were bringing with them over the frontiers had long since ceased to be even a pretence of liberty, equality and fraternity. As a student in Tübingen Hölderlin had hoped that the New Republic would be imported into Swabia; but by the time he began to write the great elegies and hymns such hopes had long since foundered. The personal and the political context of Hölderlin's mature poetry is one of disappointment ('Enttäuschung'), loss and absence.

Naturally then the tenor of much of his poetry is lament. He speaks of the 'elegiac character' of his hero Hyperion (III, 5) and had such a character himself. He wrote odes, hymns and elegies and was conscious of the nature and requirements of each of those genres; but the tone of the last, of elegy, is very often audible in the other two, and may be called most peculiarly his. The cause for lament is the simple fact that everything necessary for cultural and personal happiness must be viewed as absent and in the past. He fixed on Periclean Athens as the location and image of that lost life. In an early poem ('Griechenland. An St.') he says it with a recklessness he would not permit himself again: 'mein Herz gehört den Todten an!' (I, 180).

Lament. But lament is only one principle, one pole, of the mature Hölderlin poem. Against the past, against the almost irresistible pull of the beautiful lost life in the past, he consciously and determinedly sets the future. In other words he counters lament with hope. He strives to bring over into a better future those things simultaneously indispensable and in the past. How hard that is, almost overwhelmingly hard, the reader can feel in nearly every poem. In 'An die Hoffnung' (one of the 'Nachtgesänge') hope itself has to be prayed *for*. The poem struggles to generate the energy necessary for life.

The pull of the future and the past is contained in one of Hölderlin's favourite words: 'einst'. The word can point in both those directions. For example, in 'Heimkunft': 'Anmuth blühet, wie einst' (l. 35) and 'damit nicht/ Ungebeten uns einst plözlich befiele der Geist' (ll. 39–40). Used in ll. 131–32 of 'Brod und Wein' with past sense the word cries out to be repeated for a near future: 'Ließ zum Zeichen, daß einst er da gewesen und wieder/ Käme, der himmlische Chor einige Gaaben zurük'.[2] The poems oscillate, are driven, often very abruptly and violently, to and fro between past and future, between lament and hope, whilst the poet, and with him the reader, seeks to keep a foothold, 'eine bleibende Stätte' (I, 307) in an extremely precarious present. Many Hölderlin poems have to be read as a struggle on the edge of dissolution, as resistance to the undertow of a desperate nostalgia. 'Germanien' actually begins with that anxiety: 'Nicht sie, die Seeligen, die erschienen sind,/ Die Götterbilder in dem alten Lande,/ Sie darf ich ja nicht rufen mehr...' And why not? 'Denn euer schönes Angesicht zu sehn,/ Als wärs, wie sonst, ich fürcht' es, tödtlich ists,/ Und kaum erlaubt, Gestorbene zu weken.'

We live neither in the future nor in the past, but in the present; and Hölderlin never lets himself forget that fact. To the word 'einst' we must add the word 'indessen' fully to characterise the spirit and the dynamics of his work. We live in a meanwhile, and have to make do there the best we can. 'Indessen dünket mir öfters/ Besser zu schlafen, wie so ohne Genossen zu seyn...' Torn between a past and a future 'einst' most poems turn in the end to some equivalent of the phrase 'Aber indessen...' [3].

———*∿∿*———

Poetry puts things into words. In more poets than one might imagine that primary impulse coexists with some sense of the impropriety of speech. The coexistence in Hölderlin is exceptionally tense. In 1801, in a letter to his half-brother Karl, he diagnosed the ills of the times in these terms: 'Es fehlt nur oft am Mittel, wodurch ein Glied dem andern mittheilt, es fehlt sehr oft noch unter uns Menschen an Zeichen und Worten' (VI, 420); and he felt that it was his responsibility as a poet constantly to increase the usable signs and words. His later work is obsessively concerned with showing and bodying forth, with reading, interpreting, translating. He reads the courses of the rivers and the mountains; interprets legends and Scripture; translates Pindar; translates and – in the act of translation as well as in a following commentary – interprets Sophocles. The words 'Zeichen' and 'zeigen', always favourites, crowd into his late poems and into his compulsive revisions; and with them odder usages having a similar sense: 'Wink', 'Merkmal', 'Merkzeichen', 'Maalzeichen', 'sinnig'. The last stratum of work on 'Brod und Wein' is richly and, as it seems, compulsively strewn with such words: 'Göttliches Feuer' (l. 40) becomes 'Zeichen des Himmels' (II, 598). 'Wo, wo leuchten sie denn, die fernhintreffenden Sprüche?'(l. 61) becomes 'Wo bedeuten sie denn, die bäurisch sinnigen Sprüche?' (II, 600). In 'Stutgard' 'Dort von den äußersten Bergen' (l. 59) is revised, doubtless at this time, into 'Dort von den uralt deutsamen Bergen'.[4] One sense of the word 'deuten' given by Grimm is 'dem Volk, den Deutschen verständlich machen, verdeutschen', and those two words 'deuten' and 'verdeutschen' would serve as 'Merkmal' (to use his own word) for all that section of Hölderlin's work from the winter of 1803/4 to his incarceration in the clinic in September 1806.

The impulse towards clear utterance, which may be understood as a longing for presence, for realisation in the here and now, is accompanied and contradicted by one towards reticence, circumlocution and even secrecy. The two work in the poem in a perpetual and restless dialectic, but not as mechanical thesis and antithesis. They are closer than that, they inform one another ceaselessly and constitute between them the peculiar fluidity and movement of the Hölderlin poem. The will to expression can assert itself to the point of hubris: there is nothing the poet, through his poem, cannot bring about. The contrary movement is a backing off; he fills with anxiety, loses all courage and self-confidence. There is 'a kind of fighting' in the poems, and some characteristic structures, images and procedures embody it. I shall mention five.

## THE JOURNEY

Several of the largest poems are structured by a journey. The poet-traveller quits the landscape of disappointment and absence and visits that of presence and fulfilled life. He goes from our time and place into the light of Ancient Greece. But the journey is only permitted for the benefit of our benighted age and on condition that the poet traveller will return. 'Und wohlgeschieden...Die ruhn nun', he says, with all the determination he can muster, of the happy Greeks. And arrived in their land: 'Nicht zu bleiben gedenk ich' (II, 127, 128, 141). The poem conjures up the condition of fulfilled humanity, and backs away. It is very striking that the goal of the journey and the ending and goal of the poem never coincide. 'Patmos' is the boldest example of this. Asia is evoked or arrived at almost at once, in unforgettable brilliance. It is perhaps the most intense vision and climax in all of Hölderlin; and what follows is a long contenting of oneself with less, a backing away from what the poem has at the outset proved itself capable of.

## 'HOMELESS AT HOME'

The wanderer, in Hölderlin's poem of that name (the second version), comes home after much suffering abroad and finds a landscape which has survived in undiminished beauty; but he himself cannot be taken up into it. His parents are dead, he has aged and changed. A real home, a place of presence, is there and he cannot enter. Presence and absence coexist in the poem. The condition of immanence is made palpable, and withheld. The homecomer realises: 'Und so bin ich allein' (II, 83). It is much the same in *Hyperion*. The hero comes home into a landscape as beautiful as it was in ancient times; and for him it is the location of disappointment and absence. In a late rewriting of the eighth strophe of 'Brod und Wein' home appears as a place unable to be lived in. For an interim, which is our present age, the spirit must wander abroad, or be 'consumed' by the homeland: 'ihn zehret die Heimath' (II, 608).

## EVASIVE SAYING

Glance again at the lines from 'Germanien'. They fall towards the end of a poem whose premise was the imminent coming of the New Age and whose *Gestus* was that of annunciation. But they themselves are anything but annunciation. What they give with one hand they take back with the other. They are remarkable chiefly for the quarrelling of their gestures and tones. 'Friedensfeier' is a magnificent example of the same evasiveness. The many syntactic difficulties and the whole uncertainty attaching to the identity of the 'Fürst des Festes' are symptomatic of the painful tension between what the poet would like to be able to say and what in the world's real circumstances he honestly can say. (The meaning of the poem lies precisely in that tension.)

## METAPHOR UPON METAPHOR

In the winter of 1803/4, whilst completing his Sophocles translations, Hölderlin rewrote 'Der gefesselte Strom' and 'Der blinde Sänger' to publish them, with seven other poems, as his 'Nachtgesänge'. Those rewritings, akin to translation into a strange and radical language, involve in each case, to produce 'Ganymed' and 'Chiron', the enriching of the poem with another layer of metaphor. The poem was opened up, enriched, and closed again around an intensified and multiplied total sense. In the first, for example, to the image of the melting river, figurative of reanimation and renewal, Hölderlin added his own version of the legend of Ganymede in which the beautiful youth, after a period of exile from heaven, now, as spring comes and the river unfreezes, returns to his blessed state. The released river becomes a metaphor of the released youth, and both body forth a condition of ecstatic reanimation. The grafting of Chiron on to the metaphorical stock of 'Der blinde Sänger' works similarly. Total sense is multiplied, almost beyond what a reader can comprehend. It is like standing between mirrors, seeing endless reflections. It is true that metaphor, in contradistinction to simile, will most often resist being used, as mere illustration, to facilitate passage from the less to the more familiar; but here *any* such function is completely annulled. The metaphors do not lead us out of the poem into anything as graspable (and comforting) as unequivocal meaning. Instead they multiply our questions. Simile itself, in late Hölderlin, sometimes attains considerable autonomy and refuses its traditional function. Those late pieces 'Wie Vögel langsam ziehn...' and 'Wie Meeresküsten...' are intact in themselves. The context into which, as extended similes, they might have fitted is absent. An autonomous simile is in itself a striking image of a further sense unknown, absent, withheld.

## EXEGESIS THAT IS NO SUCH THING

Hölderlin's 'Pindar-Fragmente' take the form of exegesis – doubly so. First a difficult text in a foreign language is translated. Then follows, ostensibly at least, a commentary or interpretation. However, this form, which raises expectations of a double clarification (first translation, then exegesis), is contradicted. The text is translated in such a way that much of its foreignness still adheres to it. Then the commentary itself calls for elucidation. Thus:

> Vom Delphin
> Den in des wellenlosen Meeres Tiefe von Flöten
> Bewegt hat liebenswürdig der Gesang.
> Der Gesang der Natur, in der Witterung der Musen, wenn über Blüthen die Wolken, wie Floken, hängen, und über dem Schmelz von goldenen Blumen. Um diese Zeit giebt jedes Wesen seinen Ton an, seine Treue, die Art, wie eines in sich selbst zusammenhängt. Nur der Unterschied der Arten macht dann die Trennung in der Natur, daß also alles mehr Gesang und reine Stimme ist, als Accent des Bedürfnisses oder auf der anderen Seite Sprache.
> Es ist das wellenlose Meer, wo der bewegliche Fisch die Pfeife der Tritonen, das Echo des Wachstums in den waichen Pflanzen des Wassers fühlt. (V, 284)

'Das Belebende' is still more mysterious, and almost as beautiful.[5]

Presence coexists with prohibition, annunciation with retraction and evasiveness, and gestures and structures intrinsically suggesting clarification only increase the need for it.

I repeat: the premise of the Hölderlin poem is absence and what drives it is the longing for presence. The poem engenders image after image of fulfilled life, and simultaneously resists their immense persuasive power. If we consider that Hölderlin, at his most confident or hubristic, actually viewed the poem as a means by which a sense of the divine could be induced to re-enter lives being lived without it then the religious and existential serious-ness of Saying or Not-Saying should become apparent. The poem itself is an act of incarnation. By the 'Stab des Gesanges' (II, 170) the gods will be conducted into our disillusioned lives. In the process of the poem, by its workings (its syntax, rhythm, articula-tion) divinity will be induced – almost forced – into appearance. Or, more precisely, the poem will render it 'fühlbar und gefühlt' (IV, 243); but the commonest image of that palpable state is *appear-ance* ('Erscheinung'). The poem, an act of saying, will induce God to appear; it will be the flesh, or metaphor, of God, as Christ was. Being a Romantic, Hölderlin was inclined to view the imagination as a creative and not merely mimetic power. He would have agreed with Keats: 'What the imagination seizes as Beauty must be truth – whether it existed before or not... The Imagination may be compared to Adam's dream – he awoke and found it truth...'.[6] The imagination works in man as an equivalent of the act by which in the beginning God created heaven and earth and man.

These titanic claims for poetry are shadowed in Hölderlin, as in many Romantics, by an equal scepticism, humility and anxi-ety. Always at the back of his mind and often pushing to the fore-front is the question: What status, what validity do these images engendered by the imagination actually have? What does it mean to speak of the incarnation of God in a work of art? It is a fantastic hubris or, if there is no God, nonsense. Can a thing be induced or forced into existence merely by the power of human thought? When Rimbaud was done with being a medium and a seer his verdict was: 'Enfin, je demanderai pardon pour m'être nourri de mensonge'.[7]

The tension between hubris and scepticism is built into Hölder-lin's poems. Indeed, what they incarnate is not God but, needless to say, precisely this tension. The beautiful persuasive images, the moments when the condition of fulfilled life is rendered palpable, are revealed in the inexorable process of the poem to be only illu-sion ('Schein'). In almost every poem a dis-illusioning ('Ent-täuschung') is experienced which matches the disappointments in Hölderlin's own life and serves as their apt expression. Scepticism about the validity of the whole poetic enterprise matches a scepticism about the realisability of ideals in his own life and times. What hopeful annunciation could any honest poet make? We come back again and again to Hölderlin's characteristic 'Aber indessen...' His desire is to celebrate – 'feiern möcht' ich...' (II, 77) – but he is not permitted to. Poems whose hubristic ambition is to be the body of God become instead a temple, a house, a structure – perhaps only that: syntax, a grammatical structure – into which some sense of divinity, perhaps only the longing for it, the powerful sense of its absence, may be induced to enter. In 'Der Gang aufs Land' Hölderlin tried to fit a very ordinary and secular structure, a new 'Gasthaus' on a hill-top near Stuttgart, to be a temple for the incoming gods; and could not finish the poem, perhaps because of that disproportion. 'Friedensfeier' opens with a hall fit for any epiphany, and nothing else in the poem is as *realised* as that initial readiness and expectation.

Saying, in the particular sense of causing to appear, announcing as present, is a temptation in Hölderlin's later poetry. Again and again he seems on the brink of being seduced by the beauty of the images his own verse has engendered. That beauty itself is *nefandus*. To say what they are inducing him to say would be an impropriety. He resists, he withdraws either into lament that the ideal is lost or into an ecstatic 'Vorgefühl' of its being realised, which is to say into postponement.

—◦◦◦—

A poem works – Hölderlin's word is 'glükt' (II, 119) – when things are so well expressed in it that the reader feels them. They are then, in a certain sense, really there; made present. The poem realises them. This is a quite normal and quite secular poetics, but it will be seen how easily it can be given a religious dimension. We experience particular states when reading a poem. Nietzsche speaks of the kingdom of heaven as a 'Zustand des Herzens',[8] and such states are what the poem is suited to producing in a reader.

The states realised in Hölderlin's poems are often of a peculiar intensity. They are very persuasive, they carry the reader away. I mentioned earlier how abruptly a poem may swing between hope, anticipated joy, disappointment, lament and near despair. The reader is exposed to these violent shifts, and suffers them. Thus when 'der Gesang...glükt' states of being are realised which in their instability and ecstatic intensity may even be thought dangerous.

I mentioned Empedokles' 'Wortschuld'. He utters what it is not permissible to utter. He commits *nefas*. Put more exactly, in the fullness of his heart, in the persuasion that he, like a Hölderlin poem, has God within him, he commits a sort of identification of the divine with the medium, sign or bodily form of the divine, and calls himself a god (IV, 10). At once his sense of divinity abandons him, the strength goes from him (IV, 94). He is punished 'mit gränzenloser Oede'; 'da sizt/ Er seelenlos im Dunkel' (IV, 11, 10):

> er trauert nur
> Und siehet seinen Fall, er sucht
> Rükkehrend das verlorne Leben,
> Den Gott, den er aus sich
> Hinweggesschwätz. (IV, 98)

He inhabits then, as a typical Hölderlin hero, a condition of absence. But when he laments it, in the process of lament itself the condition of presence which was formerly his is recovered (IV, 14–15). That is the characteristic procedure and effect of elegy: it laments lost happiness and in so doing brings the happiness back, in the verse, lament goes over into celebration until the point, which must inevitably come, where this presence is recognised for what it is – an illusion, 'only in the poem', and grief returns with a vengeance. Thus in *Empedokles* and in the elegy 'Menons Klagen', again and again, with an implacable 'aber', grief sets in. And the higher the ascent into celebration the lower the descent into grief. We can express it so: the more 'der Gesang... glükt', the more powerfully, beautifully, persuasively lost happiness is rendered present in the poem, all the more exposed is the poet to the danger of succumbing to grief. He creates and increases that danger by his own poetic ability. In the *nefas* then, in the uttering of things which are *nefandus*, there resides not only an impropriety but also a risk.

This risk was already addressed in 'Am Quell der Donau'. The hymn finishes with a rather anxious prayer to '[die] guten Geister' who, as the powers of inspiration, gave him the poem in the first place: 'ihr Gütigen! umgebet mich leicht,/ Damit ich bleiben möge, denn noch ist manches zu singen' (II, 128–9). Three years later, after the death of Susette Gontard and the first advances of mental illness into his life, nearly all the poems – many of them rewritings into strange and radical speech – are pulled towards this danger. 'Thränen' falls almost helplessly prey to the temptation of the beautiful lost islands ('Ihr nemlich geht nun einzig allein mich an...') and ends in the fear of extinction. Let me mention again the close connection between utterance and epiphany. The poet waits in his meanwhile for the coming or return of a life 'voll göttlichen Sinns' (II, 111). In the 'Nachtgesänge' this longed-for moment, which the poetry itself is actively engaged in conjuring up, begins to assume an aspect of catastrophe. Joy itself in 'Menons Klagen' and even more so in 'Heimkunft' has a dangerously ecstatic edge to it; but two or three of the 'Nachtgesänge' seem to be courting total dissolution. Against the dead state expressed in 'An die Hoffnung' something perilously lively has to be summoned up. The hope the writer appeals for in that poem consists in being violently reanimated:

> O du des Aethers Tochter! erscheine dann
> Aus deines Vaters Gärten, und darfst du nicht
> Ein Geist der Erde, kommen, schrök', o
> Schröke mit anderem nur das Herz mir.

The risks of this 'other' are obvious; but in his dread of insensibility Hölderlin must conjure it up. His hero Ganymede, in the image of the frozen, shackled but now liberated river, returns to the gods, which is doubtless a happiness ('himmlisch Gespräch ist sein nun'); but his departure stands under the sign of going astray: 'irr gieng er nun', and seems like an ecstasy that human beings would do well not to imitate, 'denn allzugut sind/ Genien'. That prefix 'allzu' is a sort of signature on the later poems: 'allzubereit' in 'Stimme des Volks'and 'Chiron'; 'allzudankbar' in 'Thränen'.[9] The attraction of unrestraint is frankly admitted: 'das Ungebundne reizet'(II, 51); 'immer/ Ins Ungebundene gehet eine Sehnsucht'(II, 197); 'immer jauchzet die Welt/ Hinweg von dieser Erde, daß sie die/ Entblößet' (II, 163). Add the exchanges between Pausanias – Panthea – Delia in *Empedokles* (IV, 84–5, 115) and this from 'In lieblicher Bläue': 'Wie Bäche reißt das Ende von etwas mich dahin, welches sich wie Asien ausdehnet...' (II, 373), and it should be clear that Hölderlin knew 'das wunderbare Sehen dem Abgrund zu' (II, 51) as well as any other Romantic before or since.

Chiron, 'der blinde Sänger', longs for the return of a daylight that would also be the recovery of sight, and the poem rises to an ecstatic anticipation of that moment: 'Tag! Tag! Nun wieder athmet ihr recht; nun trinkt,/ Ihr meiner Bäche Weiden! ein Augenlicht,/

Und rechte Stapfen gehn...'(II, 57). But we know from the myth that the release Herakles will bring him is the release from immortality, the permission to die. Hence the lines: 'Den Retter hör ich dann in der Nacht, ich hör'/ Ihn tödtend, den Befreier...' (II, 57). This running together of epiphany and extinction is one of the most disquieting tendencies of Hölderlin's late work. Both can be seen hurrying nearer in the act of saying, in the ecstatic annunciation to which, again and again, his own verse pulls him. Among the words forcing themselves forward during the late rewriting of 'Brod und Wein' are many that have to do with burning and being consumed. The gods come down, in this last version, 'wie Flammen...Leben verzehrend'; their presence, 'das blühende Gut', is further characterised as 'das Verzehrende' (II, 600). Indeed, the one most at risk from this gift, from the very fullness of life the gods represent, is, needless to say, the man engaged in summoning it up, the man to whom this act of summoning up is a fatal temptation: 'Himmlischer Gegenwart zündet wir Feuer.../ Eine Versuchung ist es...' (II, 605). 'Fast wäre der Seher gebrannt...' As an alternative to 'der Seher' Hölderlin tried 'der Beseeler': 'Fast wär' der Beseeler verbrannt...'.[10] That which animates and inspirits also threatens to annihilate. The act of saying counters the living death of insensateness with more presence, life – or reality? – than a man can bear.

———*◊◊◊*———

Translation and rewriting so radical that it is akin to translation are the chief part of Hölderlin's poetry in the two or three years before his incarceration in the clinic. In the winter of 1803/4, shifting 'Der gefesselte Strom' into 'Ganymed' and 'Der blinde Sänger' into 'Chiron', he was also completing his versions of Sophocles. This was a translation which, especially in its last phase, was simultaneously an interpretation of texts as sacred in Hölderlin's world as Holy Writ. I shall conclude with a brief discussion of his *Oedipus*, and arrive in so doing at perhaps the most extreme instance there is of that which must not be said. In this work utterance, revelation and epiphany come together in the monstrous image of the blinded king.

In Hölderlin's doubtless rather idiosyncratic view of the tragedy Oedipus' guilt resides less in the murder of his father and in marriage with his mother than in his compulsion to bring the whole truth into the daylight. Utterance, compulsive revelation, are themselves the crime.

Hölderlin describes as follows the role of the seer Tiresias in the development of the tragedy: 'Er tritt ein in den Gang des Schiksaals, als Aufseher über die Naturmacht, die tragisch den Menschen seiner Lebenssphäre, dem Mittelpunkte seines innern Lebens in eine andere Welt entrükt und in die exzentrische Sphäre der Todten reißt' (V, 197). He, the blind seer who has the clearest sight, offers his fellow men a revelation they will be unable to bear.

Oedipus is advised by the Delphic Oracle that he must purify his plague-ridden country: 'Man soll des Landes Schmach, auf diesem Grund genährt,/ Verfolgen, nicht Unheilbares ernähren...' Hölderlin comments (soundly or not is immaterial): 'Das konnte heißen: Richtet, allgemein, ein streng und rein Gericht, haltet gute bürgerliche Ordnung...' (V, 197). But Oedipus at once gives way to the temptation to interpret this instruction 'zu unendlich' and 'ins besondere'. That is, he brings his country's present sickness into connection with the murder of Laius committed years before. In doing so he is, in Hölderlin's view, 'zum *nefas* versucht'(V, 197). Thus even more than the deed utterance is represented as being something impermissible, monstrous. Oedipus pushes compulsively into the *nefas*. His striving for enlightenment and the truth is characterised, very disquietingly, as 'die wunderbare zornige Neugier' (V, 198), 'das närrischwilde Nachsuchen nach einem Bewußtseyn' (V, 199), 'das geisteskranke Fragen nach einem Bewußtseyn' (V, 200). In the end he utters the unutterable: 'Er [spricht] das *nefas* eigentlich aus' (V, 197). His wanting to know and to understand – 'diß Allessuchende, Allesdeutende' (V, 201) – brings him to grief. Hölderlin comments: 'das Wissen, wenn es seine Schranke durchrissen hat... [reizt] sich selbst, mehr zu wissen, als es tragen oder fassen kann' (V, 198). The unstoppable craving for revelation ends in horror and catastrophe.

Hölderlin's translation is, as I said, also an interpretation of the text, and deliberately reinforces the view of events outlined above. The German is shot through with repeated words: 'deutlich', 'deuten', 'bedeuten', 'zeigen', 'anzeigen', 'offenbar', 'offenbaren', 'kund', 'künden', 'verkünden' etc. Naturally such repetitions occur in the Greek too, but Hölderlin intensified this effect by again and again choosing the same or allied German words even where the Greek was more various.[11] Thus the words 'forschen', 'ausforschen', 'erforschen', 'nachforschen' occur with an almost insane emphasis.

Oedipus, who got control of the city of Thebes by solving the riddle of the Sphinx, energetically sets about solving the riddle of himself. He sends Creon to Delphi, for Apollo's advice. (His father Laius was going to Delphi when Oedipus killed him.) He sends for Tiresias and for the shepherd who was Laius' servant, and interrogates them. He insists that the whole enquiry be held in public. He is possessed by the need to say everything, to drag everything into the daylight. He meets with a resistance which is a sort of shame and horror in the face of the *nefas*, first in Tiresias – 'Daß ich nicht/ Das meine sage! nicht dein Übel künde!'; then in Jokasta – 'Bist du besorgt ums Leben,/ So suche nicht'; and in the shepherd – 'Nicht, bei den Göttern, frage weiter, Herr!' (V, 136, 172, 178). The shepherd's dread is palpable: 'Oh! Oh! das Schrökliche selbst zu sagen, bin ich dran.' Oedipus replies: 'Und ich zu hören. Dennoch hören muß ich' (V, 178). Then when it is over and everything has come out Oedipus, who has been so forthright, adopts a language whose every syllable recoils in horror from the appalling solution of the riddle:

> Man sagt, ich sei gezeugt, wovon ich nicht
> Gesollt, und wohne bei, wo ich nicht sollt', und da,
> Wo ich es nicht gedurft, hab' ich getödtet. (V, 179)

The messenger cannot bring himself to repeat what Oedipus utters off stage: '[er] spricht/ Unheiliges, was ich nicht sagen darf' (V, 185). There follows then a revelation whose horror has perhaps never been outdone in all the history of theatre. Centre stage the great doors are swung open and Oedipus enters. He has put out his eyes. He has become in himself the superlative horror, he incarnates it, makes it manifest, forces it on our sight. Creon's efforts to usher him away, back indoors, out of sight, are entirely understandable. The phenomenon insults the gods and soils their elements:

> Nicht darf man unbedekt ein solches Unheil
> Aufzeigen, das die Erde nicht, und nicht
> Der heilge Regen und das Licht anspricht. (V, 188)

The craving for revelation, for utterance in this play is characterised by its translator Hölderlin as 'geisteskrank', and he translated the play in such a way that the irresistibility of the craving is accentuated. In that winter, when Hölderlin was working on the 'Nachtgesänge', King Oedipus appears almost as his alter ego there on the edge of the abyss. He wrote later: 'Der König Oedipus hat ein Auge zuviel vielleicht' (II, 373). That is, he was forced, even though it meant his own undoing, to gaze at the *nefas*, and to utter it. Among those often very shocking alterations to the 'classically' finished 'Brod und Wein' are the lines: 'daß sich krümmt der Verstand/ Vor Erkenntniß...' (II, 606). Hölderlin's Chiron looks forward ecstatically to the moment when 'einheimisch aber ist der Gott dann/ Angesichts da, und die Erd' ist anders' (II, 57). However, Oedipus too is 'angesichts da' when, after too much insight, he appears centre stage with bloody eyes.

The final apparition may be bliss or horror. In late Hölderlin it is sometimes hard to tell, as that apparition approaches, what its nature or aspect will be. Another possibility is that nothing will come. The epiphany will be merely 'the desolation of reality', finally confronted. Although after hopes such as Hölderlin's that disappointment would itself be as bad as whatever Conrad's Mr Kurtz saw on his deathbed.

## NOTES

1. Hölderlin, *Sämtliche Werke* (Große Stuttgarter Ausgabe), ed. F. Beißner and A. Beck, 8 vols, Stuttgart, 1943–85, IV, 97. Hölderlin's works are referred to throughout in this edition and all further references are incorporated into the text.
2. It is true that the sense Hölderlin most gives to 'einst' is past, and in poems such as 'Elegie' (ll. 31, 32, 33, 76, 77, 78) and 'Der Archipelagus' (ll. 18, 29, 58, 166, 239) 'the very word is like a knell' in its insistence on loss; but there are half a dozen significant uses with future sense – 'Dichtermuth', ll. 25, 27, for example – and if the words 'einmal', 'einsmal' and 'dereinst', in their future sense, are added the oscillation is pretty even. The *Wörterbuch zu Friedrich Hölderlin*, I, *Die Gedichte*, compiled by M. Dannhauer *et al.*, Tübingen, 1983, is invaluable in following these things up.
3. II, 94. The poems have more than a dozen instances of 'indessen' or 'indeß' in this critical sense. The most striking are 'Brod und Wein', ll. 119, 121, 155; 'Der Archipelagus', ll. 255, 278; 'Der Wanderer', ll. 43, 75, 82; 'Der Mutter Erde', l. 31.
4. II, 586. 'Deuten/bedeuten' is added four times to 'Brod und Wein' during that late rewriting, at ll. 61, 69, 97, and, most strikingly, at l. 135: 'Untheilbares zu deuten'. Cf also the addition of 'zeigen' at l. 124: 'zeigen/ Göttliches' and 'Witterungen', in the sense of 'signs', at l. 41 (II, 598, 600, 604, 606). 'Merkmal' is in 'Wenn aber die Himmlischen ...' (l. 52), 'Merkzeichen' (variant: 'Maalzeichen') in the late version of 'Patmos' (II, 184), 'Wink' in the much earlier 'Rousseau' (l.

31). As for 'Zeichen', let one extraordinary usage stand for several: 'Ein Zeichen sind wir, deutungslos' (II, 195).

5. See my 'Translation and Exegesis in Hölderlin', in *Modern Language Review*, 81 (1986): 388–97.

6. *Letters of John Keats*, ed. R. Gittings, Oxford, 1970, 37.

7. A. Rimbaud, 'Une Saison en enfer', *Oeuvres*, Paris, 1962, 198.

8. In *Der Antichrist*, 34, in *Werke*, ed. K. Schlechta, 5 vols, Frankfurt a.M., 1981, III, 1196.

9. Hölderlin first had 'allzuliebend' for the 'allzugut' in 'Ganymed'. The danger the prefix conveys is apparent in 'Wo aber allzusehr sich/ Das Ungebundene zum Tode sehnet...' ('Griechenland', 2. Fassung, ll. 14–15). The opposite condition, that of lifeless torpor, is in 'allzugedultig' ('Der Ister', l. 58; 'Die Wanderung', l. 105) and 'allzunüchtern' ('Elegie', l. 69).

10. II, 608. To get some clear view of these strange rewritings it is essential to use the Frankfurt edition of Hölderlin's works, edited by D. Sattler, Frankfurt a.M., 1975, and/or *Friedrich Hölderlin, Bevestigter Gesang. Die neu zu entdeckende hymnische Spätdichtung bis 1806*, ed. D. Uffhausen, Stuttgart, 1989.

11. For example Hölderlin has 'erforschend' at l. 64, 'nachzuforschen' at l. 127, 'forschen' at l. 223 and 'geforscht' at l. 225 where the Greek at those places has four different verbs: σκοπῶν, ἐξειδέναι, ἐξερῶ, ἰχνευον.

# 4

## TABOOS IN POETIC-REALIST WRITERS

*David Jackson*

It is tempting to imagine the writer-taboos relationship as one where a critical dissident is confronted by a state and/or society determined to outlaw certain topics. Having assessed risks and responses, he/she opts for the most appropriate artistic strategies. However, the situation is obviously much more complex than that. In this paper I shall first look at categories and beliefs which after 1848 acquired the status of inviolable articles of faith for certain Poetic-Realist writers. Then I will examine new taboos which emerged once the official opinion-makers of the North German Confederation and then the Second German Empire either dismissed these norms or perverted them to their own purposes. Having considered the predicament of dissenting writers, I will discuss their intellectual turmoil and intense heart-searching when reality refused to conform to their earlier expectations. Hopefully a picture will emerge of how they were torn between inhibitions about jettisoning hallowed categories and a compulsion to explore these and other taboo topics even at the risk of falling foul of relatives, friends, editors, and readers. I shall argue that because of their social position writers' attitudes were often shot through with ambivalences. They were both critics and upholders of taboos. Self-censorship and the observation of specific artistic parameters thus often reflected, not just a response to external pressures, but also a refusal to push questions to the point where the conclusion was inescapable, namely that the Poetic-Realist credo was bankrupt.

The context in which Poetic Realism came into its own after 1848 helps explain why key premises and principles came to enjoy taboo status.[1] In the dispiriting aftermath of revolution what was needed to sustain confidence in the course of German history and culture were absolute certainties. Long-term political, social, and economic trends were thus diagnosed which, when complemented by supposedly incontrovertible scientific, historical, ethical, cultural and aesthetic laws, provided an apparently irresistible dynamic.

The alliance of state and church – especially in Prussia – could not halt the long-term trend away from orthodox Christianity, and fictional critiques of religion and evocations of humanitarian alternatives loom large in the works of key Poetic-Realist writers. Ludwig Feuerbach's philosophy with its optimistic trust in nature exerted far greater influence than Schopenhauer's pessimism.[2] Pessimism like *Weltschmerz, Zerrissenheit*, scepticism, and resignation, was denounced as a luxury of a romantic, aristocratic past. Subjectivity, genius, originality, and eccentricity were held in low esteem. Keller, for instance, conceived *Der grüne Heinrich* as a Feuerbachian rejection of narcissistic individualism.[3] The 'normal' tended to become the norm. In a reaction against the critical speculations of Young German and *Vormärz* writers and their satirical depictions of the German *Bürger* as a materialistic philistine, thinking on moral and ethical issues tended to be uncomplicated: 'deep', 'honest', 'healthy' moral feeling was attributed to the 'practical', 'solid' middle classes (which did not include intellectuals, wild theorists and bohemian artists!), to craftsmen and to rural folk and farmers.[4] It was confidently predicted that the precepts of reason and conscience would prove to be identical with human beings' 'true' sensuous and sexual needs once the distorting effects of ignorance and alienation had been overcome.

In this scheme of things there was no place for fictional characters who were by nature evil, sadistic or perverse.[5] If one were allowed to obey one's natural aspirations – albeit with orderly guidance! – this could not of itself result in unhappiness, disillusionment or tragedy. Genetic disease, physical handicap and mental illness also played little part in early Poetic-Realist fictions. One had no wish to play into the hands of those who had traditionally argued that nature was fallen, that health, happiness and good fortune were precarious, and that suffering was the human lot. For the same reasons sceptical, down-to-earth views of human nature were just as taboo.

This view of nature, however, imposed strict limits on depictions of love and sex. Writers like Storm might present the current regulation of sex, love and marriage by state and society as unnatural, but, like more staid upholders of middle-class respectability, they equated the human fulfilment supposedly vouchsafed by 'true', passionate love with courtship and marriage. Monogamy supposedly corresponded to an innate, eternal instinct; in marriage two halves of an imperfect whole achieved totality. Storm did not thematise his own earlier *mariage à trois*, and homosexual love, whether male or female, does not figure in Poetic-Realist fictions. In Freytag's *Soll und Haben* (1855) Lenore von Rothsattel is presented critically as a tomboyish *Original* for dancing the gentleman's part if males are in short supply and for even appearing in amateur dramatics as a gentleman, with a whip and a little woollen beard.[6] She, too, ends up in the haven of marriage. Storm horrified members of the Rütli literary circle in Berlin by refusing to condemn incestuous love between brother and sister.[7] Treitschke accused Kleist's *Penthesilea* 'of losing itself in the mysteries of sexual life from which art was debarred', while Hettner said that Goethe's *Stella*, by commending bigamy, was the sickest of his works and proof that what was immoral was also inartistic.[8] Any attempt to challenge conventional notions of respectable middle-class married life could not be too bold. Thus in Storm's *Späte Rosen* (1859), while it is true that a middle-aged married couple rediscover their physical passion and consummate it in a summer house, Gottfried's *Tristan und Isolde* provides both the love-potion and the protective literary model. The love making is not described. In Keller's *Romeo und Julia auf dem Dorfe* (1856) the lovers, denied any prospect of order and respectable matrimony, prefer suicide to unregulated, wild love among vagrants. They make love only after concluding a suicide pact. Again everything happens 'off stage'.

Fictions often used Biblical imagery to convey alternative, humanitarian versions of revelation, conversion, and redemption. Storm's *Veronica* (1861) and *Im Schloß* (1862) depict individuals liberating themselves from the tutelage of the church and discovering true fulfilment in the love and support of understanding husbands. In the 1860s Meyer, too, gravitated towards liberal Protestantism with its stress on perfectibility and progress. The essence of Christianity was equated with the Enlightenment virtues of intellectual and ethical autonomy, tolerance, and love of one's neighbour; Jesus Christ became the ideal human being. However one had to tread warily. For the authorities in the 1850s the link between radical religious ideas and revolution was indisputable. Moreover, since the new family periodicals were commercial ventures dependent on subscribers, editors were fearful of alienating believers. Thus Storm's essay on popular belief/super-stition in Catholic Germany, although accepted by the *Garten-laube*, never appeared since Keil, its editor, feared antagonising Catholic readers. Storm did not even complete the poem 'An deines Kreuzes Stamm o Jesu Christ' where Jesus Christ is addressed as only half a human being for having neither wife nor children.[9] The manuscript of *Im Schloß* also shows self-censorship at work. The corollary of this commitment to conveying the divinity of finite, human life was that anything pointing in a different direc-tion became taboo.

It was crucial for Poetic Realists to be able to believe that their optimistic vision of life was underwritten by infallible principles and forces. They did not adopt the scientific materialism of Mole-schott, Büchner and Vogt.[10] For them the *Idee* – the Idea or Ideal Principle governing all life, culture and history – could not be reduced to chemical or physiological entities and processes. Notions of immanence and of the identity of spirit and matter served them better: the natural world, history and culture were all seen as entities both organic and spiritual, which were pro-grammed according to a blueprint more infallible even than Christian providence.[11] Indeed, despite all the polemics against Christianity and speculative philosophies, huge metaphysical assumptions of Christian provenance, secularised during the Enlightenment and in German idealist and Hegelian philosophy, underpinned Poetic-Realist notions.

In contrast, Poetic Realists had no shared detailed blueprint for state and society. They were agreed that human beings required nurture and support in an ordered, structured environment if nature was to achieve its beneficial purposes, and that it fell to state and society to provide them. However, various scenarios were compatible with this conviction and the stress both on organic, natural structures and on unity in diversity. The pro-Prussian conservative liberalism of a Schmidt or Freytag was only one option. Keller's ideal, in contrast, was that of a structured, democratic community within a federal republic. Republicanism attracted Storm, too. Nor was extraparliamentary, revolutionary action taboo in all quarters. Indeed the intransigence of the Prus-sian government during the Constitutional Struggle inclined even moderate liberals to believe that a revolutionary upheaval might be necessary after all. The idea that all the Poetic Realists yearned for a Prussian solution to the German problem is as much a myth created by Borussian-national historians and literary historians after 1870 as is the assumption that A.L. Rochau's ideas on *Realpolitik* marked a general turning away from the notion that reason and morality should operate in the public and political as well as in the private realm.[12] Not even advocates of a Prussian *kleindeutsch* solution to the German problem would have publicly suggested that the only way forward was for Prussia to wage war on Austria and the other German states. The Weimar-Classical cult of Greece had bequeathed the ideal of unity in diversity, and any future German state was expected to reflect a similar richness. There was also no general readiness among liberal or democratic writers to sacrifice demands for political freedom to the immediate primacy of unity. German national interest was not yet deemed antithetical to that of other states. On the contrary, the creation of liberal/democratic nation states with dynamic capitalist economies would, it was predicted, usher in an age of international harmony and cosmopolitanism.

What, however, was taboo to liberals and democrats alike was the Marxist idea that once the old feudal-absolutist system had been overthrown, the capitalist bourgeoisie had to be ousted by a revolutionary proletariat. For Poetic Realists private property remained sacrosanct, a basic, natural right essential for human fulfilment. As it was also vital to the Poetic-Realist project that writers should imagine themselves capable of articulating the aspirations of the entire nation, it was also taboo to suggest that their definition of *Humanität* might reflect class rather than universal human interests.

Capitalist development was a key factor in the Poetic-Realist equation. Industrial development would, it was argued, undermine the dominance of the landed aristocracy and also solve the age-old problem of poverty and want. The entrepreneur with his 'healthy', 'practical' activities and his sturdy self-responsibility became the classic modern hero. Thus Otto Ludwig denounced Dickens' *Hard Times* (1855) for presenting a caricature of reality,[13] and Fontane dismissed the idea that realism meant depicting a dying member of the proletariat surrounded by his starving children.[14] Indeed it was a cornerstone of the Poetic-Realist credo that Germany's growing economic power, when combined with its cultural and intellectual prowess and the political power which unification would bring, would create a civilisation surpassing even that of Greece. Classical genres like the epic and monumental, high drama would flourish.[15] The true writer or *Dichter* would desert inferior prose genres, i.e., the very novels and short stories which we have come to think of as quintessentially Poetic-Realist. The future belonged to hexameters and iambic pentameters.

All these sacrosanct beliefs – whether in the goodness of nature, the inevitability of progress or Germany's future civilisation – were beyond all doubt. Even more unassailable was the definition of literature's nature and role. Having in the 1830s been declared redundant until a free, united Germany could support a new classical culture, writers found a *raison d'être* for literature in anticipating and revealing the imminent ideal.[16] They declared themselves crucial agents in a grand civilisatory process. In an age increasingly marked by the division of labour and alienation, their qualifications for this were a supposed wholeness denied other professions. They could utilise the unique properties of the work of art, especially its capacity to translate abstract norms and ideas into 'concrete', 'plastic' scenes and sequences, in order to impact directly on the imagination and feelings even of the uneducated. Ideas and insights crucial to the new civilisation would crystallise out of these feelings. A tightly structured aesthetic system adapted from Weimar classicism and based on the identity of the good, the true and the beautiful catered perfectly for the Poetic Realists' need to believe that order and purposiveness underlay all aspects of reality. The aesthetic realm was part of a cosmos in which each element – whether political, scientific, ethical or psychological – co-existed with all the others in a mutually sustaining symbiosis. The 'true' writer recognised and conveyed the 'true' nature of reality; common to both writer and reality were wholeness and harmony. Any suggestion that it was impossible to avoid partiality and individually conditioned perspectives was taboo. There was truth in the singular, not competing definitions of it.

At a time when photography was beginning to pose a threat to literature in terms of its capacity to record all aspects of contemporary life, and when the sciences and history were claiming to have replaced theology and philosophy in interpreting and analysing the world, literature, it was claimed, could communicate a deeper, truer vision of reality.[17] In order to do this though it had to be true to its own peculiar, unchanging essence. It had, in Fontane's words, to offer 'die Wiederspiegelung alles Wirklichen, aller wahren Kräfte und Interessen' but – crucially! – 'im Elemente der Kunst'.[18] Only if writers recognised that *Dichtung* belonged to an autonomous realm, could it perform its civilisatory role. *Tendenz*, on the other hand, both invited the authorities' attention and vitiated the whole critical project. The 'mere' *Schriftsteller, Volkstribun* or journalist could not achieve this purpose; that was the sole prerogative of the *Dichter*. Indeed the input of the writer was deemed paramount, and it was denounced as a sign of intellectual and artistic weakness if he/she could only discern and convey contradictions, contingencies and confusion in contemporary life.[19]

The mirror held up to reality had to select, structure, purify and transfigure – in short: poeticise; only then could it capture the true nature and proportions of reality. In contrast, French realism, or naturalism as it was often termed, failed to do so. What was simply and finally repulsive, ugly or even just vulgar and common had no place in art. 'Sonderlinge, wunderliche Heilige, Kranke, zuletzt Narren und Verrückte'[20] – all came into that category. Just as life was not a hospital full of pathological cases, so too an artistic presentation could not be a clinical, anatomical diagnosis – the charge levelled against Flaubert.[21] Here science had infringed upon art's autonomy and robbed it of its humanising power. Impersonal impassivity and false objectivity, it was argued, denied literature the emotional and intellectual energy which only the creation of *Stimmung*, i.e., the attuning of the reader's sensibility, could provide.[22] Scepticism, cynicism, speculation, satire, parody and corrosive criticism, in contrast, all denied the wholeness, harmony and beauty of reality. Otto Ludwig wrote: 'Nur was geistig ist, und zwar Ausdruck einer gewisssen Idee am Stoffe, und zwar derjenigen, die als natürliche Seele in ihm wirkt und atmet, wird in das himmlische Jenseits der künstlerischen Behandlung aufgenommen; was bloßer Leib, zufällig Anhängendes ist, muß abfallen und verwesen. Soweit die Seele den Leib schafft, sozusagen, die bloße Form des Leibes steht verklärt auf aus dem Grabe.'[23] A humanly divine art communicated a humanly divine message. Challenging either the core tenets of that aesthetic or of that humanitarian philosophy would be like breaking religious taboos.

---

In the second part of this chapter I want to begin by considering factors which subjected core assumptions of this faith to increasing strain. Of course there was no fixed set of identical events and trends to which individual writers responded either uniformly or simultaneously. Particular, individual circumstances were often decisive. However, such factors acted the way they did because they occurred within a wider context. The Poetic-Realist credo of the 1850s and early 1860s had flourished as long as it was a case of trusting in potential rather than of judging achievement. There were already marked differences of emphasis among Poetic-Realist writers both in aesthetic and socio-political matters; but from the mid-1860s onwards a clear gap opened up between those who proclaimed that the ideal and the real had indeed fused and those who – at different stages and in differing degrees – were assailed by doubts.

The mode of German unification – Bismarck's wars – precipitated the first major crisis.[24] Unexpected and almost universally condemned, the Austro-Prussian War brought in the wake of Prussia's surprisingly rapid victory a belligerent campaign in the media on the part of converted liberals determined to forge a new ideology. Schmidt and Freytag followed Treitschke in declaring cosmopolitan liberalism bankrupt, substituting for it an amalgam of Darwinist and neo-Hegelian notions which legitimated a *Realpolitik* based on ethnic nationalism. The Enlightenment notion of progress was perverted to justify as natural and necessary a world-historical process which ensured that a nation's political and military might proved its moral and rational superiority. Victory and success proved the justice of a cause; might was equated with right; unity, since it enhanced national strength and survival, took pride of place over freedom. Victory over France in 1870 was attributed to German ethnic superiority in all areas. Poetic Realism, which from the outset had been a provisional art form geared to a period of transition, could now be wound up. The imperial age would generate altogether grander subjects and genres. Anyone challenging such a brash ideology could expect bruising encounters.

Both Storm and Meyer criticised the haste with which liberals revised their principles once Bismarck's policies unified Northern Germany and promised total unity. Storm denounced Prussian policy as brutal Junkerism, a return to tyrannical *Faustrecht* – but only in private.[25] As a Prussian judge he had to tread carefully. Meyer for his part found in 1870 that the patronage of exiled Germans in Zurich depended on him publicly adopting the German cause. It rapidly became taboo in middle-class, Protestant, National-Liberal circles to criticise Bismarck's policies and the Borussian interpretation of Germany's history. Such issues could only be broached behind masks and cloaks. Here the historical novel and the historical novella provided welcome camouflage. However, the drawbacks of this survival strategy are obvious: it bred artistic subtlety, but it also militated against a work exercising an immediate, powerful impact and it certainly excluded unsophisticated readers. Indeed the camouflage could be too successful. Thus although the historical novel *Jürg Jenatsch* (1874) offers a searching critique of the new ideology, its ironic treatment of Jenatsch and his admirer Waser long went unnoticed. Instead German-national critics identified with characters whose sentiments they shared.

The more trends ran counter to the progressive ideal, the more urgent it became to uphold the autonomy of art and hope that whatever happened in other areas it could still shape people's sensibilities and ideas. Yet, paradoxically, writers anxious to invite critical reflections on taboo political topics were prisoners of an aesthetic which banished *Tendenz*, analytic techniques and critical commentaries. This, together with the need to camouflage and practise self-censorship, meant that although literature's critical function was in one respect reaffirmed, writers denied themselves the basic tools of criticism and hoped to succeed, not despite but because of this. It was almost asking the impossible of *Dichtung*.

The new constellation of political forces inexorably isolated middle-class dissidents. Any viable way forward in political terms disappeared. Glowing evocations by the champions of the new order of an evolving Germanic-ethnic national community only heightened dissidents' awareness that this was far from their own ideal. The ideal of an integrated community had crumbled in Switzerland, too, where Meyer and Keller rejected the victorious radicalism of the late 1860s. Thus Keller's *Kleider machen Leute* (1874) parodies the ideal of a classical-Greek community. Whereas he too had dreamed of writing in exalted, classical genres, *Die verlorenen Liebesbriefe* now recommended as literary models – besides Goethe, Tieck, and Jean Paul – Rabelais, Cervantes, and Sterne.[26] However, eyebrows were raised even at his *Sieben Legenden* (1872), and Keller himself was too much a man of his time both in terms of his moral notions and his allegiance to the Poetic-Realist ideal to be able or willing to follow such prescriptions. Meyer, too, lost his confidence in the emergence of a 'humanised' aristocracy that would foreswear its particularism and exclusiveness. In the manuscript of *Der Heilige* (1879) the brutal Normans are referred to as Junkers.[27] In Storm's case disillusionment led him to break the Poetic-Realist aesthetic taboo in *Eine Halligfahrt* (1871). He opted instead for the techniques of Hoffmann and of the Heine of the *Reisebilder. Empfindsamkeit*, irony, satire and parody returned. The imperial public though, had no appetite for such fare; magazine editors wanted a more familiar recipe. He desisted. Henceforth hatred of the Prussian Junkers could only express itself in historical novellas such as *Aquis submersus* (1876). Although class divisions and social tensions are prominent in their works, the hallmark of the Poetic-Realist aesthetic is that writers still felt bound to balance pessimistic insights and fears with optimistic solutions or at least hopeful vistas. The framework, for instance, could relativise the inner story. Pessimism continued to be taboo.

Thus Keller was unhappy about his failure to transfigure contemporary reality in *Martin Salander* (1886) with its bleak picture of the relationship between individual and community. He planned to counteract its pessimism with an account of the life of his son, Arnold Salander.[28] The more real and ideal diverged, the more any ideal solutions proffered tended to become utopias, as unconvincing in their substance as in their artistic treatment. Reality no longer offered the imaginations of writers like Meyer, Keller or Storm the stuff out of which to construct the 'ideal-real' solutions and scenarios to which they were committed. Without them, however, their art risked degenerating into the prosaic 'negative' social criticism, the emphasis on contradictions and conflicts, which they considered inimical to true art. Meyer's later novellas present compelling images only of rulers and ruling classes trapped within the horizons of court and caste mentalities. Whenever, to right the balance, exemplary Emperors and rulers above the parties are introduced, they are rarely more than cardboard figures. In fact the insistence on plasticity and the taboo on abstract, analytic techniques heightened the effect. The compulsion to suggest the viability of the ideal by showing it incarnate only underlined its unreality. Evocations of harmony and totality were in stark conflict with contemporary reality, while past sociopolitical scenarios often captured little of the complexity of modern states and societies.

The messianic hopes attached to capitalism evaporated. As Cantonal Clerk to the Canton of Zurich Keller had ample opportunity to observe developments within Swiss capitalism where speculative practices were rife. The second volume of *Die Leute von Seldwyla* (1874) captured his growing pessimism. Meyer's *Gustav Adolfs Page* (1882) uses the camouflage provided by seventeenth-century Nuremberg to indict a mentality where consideration of the Firm prevails over all else. As social and economic tensions grew, so too did the socialist parties, and in 1878 Bismarck pushed through the

Socialist Law. Just as in the case of the *Kulturkampf* when they had supported brutal measures against the Catholic Church on the grounds of reason and progress, enlightened-humanitarian Poetic Realists found themselves in a dilemma. Sympathy for the disadvantaged and an aversion to illiberal, inhuman practices were balanced by deep-seated fears of social upheaval. Fictional presentations of the social question like Meyer's *Der Heilige* (1879) reflect these ambivalences. The problem for writers was that anyone pushing criticism of the socio-economic system too far ran the risk of being accused of doing the Socialists' spadework for them. Editors and readers would only stomach so much, and writers themselves had no wish to bring down, rather than reform, a system of which they were the beneficiaries. Storm, who was under great pressure to earn the fees paid by the great middle-class periodicals like the *Deutsche Rundschau* and *Westermanns Monatshefte*, felt so bound to distance himself from socialist criticism of the system that – quite against the usual Poetic-Realist practice – he introduced an obnoxious character into *Hans und Heinz Kirch* (1882) and labelled him a Social Democrat.[29] In *Frau Jenny Treibel* (1893), Fontane exposes cant and calculation in a bourgeois family. Even so, his ironic criticism respects definite parameters. In his last years he may have privately expressed the view that the fourth estate alone held out much hope for state and society; but his novels did not give any such unequivocal message.

The Poetic-Realist insistence on sustaining hope bred utopian idylls such as that in Storm's *Bötjer Basch* (1886) where a small master rooted in a traditional community survives by adapting new 'American' tools and work practices. Neither Keller, Storm nor Fontane followed the Naturalists into the world of the industrial proletariat in order to expose social injustice, poverty and exploitation. Storm's *Ein Doppelgänger* (1887) tackles the problems of lower-class crime, unemployment, violence and social ostracisation quite differently from naturalist works. The disturbing inner story is balanced by the optimism of the framework; its heroine is rescued by her Mr and Mrs Brownlow. The limitations of this individual, 'ethical' solution are all too obvious. Meyer's *Angela Borgia* (1892) offers an equally utopian solution to the social problem. Here, a landowner is brought through his own suffering to a new and sympathetic awareness of the plight of his peasants.

From the mid-1860s onwards the cause of enlightened, progressive humanitarianism had suffered reverses in so many areas that its core tenets inevitably came under closer and closer scrutiny.

Meyer broke one of the ultimate taboos in *Der Heilige* (1879) when he explored the hypothesis that the Christian-Enlightenment ideal of compassion and mercy – and with it the ideals of anti-racism, political equality and democratic rights – might not emanate from human beings' divine, universal essence but rather be the product of particular ethnic, genetic, sociological and psycho-physiological forces. The depiction of Thomas à Becket's imitation of Christ suggests that his master's career could also reflect impotent ethnic hatred, the frustrated will to power of the socially oppressed, and an oriental's need to believe himself the servant of an omnipotent deity. The work anticipated Nietzsche's *Zur Genealogie der Moral* (1887) – without sharing its conclusions. Its use of the fictional narrator also suggested that there might be no fixed, single truth, only perspectives. The fictional narrator comments that in making judgements as in shooting everything depends on one's standpoint.[30]

The Poetic-Realist belief in the divinity of nature also came under increasing pressure as the insights and experimental methods of modern science replaced older synthetic, idealist hypotheses about the nature of the cosmos. Darwinist categories were incompatible with final notions of the organic growth of predetermined entelechies. In Storm's case his sons' sexual promiscuity, drunkenness and fecklessness bred disillusionment and made him receptive to ideas of heredity. He revised his Feuerbachian cult of passionate love and sex, presenting them in *Waldwinkel* (1874), for example, from a bleak, Darwinist viewpoint. Henceforth he oscillated between positive evocations and darker scenarios. The Poetic-Realist need to depict reassuring solutions often pushed him towards regressive patriarchal idylls where sex and passion are defused and contained by self-sacrificing, domesticated, maternal wives. Meyer's *Die Richterin* (1885) enshrined his scepticism about the Pelagian assumptions underlying Tolstoy's *My Religion*.[31]

Whereas apologists of the new order like D.F. Strauss blithely affirmed Darwinist categories while also stressing the precepts of reason and conscience,[32] Meyer explored the relativity or absence of moral notions. In *Plautus im Nonnenkloster* (1881) Poggio, the former creator of the bawdy, erotic *Facetiae*, is preoccupied with the problem of explaining how his amoral hedonism degenerates in his sons into criminality. In *Die Versuchung des Pescara* (1887) the hero, like Renaissance Italy, can only be deepened, ennobled, and redeemed by suffering and death. Hedonism fails; Christian categories regain ground.

Both Meyer and Storm grappled with the problem of affirming notions of human responsibility in the face of determinist theories about heredity, genetic factors, and milieu. In Storm's *Carsten Curator* (1878) Feuerbach's holy human family disintegrates: the alcoholic son clings to the pole above the flood waters like Christ on the cross; he too calls in vain for his father.[33] Human beings can no longer redeem themselves or each other; father and son must each bear his cross; and the devoted wife can do nothing. Storm was uneasy about the story, however, fearing that his own worries had caused him to distort the true proportions of reality and let himself be dominated by what was *peinlich, gemein*, and *unerquicklich*.[34] He had denied hope. Typical of Poetic-Realist writers is the attempt to take on board new scientific ideas but then incorporate them into the humanitarian ideal and make them subserve the Poetic-Realist aesthetic. Thus Storm's *Der Schimmelreiter* (1888) suggests that seekers after truth and reason will always be faced by superstition and selfishness and will always have to contend with illness, ageing, and unforeseeable hereditary handicaps. Nevertheless, 'small-scale' achievements like the building of the dike may profit communities more permanently than the feted deeds of politicians; and the love and commitment of two human beings to each other and to their mentally retarded child remain unassailable human values and sources of true fulfilment. Here the framework, far from crudely relativising a bleak inner story, reinforces doubts about any belief in progress and increasing rationality. The balance is intellectually satisfying.

Whereas the official ideologues of the Second Empire used Darwinism to justify social and political hierarchies, they and the middle-class public reacted with hostility if Socialists turned the same weapons against them and accused them of degeneracy and decadence. A writer dispensing with cloaks and applying Darwinist notions critically to the upper- and middle-classes was clearly at risk. In Storm's *Der Herr Etatsrat* (1881) the hero, a dike-inspector, is described as a bear, a beetle, and a primeval monster emerging from the beach. He exploits his son and drives him to alcohol, while allowing his daughter to be seduced in the family home by the scoundrelly Käfer, i.e., beetle. He indulges in perverse, decadent bouts of drinking and music-making which end with him writhing about on the floor, like a beetle on its back, drunk and in a state of undress. Young girls are treated like whores or vaudeville girls. Notions of progress and evolution are turned on their heads. Storm protects himself though, by using as his narrator a 'decent' young man who fails to register the full horror and significance of things unthinkable und unmentionable in polite society. When he tries to find out more details about the daughter, his own sister leaves the room and an aunt remarks: 'Das sind keine Dinge für die Ohren einer jungen Dame.'[35] Westermann insisted on changes being made to the manuscript 'in usum delphini oder delphinarum',[36] and the various versions document the stylistic consequences of such censorship. In the first version Storm wrote: '...bis der Herr Etatsrath, immer noch bei Gesang und Spiel, zuletzt in greuelvoller Nacktheit [amended to Unbekleidung] dasaß.' For the magazine version this read: '...bis der Geist aus einigen weiteren Gläsern den Herrn Etatsrath über alle Schwere und Unbequemlichkeit des irdischen Leibes hinausgehoben hatte.' For the book version this was only restored to: '...bis er zuletzt in greuelvoller Unbekleidung dasaß.'[37]

The effect of works on impressionable young ladies became a prime concern since it was wives and daughters trapped in the home who were the main consumers of fiction. As reading works aloud in the bosom of the family was a vital social activity, no self-respecting *pater familias* could risk anything which might embarrass or scandalise. Since publishers depended on Christmas sales, and magazine editors on subscribers, it was fatal for writers if they were reputed to have written a work which a father could not give his daughter or allow to be left lying about in the drawing room. Meyer's *Der Heilige* (1879) provoked indignation in Zurich: 'Es ist eine starke Opposition gegen den Heiligen. Hier wurde dieselbe, wie man mir erzählt, von einer Dame folgendermaßen formulirt: Meyer hat ein Buch geschrieben, das kein Frauenzimmer in die Hand nehmen darf.'[38] The mere fact that King Henry seduces Becket's young daughter – this is of course not described! – caused even Keller offence ('der unschöne Unzuchtsfall').[39] On the other hand, Meyer's sister Betsy had already written of Keller: 'Ein sehr bedeutendes, dichterisches, ich möchte sagen, malerisches Talent. Schade daß die meisten seiner Schriften nicht wohl von Frauen in die Hand genommen werden können. So, wie man sagt, seine neuesten "Legenden".'[40] In an attempt to avoid public indignation, Meyer used Betsy to test whether a story would be acceptable to women readers; Storm too noted the reactions of women listeners when reading out drafts. As writers had families, relatives, and friends and occupied a respected place in their society, they could not afford to court scandal and perhaps blight the fortunes of their entire family. Thus Storm, mindful of his sons' future careers, the marriage prospects of his daughters, and the general reputation of the family, insisted on all sorts of middle-class conventions and on closely guarded secrecy about compromising matters. The pressures of social existence pushed writers towards conservative, conformist positions. At the same time, the strictness with which middle-class society banned certain taboo topics only heightened the readiness, both conscious and unconscious, on the part of many readers to collude with authors broaching issues which were also burning topics in their own lives. However, for this to be possible the work could not afford to deliver too rude a shock to a reader's moral standards since this would only provoke indignation and rule out any further sympathetic response. The fact that both form and content often reflected the writer's own partial entrapment in the taboos at issue facilitated empathy. A more direct, unequivocal presentation from a critical, uninvolved 'outsider' could not have had the same effect. There would have been no hope of manoeuvring readers towards positions at variance with their present stance.

Cloaks and camouflage were, however, *de rigueur*. When Meyer decided to explore in *Die Hochzeit des Mönchs* (1883/4) the sadomasochism bred by sexual repression and to hint that the Christian cult of suffering might also contain such elements, the topic obviously had to be masked. Despite his precautions relatives, friends and readers expressed their distaste. Of the forty copies stocked by a Zurich bookseller, thirty-nine had to be sent back to the wholesaler. When Meyer, whose relationship to his sister Betsy had always been close, broached the subject of incest in *Die Richterin* (1885), the historical mask was again a *sine qua non*. Profoundly uneasy about the story, he asked Rodenberg, the editor of the *Deutsche Rundschau*, to cut out or tone down anything crude or sensual that was not absolutely necessary to achieve an effect.[41] The work offers little insight into incest since, to make the topic aesthetically and morally acceptable, Meyer 'poeticised' it. High melodrama took over.

Prostitution figured very little in Poetic-Realist works. Safeguarding the purity of middle-class daughters and spouses and also the education and career of middle-class sons required prostitution and 'illicit' relationships. Precisely because they were so indispensable to society's arrangements, any serious discussion of the underlying socio-economic issues involved was taboo. In fact, even moralising, damning depictions tended to be thought inadvisable. In Keller's *Der Schmied seines Glückes* prostitutes are typically referred to *en passant* as 'verlorene Wesen'.[42] Fontane's *Stine*, despite being so removed from a work such as Zola's *Nana*, aroused such indignation because, while not containing any explicit sex scenes, it did not adopt a high moral stance.

However, there were topics which editors and readers simply would not tolerate and with which writers themselves could not cope. Reactions to the stories and novels of Leopold von Sacher-Masoch show where tolerance thresholds ended. Paul Heyse prefaced the eighth edition of his *Moralische Novellen* (1868) with an attack on prudery and conventions in 'An Frau Toutlemonde'. Yet he, too, referred to Sacher-Masoch's 'ekelhaftes Golashgericht von Wollust und Blutdurst'.[43] Respectable opinion was captured in the verdict:

> Die Nachtseiten des geschlechtlichen Lebens werden mit einer Kraßheit aufgedeckt, die auch für den Nichtprüden unanständig ist und die Grenze des Darstellbaren weit überschreitet. Das berückend schöne Weib mit Pelz und Peitsche prügelt und foltert den Mann, der in wahnsinniger Begierde zu seinen Füßen sich wälzt. Da kann man nicht mehr mitgehen. Das ist eine Literatur, welche gewisse im Handel verbotene Photographien zu illustrieren scheint, eine Literatur bestimmt nur für Männer, deren Aufgabe darin besteht, sich ein Rückenmarksleiden anzuleiden.[44]

A gay or lesbian sexual relationship was also taboo. Fontane referred in letters to homosexual friends but he did not treat homosexuality in his fiction. In Heyse's story *David und Jonathan* (1882) male friendship à la Platen is only an intermezzo: it has to be overcome for healthier emotions, more practical creativity, and heterosexual love. Storm wrote to Keller:

> Neulich wurde mir von einem Grafen Joseph Wallis aus Oestereich [*sic*] ein seltsames MS zur Begutachtung behufs Publication zugesandt; der Gegenstand war die geschlechtliche Liebe eines Mannes zu einem andern schönen und liebenswürdigen Manne, unglückliche leidenschaftliche Liebe und offenbar ein Selbstbekennntniß, in der Ich-Form geschrieben; höchst weichlich und widerwärtig; und das wollte der Mann, der übrigens ein armer, wohl von Jugend auf, Kranker ist, der Welt gedruckt vorlegen. Er hatte mir vor Jahr u. Tag schon einmal sentimental klagende Tagebuchblätter zugesandt. Der Geliebte hieß noch dazu Peter. Es thut mir leid, daß mir dieß Widerwärtige zum Schluß in die Feder kam.[45]

Equally, the social stigma attached to syphilis was such that it was banned from respectable literature. Storm, whose brother and youngest son suffered from the disease, shared the widespread almost hysterical attitude to it. In *Schweigen* (1883) fear of the insanity which can occur in tertiary syphilis is replaced by the fear of the hero – Rudolf von Schlitz (!) – that a mental breakdown caused by pressure of work could recur. Storm's Poetic-Realist concern was that the story should not become a medical and psychological case study. The issue had to be a moral one: once tensions caused by concealing the breakdown from his bride are removed, Rudolf knows himself to be permanently cured. Keller applauded the treatment. The topic is poeticised and transfigured by linking plot and presentation to Carl Maria von Weber's opera *Der Freischütz.*

High among the beliefs which Poetic Realists were most reluctant to abandon was their faith in their capacity to mould people's feelings and shape society. Increasingly, however, they were forced to adopt a much less 'idealistic' view of their relationship to publishers, editors, and readers. They gained more insight into literature's position in the political, socio-economic and ideological nexus. Meyer especially thematised these problems. Thus Dante in *Die Hochzeit des Mönchs* (1883/4) depends on patrons who demand entertainment from art. Although he tactically makes concessions to their taste, his masked criticism of their lifestyle does not have any real impact. In *Das Leiden eines Knaben* (1883) Fagon, as Louis XIV's physician, enjoys a uniquely privileged position with regard to the liberties he can take; but all his efforts to open the king's eyes to the reality of his rule fail. Nevertheless, although bruised and fragile, the hope remained that the artistic presentation might sensitise readers and suggest the need for humanitarian solutions – even if the practical, socio-political means of achieving them remained uncertain. The principle of hope survived.

Of all the sacred beliefs of Poetic Realism the one that refused to die was the belief in art's autonomy and its unique characteristics – what Keller called its *Reichsunmittelbarkeit.*[46] Rather than question its statutes, writers were, as we have seen, all too ready to accuse themselves of faintheartedness and treason if they did not succeed in naturalising prosaic or sordid topics by poeticising them. Failing to achieve the quasi-divine transubstantiation of reality into art was the supreme aesthetic sin. Structure and unity, harmony and balance, resolution of disharmonies and affirmation of optimism remained sacrosanct commandments. Without trans-figuration and reconciliation art was nothing. Thus although Fontane was prepared to accept Zola's right to have his particular opinions about the world, this open-mindedness did not extend to matters of art: 'In Anschauungen bin ich sehr tolerant, aber Kunst ist Kunst. Da versteh ich keinen Spaß.'[47] Although prepared to introduce naturalist themes, the Poetic Realists remained citizens of another kingdom. Clinging as they did to the supposedly absolute, unchanging laws of 'true' art and *Dichtung*, they were trapped in an aesthetic time-warp. Yet to the end they saw themselves as defenders of the faith. The ultimate taboo held firm.

## NOTES

1. General studies on realism in Germany include: *Begriffsbestimmung des literarischen Realismus* (Wege der Forschung, 212), ed. R. Brinkmann, Darmstadt, 1969; F. Martini, *Deutsche Literatur im bürgerlichen Realismus 1848–1898*, Stuttgart, 1962; W. Preisendanz, *Wege des Realismus. Zur Poetik und Erzählkunst im 19. Jahrhundert*, Munich, 1977. Those focussing on the period after 1848 include: *Realismus und Gründerzeit. Manifeste und Dokumente zur deutschen Literatur (1848–1880)*, ed. M. Bucher et al., 2 vols, Stuttgart, 1975–76; U. Eisele, *Realismus und Ideologie. Zur Kritik der literarischen Theorie nach 1848 am Beispiel des "Deutschen Museums"*, Stuttgart, 1976; *Vom Nachmärz zur Gründerzeit. Realismus 1848–1880* (Deutsche Literatur. Eine Sozialgeschichte, 7), ed. H.A. Glaser, Reinbek, 1982; W. Hahl, *Reflexion und Erzählung. Ein Problem der Romantheorie von der Spätaufklärung bis zum programmatischen Realismus*, Munich, 1971; H. Kinder, *Poesie als Synthese. Ausbreitung eines deutschen Realismus-Verständnisses in der Mitte des 19. Jahrhunderts*, Frankfurt a.M., 1973; *Theorie des bürgerlichen Realismus*, ed. G. Plumpe, Stuttgart, 1985; H. Widhammer, *Realismus und klassizistische Tradition. Zur Theorie der Literatur in Deutschland 1848–1860*, Tübingen, 1971; idem, *Die Literaturtheorie des deutschen Realismus 1848–1860*, Munich, 1977. See also the section on the post-1848 period in F. Sengle, *Biedermeierzeit. Deutsche Literatur im Spannungsfeld zwischen Restauration und Revolution. 1815–1848*, vol. 1, Stuttgart, 1971, 257–91.
2. See Bucher, *Realismus und Gründerzeit*, vol. 1, 34f., and Widhammer, *Realismus und klassizistische Tradition*, 57, 64, 93.
3. See *Gottfried Keller. Dichter über ihre Dichtungen*, ed. K. Jeziorkowski, Munich, 1969, 83ff.
4. Widhammer, *Realismus und klassizistische Tradition*, 70, 86; Plumpe, *Theorie des bürgerlichen Realismus*, 25.
5. It is true that in a work like G. Freytag's *Soll und Haben* (1855) the concern to establish a clear, superior national identity for the Germans already shades into racism in the respective presentation of a German, Jewish or Slav nature.

6.  G. Freytag, *Soll und Haben*, 2 vols, Leipzig, 1858, vol. 1, 230.
7.  See Theodor Storm, *Sämtliche Werke in vier Bänden*, ed. K.E. Laage and D. Lohmeier, Frankfurt a.M. 1987–88, vol. 1, 780ff.
8.  See Widhammer, *Realismus und klassizistische Tradition*, note 82, 69.
9.  See my article 'Storm at the foot of the cross', *The Germanic Review*, 59 (1984): 82–89.
10. See Bucher, *Realismus und Gründerzeit*, vol. 1, 36ff.;
11. See Widhammer, *Realismus und klassizistische Tradition*, 60ff.
12. Cf. Plumpe, *Theorie des bürgerlichen Realismus*, 11f.
13. O. Ludwig, 'Harte Zeiten von Dickens', in O.L., *Werke in sechs Bänden* (in 2), ed. A. Bartels, Leipzig, n.d., vol. 6, 344–7.
14. T. Fontane, *Sämtliche Werke* (Hanser Ausgabe), *Aufsätze Kritiken Erinnerungen*, vol. 1., *Aufsätze und Aufzeichnungen*, Munich, 1969,
15. See Widhammer, *Realismus und klassizistische Tradition*, 55–65.
16. Ibid., 59ff., and Plumpe, *Theorie des bürgerlichen Realismus*, 19.
17. Plumpe, *Theorie des bürgerlichen Realismus*, 18f., 161–83.
18. Fontane, *Aufsätze und Aufzeichnungen*, 242.
19. R. Prutz, 'Friedrich Hebbel', *Deutsches Museum*, 14(1864), no. 1: 6–10, 67–73. Quoted here from Bucher, *Realismus und Gründerzeit*, vol. 2, 446.
20. J. Schmidt, 'Der neueste englische Roman und das Prinzip des Realismus', *Die Grenzboten*, 2. Sem, 4(1856): 466–474. Quoted here from Plumpe, *Theorie des bürgerlichen Realismus*, 116.
21. Ibid., 185–209.
22. T. Storm to I. Turgenjew, 9.12.1864, in K.-E. Laage, *Theodor Storm. Studien zu seinem Leben und Werk*, Berlin, 1985, 91.
23. Ludwig, *Werke*, vol. 6, 'Der Poetische Realismus', 156–9, 156f.
24. See K.-G. Faber, 'Realpolitik als Ideologie', *Historische Zeitschrift*, 203(1966): 1–45, and my D.Phil. thesis, *The Presentation of Political, Social, and Religious Issues in the Work of C.F. Meyer*, Oxford, 1969, 128–66.
25. See my *Theodor Storm. The Life and Works of a Democratic Humanitarian*, Oxford, 1992, 137–50.
26. G. Keller, *Sämtliche Werke und ausgewählte Briefe*, ed. C. Heselhaus, 2 vols, Munich, 1958, 1963², vol. 2, 325.
27. C.F. Meyer, *Sämtliche Werke. Historisch-kritische Ausgabe*, ed. H. Zeller and A. Zäch, Berne, 1958ff., vol. 13, 320.
28. See E. Swales, *The Poetics of Scepticism. Gottfried Keller and "Die Leute von Seldwyla"*, Oxford and Providence, 1994.
29. Storm, *Sämtliche Werke*, vol. 3, 128f.
30. Meyer, *Sämtliche Werke*, vol. 13, 24.
31. See my article 'C.F. Meyer's *Die Richterin*. A tussle with Tolstoy', *Trivium*, 9(1974): 39–49.
32. D.F. Strauss, *Der alte und der neue Glaube*, Leipzig, 1872, passim.
33. Storm, *Sämtliche Werke*, vol. 2, 518f.
34. Ibid., vol. 2, 953ff.
35. Ibid., vol. 3, 54.
36. Ibid., 770f.
37. Ibid., 13, 783f.
38. See Meyer, *Sämtliche Werke*, vol. 13, 291.
39. Ibid., 293.

40. Betsy Meyer to H. Haessel, 26.4.72., in M. Nils, *Betsy Meyer. Die Schwester Conrad Ferdinand Meyers*, Frauenfeld and Leipzig, 1943, 126.

41. See Meyer, *Sämtliche Werke*, vol. 12, 346f.

42. Keller, *Sämtliche Werke*, vol. 2., 318.

43. Heyse to Storm, 6.9.75, *Theodor Storm – Paul Heyse. Briefwechsel*, ed. C.A. Bernd, vol. 1, 1969, 89.

44. F. Lemmermayer, 'Leopold von Sacher-Masoch', *Moderne Dichtung*, 1, Bd 2, Heft 5, Nr 11, 680–6. Here quoted from *Leopold von Sacher-Masoch. Materialien zu Leben und Werk*, ed. M. Favin, Bonn, 1987, 136.

45. Storm to Keller, 27.11.82, *Theodor Storm – Gottfried Keller. Briefwechsel*, ed. K.-E. Laage, Berlin, 1992, 99.

46. Keller to Rodenberg, 2.12.1880, in G.K., *Gesammelte Werke* (Schweizerische Klassikerausgabe), 2nd supplementary vol., *Briefe von 1856 bis 1890*, Zürich, 1944, 345.

47. Fontane to Emilie Fontane, 12.6.1883, in T.F., *Werke, Schriften und Briefe* (Hanser Ausgabe), Section 4, *Briefe*, vol. 3, Munich, 1980, 255.

# 5

## OF MADNESS AND MASOCHISM:
## SEXUALITY IN WOMEN'S WRITING AT THE
## TURN OF THE CENTURY

———⟋⟍⟍⟋⟍———

### *Chris Weedon*

Das Weib, die Mutter künftiger Geschlechter…Die Wurzel, die den Baum der Menschheit trägt…Ja – aber erhebt ein Mädchen nur die Hand, will sie nur einmal trinken aus dem Becher, den man ihr von Kindheit an fortwährend lockend an die Lippen hält – zeigt sich auch nur, daß sie durstig ist…Schmach und Schande! Sünde – schamlose Sünde – erbärmliche Schwäche – hysterische Verrücktheit! (GR, 374)

Romance, love and the unspoken promise of sexual passion were central to the culture of middle-class femininity in late nineteenth- and early twentieth-century Germany. Fed by a diet of popular fiction, young women longed for love and passion, while their families looked for suitors who would provide good social and economic alliances. The middle-class woman's destiny was as wife and mother, often in a relationship where sex was experienced as duty rather than pleasure. Taboos around sexually active women, lack of knowledge of female sexuality, taboos on contraception, venereal disease, and the incessant chain of debilitating pregnancies rendered the reality of sex in most married women's lives far from any romantic ideal. Yet for those women confined to an often lonely life of celibacy for lack of a willing suitor and for those subject to sexual exploitation as servants or prostitutes, marriage seemed by far the more desirable option.

The emergence in the 1890s of a climate in which issues of female sexuality could be raised at all owed much to developments in German feminism. Ideas about men and women in the older German feminist movement were coloured by traditional notions of femininity. These included the assumption that women did not have sexual needs comparable with those of men. While women's organisations concentrated on girls' education and charity work, double standards of sexual morality prevailed unchallenged. These allowed men an active and promiscuous sexual life while women's sexuality was sanctioned only within the confines of the marital chamber and then primarily for the purposes of procreation. Women's rights to the free expression of sexuality and their rights to protection from exploitation by men would not become live issues within the women's movement until the 1890s.

In 1894 a new feminist umbrella organisation, the Bund deutscher Frauenvereine was founded. Radicals such as Minna Cauer, Anita Augspurg, Maria Stritt, Helene Stöcher, Lida Gustava Heymann, and Adele Schreiber, gradually gained influence. The newly emerging radical wing of the women's movement was anxious to reform the marriage laws and bring in a more liberal attitude to sexuality.[1] The term *neue Ethik* came into circulation. It was used to refer to a liberalisation in sexual matters and the right to determine one's personal life for oneself. It also included demands for equal rights for wives where their children were concerned, easier divorce, an improvement in the position of unmarried mothers and illegitimate children, and the rights of unmarried women to sexual relations. The programme for this new ethic was mainly represented by the Bund für Mütterschutz und Sexualreform.[2] Beyond the ranks of the women's movement, debates about female sexuality and the related issues of contraception, abortion and venereal disease remained tabooed.[3] Despite the best efforts of radical feminist activists, the turn of the century was a period dominated by unyielding social norms governing the education and lifestyles of middle-class girls and women. Meanwhile working-class girls, many of whom were employed in domestic service, remained the victims of sexual abuse which often drove them into prostitution. Rates of prostitution in Berlin at this time were extremely high, as were rates of venereal disease, which was often brought home to middle-class wives by their husbands.[4] Tabooed in respectable middle-class society, these issues were none the less central to women's lives.

How then did issues of sexuality surface in women's writing between 1890 and 1914, a period in which many women writers were publishing novels, poetry and non-fiction and had large female readerships? In this chapter I will examine how female desire figured in prose writing by Gabriele Reuter, Hedwig Dohm,

Helene Böhlau, Lou Andreas-Salomé and Franziska zu Revent-low. These authors illustrate a range of positions on the question of female sexuality. They demonstrate attempts to negotiate or challenge dominant thinking about women within the limits of what could be said at this time.

—*◆◆◆*—

In 1895 Gabriele Reuter published a novel, *Aus guter Familie. Leidensgeschichte eines Mädchens*, which immediately became a best-seller. It tells the story of Agathe Heidling from her confirmation at the age of seventeen to her nervous breakdown in her early thirties. Agathe is unable to marry since she has no dowry: her mother's fortune has been dissipated paying off her brother's gambling debts. At this time spinsters were a widely disparaged social group who were seen to have failed as women. While the culture of femininity for middle-class girls focused their aspirations on romance, love and marriage, society at large privileged motherhood as woman's mission in life. From conduct books to popular fiction a clear message rang through: fulfilment lay in meeting, marrying and satisfying the needs and desires of a man and in bearing and raising his children. Reuter's novel explores the psychological and emotional consequences of spinsterhood and enforced celibacy for women.

Confined to the parental home, Agathe is thwarted by her father in her attempts at self-education. He deprives her of books that he considers incompatible with his ideas of true woman-hood: 'Er schätzte eine positive Frömmigkeit an dem weiblichen Geschlecht. Für den deutschen Mann die Pflicht – für die deutsche Frau der Glaube und die Treue'(GR, 18). In the novel religious faith functions not only as a substitute for knowledge, but also as a channel for sexual feelings. Agathe is subject to a strict religious education which stresses renunciation of the world of physical pleasures. Yet this religion sends out mixed messages. The hymns, for example, use erotic language and start what becomes for Agathe a habit of displacing sexual needs and feelings into religious pietism.

Despite her father's best intentions, Agathe does not remain ignorant of sexuality. At an early age her precocious friend and later sister-in-law Eugenie, who has been spared a repressive religious upbringing and has learned a relaxed attitude to sexuality in her flirtatious encounters with young men in her father's factory, teaches her about sex. Throughout the novel Eugenie represents that physicality which both fascinates and horrifies Agathe. Unlike Eugenie, Agathe cannot see sexuality as something natural and wholesome. Yet she is aware that the demands made on her by religion are contradictory:

> Besitzet, als besäßet Ihr nicht – genießet, als genösset Ihr nicht! – Auch der Tanz – auch das Theater sind erlaubt, aber der Tanz geschehe in Ehren, das Vergnügen an der Kunst beschränke sich auf die reine, gottgeweihte Kunst. Bildung ist nicht zu verachten – doch hüte Dich, mein Kind, vor der modernen Wissenschaft, die zu Zweifeln, zum Unglauben führt. Zügle Deine Phantasie, daß sie Dir nicht unzüchtige Bilder vorspiegele! (GR, 20)

Agathe's own sexual awakening comes at school where she develops passionate feelings for Eugenie who rejects her for other friends. She transfers her feelings to her cousin Martin but is profoundly shocked when he tries to kiss her. Already she has learnt to despise real physicality and sexuality, indulging instead in an imaginary anticipation of her future husband: 'Sie wollte auch immer streng und abweisend bleiben – bis – ja bis Er kommen würde, der Herrlichste von allen!'(GR, 64). The opposition which the novel sets up between an intellectual and emotional desire for love and sexual contact and a profound hostility to sensuality and physical contact sows the seeds of mental illness in Agathe. Her hatred of the physical extends to her own body: she is ashamed of its fullness. She does not trust or approve of her own attractiveness, yet wants male approval and success. To escape these contradictions she turns to obsessive imaginary romantic relationships with the poet Byron and a painter called Adrian Lutz. Despite his bad reputation, Lutz is for Agathe an ideal drawn from fairy tales and religion. Her image of him is only broken when she discovers that he has a child by an actress. Unable to cope with her jealousy, she falls seriously ill in a gesture that prefigures her future mental illness. On her recovery she turns to pietism.

Despite her puritanical attitudes to the physical, spinsterhood is a future that Agathe wishes to escape at all costs. At twenty-four, therefore, she determines to marry a friend of her father's, Raikendorf, whom she does not love but respects. His proposal fills her with masochistic feelings of devotion: 'Nie – nie wollte sie Raikendorf vergessen, daß er ihr den Abend – die Fülle von freundlichen Hoffnungen gegeben. Ihr ganzes Leben sollte ein

Dienen dafür sein. Nicht genug konnte sie sich darin thun, ihn als ihren Herrn zu erhöhen und sich zu erniedrigen'(GR, 262). However, Raikendorf, like other potential suitors, will not marry her without a dowry. This encounter reawakens her desire for sexual contact: 'Seit Raikendorf sie beinahe geküßt hatte, träumte sie nur noch von diesem Kuß – nicht mehr von ihm, von seiner Persönlichkeit, sondern einzig von dem Kuß, den sie schon zu fühlen meinte und der ihr dann in Luft verhauchte. Er war ihr letzter Gedanke beim Einschlafen, ihr erster beim Erwachen'(GR, 269). She dreams of experiencing passionate adventures while remaining 'das vornehme, zurückhaltende Mädchen': 'Sie spielte mit der Gefahr, nach der sie sich sehnte, bis sie vor der leisesten physischen Annäherung eines Mannes instinktiv zurückschauerte'(GR, 271).

The climax of the novel comes after the death of Agathe's mother. Agathe has taken over the running of the household and her life is reduced to a never-ending succession of tedious and unrewarding tasks. Her answer to her own desires and needs is a vigorous attempt to suppress them in an act of sheer willpower. This resolve, which inevitably takes its toll on her health, is broken on a holiday ordered by her doctor, when, in a Swiss hotel, she meets her cousin and childhood sweetheart Martin Gressinger, now a respected writer. They re-establish their previous closeness and Martin urges her to break loose and stay in Switzerland. Yet, unacknowledged by herself, Agathe's interest in Martin is first and foremost sexual, whereas his interest in her does not extend beyond liberating her from the confines of a narrow bourgeois lifestyle. Yet Agathe is not only financially and emotionally tied to her repressive father, she has internalised social conventions of femininity which make it impossible for her to act solely in her own interest. Repressed sexual desire resurfaces in her when Martin engages in a flirtatious interchange with a waitress. As before it takes the form of repudiation: 'Er war ihr widerwärtig geworden, aber noch widerwärtiger war sie sich selbst. Was hatte sie an einem solchen Manne finden können? Wie war sie zu der Verirrung gekommen, ihn für groß und bedeutend zu halten? Und warum riß ein so grausamer Schmerz an ihrem Herzen?'(GR, 357). The relationship comes to a climax on the following evening when, filled with murder and suicide fantasies, Agathe is accused by Martin of being 'klein und sentimental und weiblich eitel'(GR, 360). Finally acknowledging her feelings, she screams that she loves him and runs off into the night. He leaves the next morning. She has a nervous breakdown.

During her mental illness, Agathe is cared for by Eugenie, who takes her against her will to a spa resort. In the women's sanatorium there are hundreds of women from all parts of Germany: 'Fast alle waren sie jung, auf der Sommerhöhe des Lebens. Und sie teilten sich in zwei ungefähr gleiche Teile: die von den Anforderungen des Gatten, von den Pflichten der Geselligkeit und den Geburten der Kinder erschöpften Ehefrauen und die bleichen, vom Nichtstun, von Sehnsucht und Enttäuschung verzehrten Mädchen'(GR, 369f.). Agathe's hatred of her sexually secure and attractive sister-in-law grows to the point where Eugenie's openly flirtatious relationship with the head doctor provokes Agathe to attempt to murder her. Symbolically she is murdering the sensuality and physicality that she both desires and despises. There follow two years in mental hospitals, after which she is returned to her father, docile, brain damaged, no longer knowing what she is missing in life. Her future will be a home for women. In *Aus Guter Familie* madness is the symptom of repressed sexuality, distorted by religion, which can find no legitimate expression. That a respectable, middle-class spinster should have sexual needs and desires was unthinkable in Germany at this time. Equally unthinkable was the possibility that a widow approaching sixty, who had led a life of utmost respectability, might also experience strong sexual feelings for a young man.

—*ᴗᴗᴗ*—

In Hedwig Dohm's 1894 novella, *Werde, die Du bist*, madness again figures as the vehicle for the expression of female sexuality.[5] Judged by the social norms of the day, the heroine Agnes Schmidt, who has been confined to a mental hospital for two years, has led an exemplary life as housewife and mother. In her own eyes, in contrast, she has lived a life devoid of love or self-fulfilment. Her case completely mystifies her doctors. The key to her condition is to be found in the diary which she kept from the death of her husband to the onset of her madness. It traces her growing self-awareness and critical attitude towards herself and society.

After her husband's death Agnes travelled to the North Sea and to Italy. She saw herself as fighting for her individual identity against her former 'little housewife's soul'. This new identity included sexuality. On Capri she finally experienced the passion that was lacking throughout her married life when she fell in love with a young doctor. Aware of social attitudes to sexual feelings in older women, she was ashamed to express her feelings and was driven to fantasise that her old age was a dream from which she would awake once more young and beautiful. This fantasy was reinforced when the young man gave her a bunch of myrtle. When he betrayed her fantasy by jokingly calling her 'Grandmother Psyche', she returned to Berlin and fell ill. During her illness Agnes clings to the symbols of her more youthful, sexual self. This discovery of her sexuality both enhances her appearance and gives her a visionary quality that brings her a sense of fulfilment missing in the rest of her respectable life. Her recovery is brought about by the chance visit of the young doctor to the hospital. Yet returned to normality and on the verge of death, Agnes values her madness over her former asexual respectable life.

If it were only the conventions of bourgeois life which denied women the space in which to realise their sexual desires and needs, the problem might be fairly easily resolved. Even the internalisation of repressive attitudes to sexuality in young women could be transformed by a more liberal sexual climate in which sexuality would be seen as integral to a healthy woman and not by definition taboo or immoral. Yet certain texts by women writers of the period suggest that the problem goes much deeper. The way in which men see and define women as not their equals and not fully human makes the combination of sexuality and reason, knowledge and artistic creativity in a woman impossible. While society dictates that women remain unmarried if they are to have a life beyond domesticity and that, if unmarried, they forego their sexual needs, male views of women continue to define them only in terms of their sexual and procreative roles.

—◦◦◦—

In 1899 Helene Böhlau published a radical novel *Halbtier* which, despite its negative depiction of German feminism, reads as an explicitly feminist text. Like *Aus guter Familie*, it became a controversial bestseller. It tells the story of Isolde Frey and her elder sister Marie, *höhere Töchter* brought up in a repressive patriarchal family of very limited means. The family's fortunes change when the girls inherit a legacy which can ensure financial independence and attract suitors. As in other novels of the period, the father, Herr Frey, is presented as a man who treats his wife callously while behaving with the license of a bachelor outside the home.[6] Frau Frey, for her part, had married for love, against the wishes of her family, but she is destroyed by the never-ending tasks of making ends meet and trying to please an ungrateful and domineering husband. Her daughter, Isolde, however, who is the central focus of the narrative has little sympathy with her, identifying rather with her father. Moreover, Frau Frey has internalised patriarchal values: 'Die Frau hat sich nach dem Mann zu richten, und wie der ist, so ist er, und was der tut, das tut er' (HB, 164). She is instrumental in perpetuating the social mores which have destroyed her. Thus, as a mother she keeps her daughters in ignorance of life and in particular of sexuality and of the negative sides of her marriage: 'Sie hatte auch "von nichts" etwas gewußt. Dann waren die Überraschungen gekommen! Weshalb das so sein mußte, wußte Mama nicht. Es war hübsch so – und anständig. Alle Mädchen aus gutem Haus mußten so ins Leben hinausgehen'(HB, 110f.).

From early adolescence Isolde aspires to the respect and the full life that are enjoyed solely by men. She has a romantic view of an alternative life in which people walk naked and free without shame in a world of gold, ivory and mother of pearl. This ideal springs from her experience of an exhibition of paintings by Henry Mengersen which she saw in Munich at the age of fifteen. Mengersen inspires in her an almost religious and masochistic devotion: 'Wie Gottes Sohn empfand sie ihn. Und ob er schön und elegant, oder häßlich und verschabt war, was ging das sie an? Wie einen Teppich hätte sie sich vor seine Füße breiten mögen'(HB, 61). He, on the other hand, finds her novel: 'Ja, das war etwas Urweltliches; und so etwas lief in modernen Kleidern umher, ließ sich höhere Tochter nennen, benahm sich ganz ehrbar, wie andere auch. – Wie sie dastand! – Die verkörperte Liebes – und Lebenssehnsucht. So, in dieser Gefühlssituation hatte er das Weib noch nie gesehen. Das war ihm neu'(HB, 71). What Mengersen sees is a sexual woman and for him sex is the essence of woman. Intellect is misplaced in a woman: '"Entsetzlich," denkt Henry Mengersen und sieht wieder auf Isolde, das Weibliche in der Natur! Dies blinde, Sich-ins-Elend-stürzen-wollen, dies Gedankenlose, Nie-die-Folgen-überschauende. Egoistisch wie der Mann, aber so unsäglich dumpf, unbewußt, so instinktiv, so elementar'(HB, 86). In his eyes women are also masochistic: 'Ein Tier, das gejagt würde, wie das Weib gejagt wird, dem wüchse irgend etwas, ein Horn, ein Giftzahn – dem Weib wuchs nichts. Es wurde zahm und zahmer, widerlich zahm, das Haustier im vollsten Sinne!'(HB, 86f.)

Misinterpreting Mengersen's interest in her as love, Isolde agrees to pose naked for him. After the drawing session she feels an enormous longing for sexual contact and interprets the fact that he did not touch her as a sign that he is better than her. Mengersen, however, is looking for a wife with a fortune who will not challenge his view of women. Thus he chooses Isolde's sister Marie. Marie, too, soon discovers the full force of Mengersen's sexism which destines her for a life like that of her mother: '"Nichts bin ich ihm! Gar nichts! Das, was ich ihm bin, haß' ich!"'(HB, 127). Gradually the marriage destroys her, too. Isolde's encounter with Mengersen brings home to her for the first time the way in which women are regarded by men in this society: 'Das dumme, dumpfe, ins Ekelhafte gesteigerte Weibgefühl...das Gefühl, ein Wesen zweiter Ordnung zu sein, ein Wesen, das nicht Mensch sondern Weib ist, ein Wesen, das nicht wie ein Mensch fühlen und handeln kann, das nur geschlechtlich ist'(HB, 120). She is made to realise that the free expression of sexuality in a woman confirms her position as something less than fully human. Sexuality cannot be one aspect of a woman. According to patriarchal thinking, it is her essence. This confining definition of woman's nature is the basis for her exclusion from all areas other than wife and motherhood: 'Alles, was je gedacht, war vom Mann gedacht worden; alles, was je getan, war vom Manne getan worden. Nie war ihr das noch klar geworden, – ganz neu starrte sie das an. Das Weib und das Tier haben nichts getan und nichts gedacht, von dem man weiß'(HB, 121). This realisation produces in Isolde a single-minded determination to refute this view of women.

At this point the narrative jumps five years during which time Isolde dedicates herself to becoming a successful artist. Wanting to be recognised for more than her sexuality, she finds that she must repudiate her own sexual needs and desires. This has its costs. At times she feels that she has nothing from life, that one can only really feel whole in another person. She also desires a child. She knows she is beautiful and desired by men, enjoys this knowledge and longs for love but her desire to be recognised as more than sex enforces a life of celibacy. She must become like a man in denying those aspects of herself that make her a women in the eyes of society while foregoing the pleasures that men enjoy. She is indeed critical of the way that love becomes the single goal of women's lives: 'Wir haben die Liebe zu einer Art Untier gezogen, zu einer Bestie. Sie hat unsern Geist gefressen. Wir haben uns an ihr arm und dumm gefüttert'(HB, 181). Yet the novel suggests that to be without love, to be a spinster is to be sexually repressed and hypersensitive. *Halbtier* offers no solution to this state of affairs. By the end of five years of dedication to her art, Isolde has reached the stage where even Mengersen must recognise the value of her work. While she appreciates this, she continues to hate him as a man who has degraded her and destroyed her sister's life. The plot comes to its melodramatic climax when Mengersen, for whom all women remain sex by definition, whatever the evidence to the contrary, attempts to rape Isolde. She shoots him and as she faces her own death, becomes a martyr to the cause of women: 'Sie steht hier als der Begriff des ewigen bedrückten Weibes, des geistberaubten, unentwickelten Geschöpfes, dem alles geboten werden darf, das alles hinnimmt, waffenlos und rechtlos jeder Erniedrigung gegenüber' (HB, 178f.). There is no space in this society for women who lay claims to sexuality, intellect and creativity. At best a woman can live like the wealthy society hostess Mrs Wendland: 'Diese Frau hatte sich in Nichts nachgegeben, das sah man. Sie hatte ihr Leben mit sich selbst durchdrungen'(HB, 50). Yet Mrs Wendland is exceptional in more ways than one. She is a widow of independent means, but – and this is perhaps more important to the argument of the novel – she is also a foreigner who has not been subject to the processes of education and socialisation inflicted on German girls. She sees through Mengersen. For example, when he paints her as if she were a beast of prey, she sees this as a reflection of his attitude to women: 'Ich weiß, ich bin Herrn Mengersen ein Dorn, trotzdem er sehr liebenswürdig zu mir ist, weil ich ein wirklicher Mensch bin, lebe wie er lebt und bin so klug wie er ist. Wenn sich Herr Mengersen auch als Raubtier ausmeißelt, bin ich zufrieden'(HB, 59). Her autonomy lies in not being subject to or dependent on men: 'Mir geht es so wohl, Henry; wenn ich wieder zu Erde komme, werde ich wieder als unabhängige Witwe geboren. Ich bin ein freier Mensch'(HB, 66). For the ordinary or even exceptional German woman, however, the novel offers little hope.

—⟨∿∿⟩—

Patriarchal constructions of woman as sex, destined only for wife and motherhood or for prostitution, ruled out the possibility of woman being a rational, creative and sexual being. Women's internalisation of their patriarchally defined difference led to forms of masochism which looked to religion, society and nature for their guarantee and justification. The masochistic construction of femininity in Germany at the turn of the century is a repeated theme in women's writing. It is the key psychic dimension of women which accounts for their internalisation of repressive norms and it explains why they put up with their oppression and moreover extend it to their daughters. Men, mostly in the guise of fathers and husbands, play a crucial role in this process, but in the end it is the construction of femininity which is at issue.

—*ひひひ*—

Lou Andreas-Salomé turned her attention to the area of female sexuality in both her fiction and her essays.[7] Female masochism is the key theme of Andreas-Salomé's *Eine Ausschweifung*. A woman painter, Adine, tells of her first love an experience which has rendered her incapable of serious relationships with men. Despite her unusually liberal upbringing and her father's support for her artistic aspirations, Adine grows up with a masochistic attitude to erotic relationships between women and men. After her father's death, she falls passionately in love with and becomes engaged to her cousin Benno Frensdorff. She tries to become what he expects of her, a good traditional housewife, even giving up her art from the fear that it will spoil her relationship with him. Her attempt makes her ill and Benno eventually dissolves the engagement. Heartbroken, Adine goes abroad with her mother and becomes a successful painter in Paris.

After six years, at her mother's and Benno's request, Adine returns to Brieg to discover that Benno has asked her to come home because he still loves her, wants to marry her and to have a relationship with her in which they are equals. However, for Adine this is no longer possible: equality rules out sexuality which remains tied to masochism. Indeed, masochism is the predominant feature shared by all but one of the female characters in the story. Adine's mother sacrifices her own needs for her husband and daughter: 'Auf die Länge lieben wir keinen Mann so recht, wie den, der uns befiehlt'(A-S, 119). Similarly the eighteen-year-old crippled Baroness Daniela has a masochistic relationship with Benno: 'Aber das ja ist gerade das Herrliche und Merkwürdige: daß es so glücklich macht, sich ihm gegenüber klein und gering

vorzukommem und nur sein Mitleid zu verdienen'(A-S, 100).
Adine neither resists nor responds to Benno's passionate kisses:
'Und während ich seinen unsinnigen Küssen nachgab, regte sich
im mir etwas Wunderliches, ganz Zartes und beinahe Mütter-
liches – die Hingebung einer Mutter, die einem weinenden Kinde
lächelnd ihre nahrungschwellende Brust öffnet'(A-S, 115).
Looking for a way out and not wanting to hurt Benno's pride,
Adine lets him believe that she has another man in Paris:

> 'Staub zu seinen Füßen, – jetzt bin ich ihm das wirklich!'dachte ich
> nur noch dumpf, und irgendeine unklare Vorstellung dämmerte
> dunkel in mir auf, daß sich da soeben etwas Sonderbares begäbe:
> irgendeine wahnsinnige Selbsterniedrigung und Selbstunterwer-
> fung, – irgendein sich zu Boden treten lassen wollen –.
> Und doch löste sich dabei etwas in meiner innersten Seele, was
> sich bis zum äußersten gestrafft und gespannt hatte wie ein See-
> lenkrampf, – und es überflutete mich mit einer zitternden Glut, und
> es schrie auf und frohlockte –. (A-S, 118)

Adine traces her own masochism back to an incident in early
childhood when she saw her nanny's pleasure in being beaten by
her husband. The nanny had looked at him with 'verliebter
Demut'. She believes that it is an inherited attitude from which
women are only now beginning to liberate themselves.

There are examples in the literature of the period of women
who lay claim to respect as an individual, to a career outside the
home and to non-masochistic sexual relations with men. Such a
heroine is Fenitschka in Lou Andreas-Salomé's novella of the
same name in which she raises the question of whether it is possible for women to have sexual relations with men without losing
their hard gained independence and individual sovereignty.

*Fenitschka* is the story of a Russian woman who has studied in
Zurich and returns to St Petersburg to take up a teaching post.
There she falls in love and has to choose between marriage and a
career. She chooses her career. The story is told from the perspective of a German psychologist, Max Werner, who first meets Fenitschka in Paris and then over a year later in Russia. In Paris he is
attracted to her because she seems different from other women he
knows. She appears intelligent and has a 'von Geistesanstreng-
ungen zeugendes Gesicht' which, from his perspective, is at the
same time asexual (A-S, 8). In a West European context she appears
unconventional in her spontaneity. Yet, in her home setting in Russia in contrast she appears as essentially womanly. Her femaleness

transcends education: 'Der Ausdruck ihres Naturwesens war viel stärker als irgend etwas Angelerntes'(A-S, 23). Whether 'natural' or learned, Fenitschka's attitude to love is that it is something completely natural, healthy, all consuming and exalted:

'...da kommt nun etwas und nimmt einen hin, und man gibt sich hin, – und man rechnet nicht mehr, und hält nicht mehr zurück, und begnügt sich nicht mehr mit Halbem, – man gibt und nimmt, ohne Überlegung, ohne Bedenken, fast ohne Bewußtsein, der Gefahr lachend, sich selbst vergessend, mit weiter – weiter Seele und ohnmachtumfangenem Verstande – und das, *das* sollte nicht das Höhere sein?' (A-S, 47)

She despises the socially imposed conventions which deny her public access to love and force her to conduct her relationships in a clandestine fashion: 'Es ist das Erniedrigendste, was ich noch je gehört habe'(A-S, 38). In contrast, sexual double standards allow men to find secrecy engaging.

Much of the critical edge of the story comes from a confrontation between Werner's traditional views of women and what he learns from his relationship with Fenitschka. For example, after he sees her with her secret lover he is forced to ask himself (thinking back to Paris): 'Warum hatte er in beiden Fällen ihr Wesen so typisch genommen, so grob fixiert?... Es war ganz merkwürdig, wie schwer es fiel, die Frauen in ihrer rein menschlichen Mannigfaltigkeit aufzufassen und nicht immer nur von der Geschlechtsnatur aus, nicht immer nur halb schematisch'(A-S, 36). Nonetheless, Fenitschka's way of talking to him as an equal disturbs him profoundly. This and her sexual behaviour are for him examples of her behaving like a man. She finds the fact that he continues to treat her like a respectable woman patronising: 'Sie glauben, mich mitleidig ignorieren zu müssen, – und jetzt wieder – mich schützen, – ich bin doch kein Verbrecherin, die man aus lauter ritterlicher Schonung nicht erkennt'(A-S, 42).

As with Werner, so too in her relationship with her lover, Fenitschka comes up against men's inability to enter into equal relations with women. She is confronted by his desire to possess her completely and domesticate her. Yet she is not prepared to conform to traditional masochistic modes of relating to men. When her lover asks her to marry him, give up her career and move away from St. Petersburg she refuses: 'Nein! Ich kann es mir einfach nicht als Lebensziel vorstellen, – Heim, Familie, Hausfrau, Kinder, – es ist mir fremd, fremd, fremd! Vielleicht nur jetzt, vielleicht nur in dieser Lebensperiode. Weiß ich's? – Vielleicht bin ich überhaupt untauglich gerade dazu. – Liebe und Ehe ist eben nicht dasselbe'(A-S, 56). In drawing this distinction between love – which she sees as demanding equality – and marriage which remains essentially patriarchal, Fenitschka takes the only path open to her in this society. Yet, unlike for men, the price of maintaining a degree of autonomy and an identity outside of marriage is to forego marriage itself. If a woman is to maintain the respectability essential for a career, this means celibacy.

—◦◦◦—

Most women's writing in Germany at the turn of the century suggests that women cannot be both sovereign and sexual individuals. One exception is the work of Franziska zu Reventlow. In her prose writing, the alternative to a celibate independence and the respectable expression of sexual needs within the confines of a patriarchal marriage is unrespectable promiscuity.[8] Women can only afford such life-styles if they have independent incomes. Seen as scandalous by both mainstream German society and by feminists, zu Reventlow portrays women who subscribe to what were regarded as quite immoral views of female sexuality and women's place in society. Her heroines can combine sovereign individuality and sexuality, but only if they are willing to behave like men and forgo social approval. Like men they must divide the opposite sex into two groups: those to talk to and form friendships with and those for the bed. Like Andreas-Salomé, zu Reventlow also depicts sexuality as incompatible with the equality necessary for friendship.

Whereas all the texts discussed so far have been realist, zu Reventlow draws on irony and humour to put across her outrageous message. Arguably the positive depiction of a sexually immoral woman in fiction in this period ruled out realism. It required a degree of humour and irony which could be read by critics as less than serious. Moreover, a key target of her irony is male attitudes to women. *Von Paul zu Pedro. Amouresken*, published in 1912, is written as letters from an unnamed woman to a male friend in which the writer considers questions of women's sexuality and the relations between the sexes. Herself a beautiful woman, the writer has multiple relationships with men. While she realises that she should marry well and secure her future, she nonetheless opts for an uncertain but varied life in which she continues to have a series of love affairs. Her lifestyle is unacceptable to society at large. Yet she resists being treated by her friends as a 'problem'. Her desire for autonomy is incomprehensible to the men with whom she has affairs. She does not want married men to break up and leave their families for her. She maintains a distinction between sensual attraction and personal attraction. She has relationships that function only at the level of physical attraction and those which involve personal platonic friendships: 'Sie können es sicher immer noch nicht begreifen, daß ich mich in ein *objet* verlieben kann, aus dem ich mir im Grunde gar nichts mache, mit dem man sich nach zwei, drei Stunden zu Tode langweilt und nie im Leben ein richtiges Teegespräch führen könnte'(FvR, 13). She calls the objects of such relationships 'Paul': 'Paul ist eine Begebenheit, die immer von Zeit zu Zeit wiederkehrt. Nicht etwa, weil sie besonders tiefen Eindruck gemacht hätte – im Gegenteil, Paul ist immer etwas Lustiges, Belangloses, ohne Bedenken und ohne Konsequenzen'(FvR, 16). 'Pauls' are short-lived, come in all forms but can easily be confused with one another. Pauls also take relationships lightly and are rarely jealous.

This attitude to sexual relations, which society accepts in the case of men, is disturbing for both men and women when found in a woman. Indeed, the narrator's male friends refuse to accept such an attitude and look for explanations that reaffirm woman's natural monogamy. The narrator recounts how men accuse women of lack of discrimination when they have relationships with men of whom they do not approve. They deny that women can be attracted to all sort of different features in men. The male ego suggests that only men like themselves could be freely chosen. Indeed, as in *Fenitschka*, it is male attitudes which make serious sexual relations between men and women impossible. The narrator maintains a distinction between *Liebe* and *Erotik* which her male friends find inconceivable in a woman. Men, she argues, assume that women maintain at least the illusion that they are in love when they have sex with a man. She resists male generalisations about women. Women's sexual relationships may involve love or 'great passion' but often the motivation is pleasure, adventure, the immediate situation, politeness, or boredom. Even love, as distinct from mere sexual attraction, is short-lived. She describes it as a serious lasting emotion which may last months! Her attitude to love is egotistical but unlike men unpossessive.

The narrator argues that this independence in women is something that men find intolerable. One common reaction is the desire on the part of men to rescue such women:

Der Retter sagt gerne:'armes Kind' und streicht einem dabei die
Haare aus der Stirn – eine unausstehliche Angewohnheit, man darf
nie vergessen ein Taschenkämmchen mitzunehmen.
Manchmal bietet er auch pekuniäre Hilfe an, aber mit dem
Gefühl, daß für 'sie' doch eigentlich etwas Degradierendes darin
liegt und es ihr sehr peinlich sein müsse (ach, Doktor, es ist ihr
durchaus nicht peinlich, sie tut nur manchmal so – aus guter Erziehung). (FvR, 23)

Such men believe in women's natural monogamy – 'trotz der
schlagendsten Gegenbeweise'(FvR, 24). Often they want a child
by such a woman, 'vielleicht weil sie dann in seinen Augen "ganz
anders dastehen würde" – und er nimmt es übel, wenn sie lieber
darauf verzichtet'(FvR, 25).

It is the male desire to possess and control women which rules
out marriage for the narrator. Yet zu Reventlow ironises the drawbacks of an independent, promiscuous lifestyle in a society which
operates with sexual double standards:

Manchmal finde ich es verzweifelt unbequem, einen schlechten Ruf
zu haben. Wäre ich noch einmal achtzehn Jahre alt, so würde ich
die Sache anders angreifen, mich entweder ganz in die Tiefe bege-
ben oder darauf schauen, gesellschaftlich ganz oben zu bleiben.
Der Mittelweg ist in diesem Fall an Freuden vielleicht reicher, aber
jedenfalls bei weitem der unbequemste. Die Leute wissen so oft
nicht, für was sie einen nehmen sollen.
    Und der schlechte Ruf verpflichtet. Man kann sich so vieles
nicht leisten, was eine Unbescholtene ruhig tun darf. (FvR, 32)

Her conclusion is that a woman should establish herself socially
and financially before compromising herself. *Von Paul zu Pedro*
ironises many of the social attitudes of which feminists at this time
were critical. Above all it gives a vivid picture of the male attitudes
that make serious, sexual relations with a man impossible. Unlike
feminist depictions of the issues of female sexuality, however, zu
Reventlow, celebrates a promiscuous lifestyle for women, free
from any long-term commitments. It was this suggestion which
scandalised most sections of German society, even though it had
long been tolerated in the case of men.

We have come a long way here from the plight of Agnes Heidling or Isolde Frey. Our letter writer has the means and the self-confidence to live in spite of norms of respectability. Nonetheless, the
possibilities of realising sexual feelings and desires are still circumscribed by dominant patriarchal social values which deny women
the right to be both independent and sexual, inside and outside of

marriage. The long established dualistic ways of seeing women still render it impossible to depict a woman in fiction who can successfully combine her sexuality with other aspects of her being.

## NOTES

I would like to acknowledge here the generous support received from the Alexander von Humboldt-Stiftung which enabled me to spend a long period researching in Berlin.

**Abbreviations**
GR = Gabriele Reuter, *Aus guter Familie. Leidensgeschichte eines Mädchens*, Berlin, 1895.
HB = Helene Böhlau, *Halbtier*, Berlin, 1899.
A-S = Lou Andreas-Salomé, *Fenitschka. Eine Ausschweifung*, Stuttgart, 1898, reprinted by Ullstein, Frankfurt a.M., 1982.
FR = Franziska zu Reventlow, *Von Paul zu Pedro. Amouresken*, Munich, 1912, reprinted in Franziska Gräfin zu Reventlow, *Der Selbstmordverein*, Berlin, 1991.

1. For an overview of feminist approaches to sexuality in this period and a range of primary source materials see *Frauen und Sexualmoral*, ed. Marielouise Janssen-Jurreit, Frankfurt a.M., 1986.
2. The Bund für Mütterschutz und Sexualreform combined campaigns to change public attitudes with practical social work in the form of advice and financial assistance for unmarried mothers. The movement was bitterly opposed, even within the women's movement. Moderates such as Anna Pappritz, Helene Lange and Gertrud Bäumer developed an increasingly violent resistance to the ideas of new ethics and by 1908 had successfully contested the influence of the Bund für Mütterschutz und Sexualreform within the Bund Deutscher Frauenvereine.
3. Anna Pappritz reported in her study *Herrenmoral* (Leipzig, 1903) that cases of VD in Prussia alone at the turn of the century were in the region of 100,000 daily. Every second man over thirty entering marriage had gonorrhoea and every fourth or fifth syphilis.
4. See the introduction to Janssen-Jurreit, *Frauen und Sexualmoral*.
5. Hedwig Dohm, *Werde, die Du bist*, Breslau, 1894, reprinted by ALA Verlag, Zurich, 1988.
6. Further examples of husbands who emotionally abuse their wives can be found, for example, in Hedwig Dohm's novels *Schicksale einer Seele* (1899, *Christ Ruland* (1902) and Gabriele Reuter's *Ellen von der Weiden* (1900).
7. In addition to the fictional works discussed here, see, for example, Andreas-Salomé's essays 'Der Mensch als Weib'(1899), 'Gedanken über das Liebesproblem'(1900), and 'Die Erotik'(1910), all of which are republished in Lou Andreas-Salomé, *Die Erotik*, Ullstein, Frankfurt am Main, 1992.
8. Franziska zu Reventlow also wrote essays on women's nature which assumed woman's natural promiscuity. See 'Das Männerphantom der Frau'(1898), 'Was Frauen ziemt' (1899) and 'Erziehung und Sittlichkeit' (MS) republished in Franziska Gräfin zu Reventlow, *Der Selbstmordverein*, Verlag der Nation, Berlin, 1991.

# 6

## THE DOUBLE TABOO: MALE BODIES IN KAFKA'S *DER PROCEß*

—◦◦◦—

### *Elizabeth Boa*

As originally used in Polynesia, Melanesia, New Zealand etc.: set apart for or consecrated to a special use or purpose; restricted to the use of a god, a king, priests, or chiefs, while forbidden to general use; prohibited to a particular class (especially to women), or to a particular person; inviolable, sacred; forbidden, unlawful; also said of persons under a permanent or temporary prohibition from certain actions, from food, or from contact with others.

Thus the *Shorter Oxford Dictionary* on taboo as an adjective, and for a verb the definition runs:

To put (a thing, place, action, word or person) under a (literal) taboo. To give a sacred or privileged character to (a thing), which restricts its use to certain persons, or debars it from ordinary use or treatment; to consecrate, set apart, render inviolable; to forbid, prohibit to the unprivileged, or to particular persons. To put (a person, thing, name or subject) under a social ban; to ostracise or boycott.

Within this wealth of definitions lie two ostensibly opposite senses: on the one hand the taboo object is sacred and precious, a mark of status or power; on the other hand the taboo object or person is to be ostracised or barred or avoided as dangerous or unfit (certain foods, for example, or menstruating women). The taboo object at issue here is the phallus as 'the instrument set apart for or consecrated to a special use or purpose; restricted to the use of a god, a king, priests, or chiefs, while forbidden to general use; prohibited to a particular class (especially to women), or to a particular person; inviolable, sacred'. By the phallus I mean the symbolic representation or sign of the power accruing to men by virtue of their sex as distinct from the penis or more generally the male body as a material, sensuous apparatus.

My topic is the interaction of the symbolic taboo and the male body as represented in the work of Kafka. I shall argue that Kafka's representations of male bodies are sacrilegious in effect because they mix different levels of representation and blur the distinction between the symbolic and the literal or empirical: the sacred taboo is tarnished through its association or its interchangeability with empirical male bodies, for if the phallus is seen to be but the penis, then its sacred character is destroyed. Kafka's work explores male subjectivity as the site of a painful contradiction between phallus and penis, between the symbolic taboo object and actual fleshly bodies, between the symbolic role and actual desires. These second entities – penis, fleshly bodies, desires – take on, when juxtaposed with the sacred, a taboo aspect in the second sense of taboo. The sacred object, being forbidden to general use, turns what *is* in general use into the forbidden, the prohibited and the unlawful. Thus the male body is twice over taboo: as the sacred phallus; and as the site of desires which threaten to override the phallic interdict and which are hence forbidden.

Such timeless dilemmas are inherent in the patriarchal structure which gives men power over women, children, households, animals and the realm of nature *and* gives the old power over the young. This structure produces the archetypal clash between the sacred and the forbidden in the form of the generational clash between the father as possessor of the phallus and the rebellious son. But the *inter*-personal, generational conflict becomes also an *intra*-personal, internalised tension within male subjectivity. At the time Kafka was writing, the inherent instability of the patriarchal structure was compounded by many historical factors, notably the decline of traditional family-based father-power in modernising, liberal society. This is also the context of Freud's work which addresses the same perceived crisis in patriarchal authority.

Before turning to Kafka, I shall begin with textual issues by drawing a comparison with another literary example in order to illuminate the iconoclastic effects of key formal aspects of Kafka's writing which may be described as modernist. I shall then discuss the mixing of gender, class and racist ideology in the imperialist culture of Kafka's time with a view to illuminating two passages in *Der Proceß* in which a double tabooing of male bodies mixes disturbingly with class and racist discourse.

## POST-NATURALIST MODERNISM

One way of looking at modernism is as various brands of post-naturalism: for example imagism or the Rilkean *Ding-Gedicht* where things take on numinous, hermetic meaning; or sur- or hyperrealism which deploys estranged yet ultra-precise detailed representations; or Brechtian alienation of naturalist details of behaviour or milieu; or montage and collage techniques. Comparison with Thomas Mann's *Buddenbrooks* (1900) as a work on the hinge between realism and modernism where naturalistic details act as the nails in the hinge may serve as a way in to discussing some features of Kafka's work. Among the leitmotivic nails which hold *Buddenbrooks* together is the sequence of deaths which are recounted with increasing textual elaboration. As elements in the story, these deaths contribute to the growing sense of tragic decline, but the increasing textual elaboration of the processes of death conveys a quite different and morbid pleasure in mortality. Where old Johann dies without fuss and the Konsul dies offstage to the accompaniment of a pathetically fallacious thunder storm, the deaths of Elisabeth and Thomas are narrated at length with much gruesome naturalistic detail, one a death by drowning in fluid rising through the lungs and the other a stroke brought on by the botched extraction of a bad tooth. But along with the naturalistic medical detail, these deaths are also sexualised as orgasmic breakthroughs which assume characteristically female and male forms: Bethsy's death-throes appear as sensations dispersed throughout her whole body, as she lies *supine* on her back convulsively throwing wide her limbs, whereas her son experiences a concentrated cerebral orgasm which throws him down *prone*, his head and shoulders lying lower than the rest of his body, and which climaxes in an effusion of blood through facial orifices.

The effect is of two levels of representation: naturalistic scientific precision at the level of the story; but at the textual level there is a subversive unveiling of symbolic figures as the repressed returns in these deathly orgasms to turn the Matriarch into a writhing Maenad and to topple the Patriarch in the gutter. Symbolically, the patriarchal and matriarchal figures conduct a deadly struggle which culminates in the victory of the forbidden tabooed body over the sacred phallus, the sign of patriarchal power. (This outcome is partly the result of a debilitating quarrel between the Matriarch and her Patriarch-son, but that is not my topic here.[1]) It is still not easy to assess the ideological force of such double representation, but in Mann's novel the two levels are at least discrete. This separation allows for a clear distinction between the actual persons who die their painful deaths and their symbolic roles in the social order. Thus Mann evokes pity and love for his characters as individuals, but at the same time conveys an iconoclastic mockery of bourgeois patriarchy. The deathly sequence culminates with Hanno who is afflicted by a black deposit on teeth and gums and red pustules which break out all over his feminised body, again demonstrating the double level of scientistic, naturalist detail and a highly ambiguous symbolic punishment of a male body as object of narcissistic or homoerotic desire.

## A CONFUSION OF LEVELS

The stigmata of typhoid which afflict Hanno's body find their equivalent in Gregor Samsa's insect body or in the vulva-like wound in the boy's side in *Ein Landarzt*. However, whereas the discrete levels in *Buddenbrooks* enable the reader to distinguish between realist story and subversive sub-text, in Kafka's representations the levels do *not* remain discrete but are gruesomely intermingled. The two realms in *Der Proceß*, for example, of the everyday world and the court, parallel what appear in Mann's novel as the levels of the story and the text. In *Buddenbrooks* the realist story remains remarkably prim about sexual matters and is quite distinct from a covert, textual expression of the forbidden taboo desires underlying the Law and elicited by it. This secret yet blatant commentary celebrates the collapse of patriarchy in scandalously obscene images which transform tight-laced Bethsy in a dance of death and topple upright Thomas in a grotesque parody of the sexual act, yet without obliterating the realist dimension.

However, in *Der Proceß* the arrival of the court emissaries initiates a confusion of levels as the symbolic underpinnings of the social order emerge into the empirical world. The realist story and the symbolic figures intertwine because of a crossing-over of naturalistic techniques into representation of the symbolic. Three of the men who arrest Joseph K., the symbolic harbingers of justice, are at the same time employees at the bank and are portrayed in naturalistic detail. The warders, Franz and Willem, are not depicted emblematically as messengers wearing winged sandals but are all too naturalistically embodied, as witness fat, fleshy Willem. Such naturalistic detail attached to symbolic emissaries of justice immediately becomes loaded with obscene meaning; naturalist detail turns into the forbidden taboo because the phallus only acquires its sacred uniqueness as the origin of meaning through proscriptions and exclusions which turn the generality of bodies into the forbidden and tabooed. A comparable mixing of levels to obscene effect is implied in the juxtaposing of the symbolic female figure of Justicia in a painting with Leni in the *tableau vivant* of Block's humiliation.

In the great realist novels of the nineteenth century extradiegetic moral commentary and sub-textual poetic symbolism accompany and enrich the diegesis. Here the moral commentary and the poetic subtext have descended from above and risen from below to intrude blatantly into the story and have become hopelessly contaminated: the naturalistic embodying of the symbolic produces an effect of sacrilegious profanity. Seen as a confusion of the diegetic and extradiegetic textual levels paralleling the confusion of the transcendental and the empirical, the whole of *Der Proceß* is a sustained and unsettling *mise en abyme*: what should be an abstract moral commentary has turned up embodied in the likes of Willem.[2] At the same time the moral masterplot of law and justice is sexualised, like the Patriarch in the gutter in *Buddenbrooks*, as the two kinds of taboo – the sacred and the forbidden – quarrel.

In psychoanalytic terms, the distinction between the reality principle, the Symbolic and the Imaginary has collapsed, making it difficult to use metaphors of text and sub-text: the latent subtext has come out on the realist surface and also contaminated the masterplot of crime and punishment because the Law has descended from the heights to become embodied. In sum: the sacred taboo object, the Phallus, and the forbidden taboo, the body, are both unveiled and intrude directly into the diegesis to become dangerously interchangeable. Consider, for example, the book which Josef K. finds on the table in the scene of the first interrogation: 'Die Plagen, welche Grete von ihrem Manne Hans zu erleiden hatte'(K, 76). Marital sex is supposedly legitimate as opposed to pornography which depicts the whore. This title though, places wives as whores to service their husbands' perverse lusts. The book lies on the table in the equivalent position to the candle on Fräulein Bürstner's little bedside table which served as table in the scene of the arrest. Following the wooing of the virgin, symbolised in the white candle, marital relations follow on under the sign of the sacred phallus. However, the virgin's wooing took a grotesquely vampiric form and the title of the sacred book

on licit sex is doubly scurrilous through its childishly teasing circumlocution and the proverbially innocent and ultra-Germanic
names: Hans and a grown-up Gretel offer a whiff of incest as they
are transported from a children's fairy-tale into pornography for
adults.[3] Thus wooing and marriage under the sign of the phallus
are unveiled as a dirty obscenity. Moreover it is the law, the sacred
taboo, which taboos actual bodies and forbidden desires so producing the pornographic.

## BODY CULTURE

I now want to place Kafka's representations of male bodies in an
ideological context of the early twentieth century. First some
examples of the many bodies in Kafka's work: there is Gregor's
insect body in *Die Verwandlung* which contrasts with the final
image of his sister's healthy young body, or in *Ein Landarzt* the boy
with the wound contrasts with the groom with his 'offenes blau-
äugiges Gesicht'.[4] Or there are Franz and fat Willem as against the
whipper, who has a family resemblance to the groom albeit turning his attention to men rather than to maidservants: he is 'braun
gebrannt wie ein Matrose' and has 'ein wildes frisches Gesicht'(K,
111). In addition there are many other notable male bodies, the
hunger artist's, for example, set against his beautiful animal successor, or there is athletic Georg Bendemann who effortlessly
swings himself over into the river as against his yellow-faced,
sickly friend in Russia. Grotesquely enough, one of the last narra-
torial comments, perhaps echoing one of Georg's last thoughts
before he dies, recalls his parents' pride in their son's gymnastic
prowess as a schoolboy. Georg's father has two bodily appearances: as an old weak body whose natural functions result in dirty
underwear and as a giant rearing up above the cowering son.
These bodies cannot be allocated to any fixed taxonomy, but ten-
tatively, two kinds are evident: on the one hand healthy bodies in
good trim; on the other hand bodies which are either too thin or
too fat, or sickly and wounded, or old and dirty, or ugly and exud-
ing nasty fluids.

Cumulatively, then, there is a contrast between health on the
one hand, and on the other sickness or degeneration or ageing or
unfitness or some sort. This underlying discourse of bodily health
and sickness can be seen in the context of body culture in the early
twentieth century: the cult of youth and health, of hiking, cycling

and climbing, of dieting or banting, of chewing food forty times (*fletchern* after an American Dr Fletcher), vegetarianism, exercising every morning (*müllern*, after a German Dr Müller), fresh air and open windows, bathing, naturism. As Mark Anderson, Ernst Pavel and others have noted, these were all leading interests of Kafka who was obsessed with body culture.[5] There is also an alignment between the medical and the aesthetic: between health and attractiveness or beauty on the one hand and between degeneration or sickness and ugliness on the other. Several characters make efforts to control their body-shape. Things are complicated, however, in that ascetic control, which might be expected to produce a lean, healthy body, can misfire as in the case of the hunger artist: he overdoes mortification of the flesh and in any case fails to take exercise. So no amount of dieting on its own can produce the fit, beautiful body – you also need exercise and activity. Gregor Samsa shows initial athletic tendencies in crawling up and over the walls and ceiling of his room, and he is choosy about food. Even so, like the hunger artist he takes asceticism too far and inertly starves to death.[6]

The healthy, lean male ideal was ascetic, even asexual. In British public school culture, a cold shower would at best detumescently do away with the urge or at least hygienically wash away messy consequences. In such a body culture, glorified in the Olympic movement and memorably represented at the beginning of Leni Riefenstahl's Olympic film, the male body is an instrument for performance, not a sensorium for feeling. The cult of healthy athleticism and the pursuit of ascetic control over the body and its shape made a sacred taboo of the body while at the same time proscribing indulgence of forbidden appetites for the wrong food or the wrong pleasures. In particular masturbation was seen as debilitating, and some athletes still abstain from intercourse before the supreme performance to save bodily power. Such a culture at once made the body into a sacred taboo *and* tabooed it in the second sense as unfit and unclean in as far as it fell short of the ideal. The fluids which men produced found their acceptable goal in intercourse whether in procreating or being hygienically channelled off, so to speak, in the drain of the prostitute body. If that hidden product becomes too visible in involuntary or masturbatory emissions, the sacred fluid becomes obscene. Gregor Samsa's initial nasty sliminess and big, round squelchy tummy are a case in point; by the end he has achieved a dried-out flatness, but at the cost of his life.

## MEN DO, WOMEN FEEL

Throughout the nineteenth century there is a deep paradox at the core of sexual ideology. On the one hand, middle-class respectable women were envisaged as essentially maternal with a weak sexual urge: men are the subjects of desire, women the passive object; the male agent activates the substance of life of which the female body is the passive vessel. Yet on the other hand pleasure was construed as something which men arouse in women: men are agents and the male organ an instrument which produces effects and sensations in women. Or in another metaphor, man is the player and woman the instrument – in modernist painting, for example, the guitar – on which he plays. Thus although men are the desiring subjects, women are the more pervasively sensual beings who melt in the sensations which men activate; hence Bethsy's death throes all over her body in contrast to Thomas's concentrated cerebral orgasm. So the phallus has a double paternal and sexual aspect which produces the double morality and the division of women along class lines: asexual bourgeois fiancées, wives and mothers serve the paternal aspect; sexualised lower-class women answer the sexual aspect as mistresses, prostitutes or mythically heightened *hetairas*.[7] The sacred phallus in its double paternal and sexual aspect issues interdicts and faces various threats from rebellious sons, overwhelming mothers, treacherous wives or castrating *femmes fatales*. The threat at issue here, however, comes from the very sign of phallic power, the male body itself. Although men are the subjects of desire, the male body as sacred taboo or phallus, is not sensual. Men are agents who do or perform; it is women who feel. The male body as sensual, feeling flesh is always liable to overwhelm the subject with needs, desires or fears. It threatens phallic power and control and so is placed under ban or tabooed.

The connections between sexuality and athleticism, dieting and the other features of body culture in the early twentieth century are complex. The *Jugendstil* aesthetic idealised the androgynous look: young girls were slim and lithe; conversely the young male body took on a girlish grace. However, this cross-over threatened to obliterate sexual difference at a time when the franchise campaign and the left-liberal wing of the women's movement were demanding access for women to education and the professions so threatening male dominance and clearly defined sexual difference. Karl Kraus wrote with horror at women demanding the vote; men might as well, he suggests, demand government permission to menstruate.[8] Class difference too was under threat from social democracy. One expression of the backlash against the threat to traditional class and gender authority was a reassertion of strongly marked sexual difference, evident, for example, in the pages of the journal *Die Jugend* where *fin-de-siècle* androgyny was largely displaced by a more monumental and athletic, neo-classical male body and fleshier adult female shapes.[9]

A notorious expression of sexual hysteria at the beginning of the century was Otto Weininger's bestseller, *Geschlecht und Charakter* (1903).[10] This at once stoked anxiety by decoupling gender attributes from biological sex, yet reasserted an absolute difference between men as transcendent beings rising above nature and endowed with individuality or character and women as the sex, sunk undifferentiated one from another in fleshly existence, divided only into the categories of Mother or Whore. Weininger sets character against sex and proposes an extreme ascetic ideal for men who should transcend sensual existence altogether: in Weininger's pages the male body becomes the ultimate Apollonian icon, beautiful and untouchable, purified of all fleshly lust, like the Christian *noli me tangere* which was a common motif of the age with homoerotic undertones and which sharply set off Christ's lean, ascetic manhood against the Magdalene's sensuality; John the Baptist and Salomé are another such pair. Growing militarism contributed to an ideal ascetic manhood with homoerotic undertones.[11] Notoriously Weininger aligned Jews with femininity and helped to stoke sexist and racist ideology. Muscular Christians and clean-limbed Germanic heroes alike contrast with stereotypical Jew of anti-Semitism who overlaps with the negro and, in sub-Darwinian discourse, with the ape.[12] Jews and negroes lust after Christian or white women and evince a thick-lipped, animalesque sensuality as do ape-like lower-class men who have not developed character and are especially prone to incest.[13] Hence Jews, the anti-race, posed a sexual threat to the cultural and blood integrity of true races.[14]

A final element in the brew of sexual/racial/class ideology is the sado-masochistic construction of male sexuality arising from the double tabooing of the male body. I have argued that the masculine subject as agent and the phallic male body as instrument lead to the tabooing of the male body as a sensual apparatus which feels pleasures and pains and whose desires and fears threaten to overwhelm the subject. This splitting produces the sado-masochistic

split between the roles of performing subject who inflicts sensations and the sensuous object which feels. The sado-masochistic
structure is frequently mixed with racial and class elements and
may be figured in homoerotic terms as a ritual between men or in
a heterosexual transgressive cross-over whereby the man adopts
the feminine position of object and the woman acts as dominatrix.
This field of gender and sexual ideology mixed with racial and
class elements provides a context for many of Kafka's representations of the doubly tabooed male body. These bodily motifs belong
in the ambit of a pervasive theme in Kafka's work, namely the
sense of a collapsing old order, but also of the failure of liberalism
and of European enlightenment to create a new freer world.
Instead there is the threat of regression into barbaric violence,
played out in sexual terms and fuelled by class and ethnic antagonisms. In *Ein Landarzt*, for example, masculinity divides into a
rapacious (blue-eyed, Ayrian) sexuality, unrestrained by patriarchal law or by modern scientific enlightenment (the old doctor),
and a feminised masochism incapable of agency; likewise the feminine splits into a victimised woman or else appears as the disabling wound in the boy's feminised body. I cannot here survey
the whole range of such motifs but will limit myself to two scenes
in *Der Proceß*: the whipper episode and the last visit to the Advocate Huld, the former illustrating the intermingling of class and
sex in a homoerotic sado-masochistic ritual, the latter mixing
racial and sexual motifs in a heterosexual, sado-masochistic ritual.
Both take on the quality of a static *tableau vivant*. In thus becoming
pictorial they can also be associated with Titorelli's paintings
which show male judges but figure justice as a goddess, so sexu-
alising the discourse of law and punishment.

## SADISTIC PHALLUS AND MASOCHISTIC BODY

The episode with the whipper comes across as a ritual, beginning
with and culminating in two *tableaux vivants*: the first consists of the
three men as K. first sees and then re-sees them, seemingly quite
unaltered, the next day; the second is the moment of the first blow
of the whip as the whipper plays upon Franz's body as his instrument, eliciting the scream which is 'ungeteilt und unveränder-
lich'(K, 113). Although the whipping then continues, the effect is of
an endlessly repeated sequence and of an unchanging state sig-
nalled by the scream: someone is always about to inflict pain upon

another human being; the scream of agony from a tortured body is always to be heard by whoever chooses to listen. As William Dodd points out in comparing the new critical edition with the text as we have known it, K. re-sees not the end but the *beginning* of the scene, so that he has a second chance to intervene, which, however, he fails to take up.[15] The scene seamlessly combines social and psychic meaning to uncover the human relations underlying the economic system served by banks and to reveal tabooed impulses and desires. A lumber room in a bank is intrinsically incongruous; lumber rooms belong in the domestic sphere. Seen from the outside banks were, as many still are, architecturally eclectic temples devoted to the god of money, but *Der Proceß* moves behind the facade. The architectural double aspect of temple of mammon and lumber-room corresponds to the double aspect of the male body as sacred phallus yet site of forbidden, unclean lusts. Legally, Franz and Willem are guilty of petty pilfering of food and clothes, the crimes of poor men being punished in the temple of money.

The scene uncovers punitive law, whether the literal punishments meted out by the state or the psychological pressure of moral law, as a means of class oppression which corrupts rich and poor alike. Franz tries to escape his punishment at cost of his older colleague Willem and both lust after the food K. eats and the clothes with which he covers his body. The scene uncovers the fear and envy pervading hierarchical class society through uncovering bodies. K. is the fully dressed, middle-class spectator of a scene in which the lower-class players are semi-nude, typically the situation of obscene performances. The whipper is wearing a leather costume which leaves his arms, neck and much of his breast bare. Plunging décolleté dress in both sexes emphasises the secondary sexual difference between hard muscles and soft flesh.[16] Whereas it is conventionally acceptable under defined conditions for women to display parts of their bodies, male display is taboo among the respectable professional classes though frequently practiced by body-building members of the lower orders. The whipper has an exotic yet also freshly healthy aura: he is suntanned like a sailor and has a wild, fresh face. Such butch masculinity and wild freshness make him an erotically loaded figure in the eyes of sedentary K. who spends his life indoors. I do not know whether, given where and when Kafka was writing, the figure of the sailor signified homosexuality and a penchant for flagellation, but from the context one might hazard that it did. With his longing for fine underwear and his soft, vulnerable flesh, Willem plays the feminine role to the butch whipper. Willem's delight in getting other people's breakfasts for nothing is also naively childish, and it is a typical childhood experience to be at the mercy of someone bigger than oneself as it is to have to take one's trousers down for punishment. Such ritual re-enactment of childish bodily display and punishment are a common pornographic motif. To have something done to your body, as happens to children and women, is by that token the more shameful for men. Willem's feminisation and infantilisation are all the more unsettling because he is the older of the two warders: the fat boy is a typical victim of bullying; Willem is an incongruously elderly fat boy.

The fully clothed K. shows signs of the bullying temperament and takes a prurient interest in the procedures of the whipping, participating actively towards the end: when told that Willem and Franz, already naked to the waist, will have to take their trousers off, he answers simply 'Ach so'(K, 111) and then immediately notices the whipper's sunburn and wild freshness; a little later he studies the switch and asks if it can really cause such terrible pain; and it is he who pushes Franz down on to the ground.[17] The whipper's skilled flicking of the switch and his comment on Willem's fat in which the first stripes will be lost have a gruesomely playful note, and the whipping culminates in an obscene parody of the rhythm of intercourse as Franz writhes prone on the floor beneath the regular up and down movement of the whip. K. thus flirts with the positions of both whipped and whipper when he inquires whether the switch would really inflict pain, when he plays with the idea of whipping a judge, one of his own persecutors, and when he pushes Franz to the ground. The association of judges with erotic flagellation remains to this day a subversive cartoon motif. The playful aspect of the episode could point towards a ritualistic working through in the sexual realm of social power relations: play-acting by the lower-class figures for K. as spectator, or else a scene in his imagination. Whether imaginary or actual, either way the obscene subtext heightens the horror of the episode. It reveals K.'s secret pleasure at the *thought* of inflicting and suffering pain, so implicating a sado-masochistic male sexuality in making the workings of social power tolerable, even down to cruelties of the torture chamber which are all too actual.[18]

The double taboo splits male sexuality into sadistic phallic performance and masochistically sensuous body in an episode which reduces men to being either the subject or object of power, eroticises these positions as masculine and feminine/infantile and, in

K.'s responses and the disappointed hopes of the warders that they might become whippers themselves, suggests the inter-changeability of the roles. So too does K.'s situation as the mid-dle-class observer but also involuntary initiator of a punishment which he is helpless to stop, because it is a practice in an institution which he does not control. He is thus in an ambiguous position between being powerful yet powerless, whether to control his imagination and his desires or to control the social practices from which they spring or to which they contribute. K.'s sado-masochis-tic responses comes across as an expression or outgrowth of the position of middle-class men in a class and sexual culture which promises power to successful men, but only if they accept a hier-archical structure which will frequently position them also as the objects of power and which will leave those who reflect upon how the system works racked with an impotent guilt at their collusion. Sado-masochism is not peculiar to the modern world, but its growing prominence as a literary motif following its sexological naming by Krafft-Ebing suggests that it served as a vehicle for anx-ieties induced by the social changes in a competitive society.

The scene also gestures hermetically towards a more specific sense of guilt in the author towards his fiancée, Felice Bauer, through the name of the younger warder, Franz, whose fiancée, so he claims, is waiting for him outside. However, when K. leaves the bank there is no one there: the door once shut upon the scream of the guilty, the fiancée conveniently also disappears. Franz's pun-ishment has, it seems, nothing to do with his fiancée who is exter-nal to a scene being played out between men. At most Franz may be held guilty of keeping his fiancée waiting outside while K. watches him being whipped, half trying to stop it, half enjoying it. The absence of the fiancée and the self-division into a K. observing a Franz's punishment suggest that guilt about fiancées follows from a preceding sado-masochistic temperament and from a pref-erence for writing over marriage. Franz wipes off his own tears on K.'s sleeve, a motif which suggests the secret identity of the two figures, like the acrobat's tears in 'Erstes Leid' which also flow over the face of the impresario to suggest that they are two facets of the writerly self. Detlev Kremer reads *In der Strafkolonie* as a hermetic representation of writing as indulgent self-punishment; likewise the rise and fall of the whip here may be a monstrous shadow cast by the up-and-down of the pen.[19] The scene with Titorelli takes further this subtext concerned with writing as nar-cissistic self-observation and literature as self-display. Here K.

evinces an unconscious tendency towards exhibitionism as the heat of the attic drives him to start taking off his clothes so that he ends up lounging on the bed, in the position of an artist's model, under the lewd gaze of the little girls. This reversal of the gaze, turning the man's body into an object of female eyes, as well as the homoerotic undertone of self-display before another man, a painter of images, moves K. from the dominant masculinity of the clothed observer-subject towards objectification and bodily vulnerability which are effeminate. Both voyeurism and flagellation have in common a displacement from the penis to the eye and the whip as the active organ. Such displacement signifies that the flesh being whipped and the object of the gaze are the locus of sensuality whereas the whip, not a bodily organ at all, and the eye, which is not touched and so does not feel as the penis does, become pure instruments of power. Here is the double taboo at work which alienates the male organ into the abstract phallus and by the same token makes the sensual body shameful. Even more remote alienations are the phallic pen and paintbrush. Dualistic metaphysics distinguishes between the sovereign mind and the body, and between man as the transcendent universal subject and woman as nature. The body to which something is done, even if only writing or painting it, thereby becomes effeminate while the act of writing takes on sadistic meaning so turning the writer's sado-masochistic imagination into the scene of narcissistic self-exhibitionism to the punishing eye and of self-abandonment to the sadistic pen.

## RACIALISING GENDER; GENDERING RACISM

Writing the body is said to be the path to liberation for women, but the body cannot simply be re-written by an act of will. Implicated in the meanings of the body as Kafka writes it are the class and sexual culture of his time. The contrast between the clothed and unclothed or semi-clothed in the whipper scene aligns with class difference as middle-class K. observes the semi-naked whipper and the demeaning striptease which Willem and Franz are forced to perform. In Tiorelli's attic the positions are reversed as slum girls threaten to intrude into the commerce between their male social superiors. The threat from lower-class women is realised when clothed K. observes the humiliation of middle-class, shirt-sleeved Block at the hands of the maidservant, Leni, draped in her long white apron, while Huld is just a voice emerging from under a huge quilt. In this scene, however, racialist discourse mixes with class and gender motifs to modify their meaning. The scenes with the whipper and Titorelli are sado-masochistic and homoerotic (or narcissistic) variations on the standard situation of the clothed male observer of female nudity whether in paintings (the tradition to which Manet's *Déjeuner sur l'herbe* alludes), or erotic performance. Block's humiliation is a masochistic heterosexual derivate with strong racist undertones. Nude painting and striptease uncover the female body as the site of erotic sensuality whereas the observer's body remains covered; only the scopophiliac eye is implicated.

The sexual culture of nineteenth century bourgeois society through to the First World War saw the saturisation of the young, non-maternal female body with sexuality in contrast to an ascetic masculinity necessitated by the pursuit of social and imperial ambition which might at most allow for a cleanly thrusting assertion of phallic power. Sensuality *per se*, and, *a fortiori*, non-genital sensuality, was thus frequently perceived as exotic or effeminate: others are sensual, whether it be the coarse sensuality of the lower classes – a favourite motif in Naturalist literature – the exotic sensuality of the odalisque or the perverse sensuality of other races. Unlike the exotic African, Arab or Asian Other of European colonialism, the Jewish racial Others of the hegemonic German culture in Central Europe were not geographically distant but were familiar neighbours who increasingly were moving into the cities and moving out of the ghettoes, were engaging in trade, and were socially ambitious.[20] As such they were represented as an insidious threat, insinuating themselves everywhere and aping the culture of the dominant Germans as they tried to assimilate yet remained different.[21] Their creeping and crawling was presented as the unmanly and hence effeminate behaviour of the weak, and behind their flattery lay a perverse lust for Christian women.[22] Nietzsche, not himself anti-Semitic, nonetheless provided the imagery of this creeping weakness.

Block evinces some of the features of the stereotype in which age too is an element, as it is also in the scene with the radiantly youthful whipper whose freshness of visage suggests the healthily Germanic beauty of a Siegfried in leathers. Youth denoted strong nationalist identification from the liberal movements of the nineteenth century, prefixed by the adjective 'Young', through the *Jugendstil* to the iconography of the Third Reich, albeit with varying connotations.[23] Ageing Block suffers many humiliations beginning with the disadvantage of facing a fully clothed and younger K. when only semi-clothed himself, a motif recalling K.'s arrest when lying trouserless in bed. K.'s sense of superiority because of his greatcoat is expressed in his straddling posture and aggressive questioning of Block, postural signals which have reappeared endlessly in cinematic depictions of sadistic power relations. Later K. holds Block by the braces like a dog on a lead, just as Leni jerks him by the collar at the end of the episode. K. jealously imagines Block to be Leni's furtive lover, forgetting how furtive his own behaviour is. He also quizzes Block about his name, an allusion perhaps to the practice of some assimilated Jews to take non-Jewish names. K. feels his own status to be enhanced through contrast with Block, just as one does when abroad talking to low-class people; this comment by the narrator positions Block as a low foreign body, at least in K.'s eyes, even though he is a local business man, a grain dealer as it turns out. Moreover Block lies to Huld, for he confesses to K. that he secretly goes to other lawyers, evincing that rootless lack of loyalty or true national identity of which the Bohemian Jews were accused because, it was claimed, they sided now with the Germans, now with the Czechs, depending on their interests of the moment.[24] Block is portrayed, in refraction through K.'s eyes and indeed his own, as a ludicrously timorous creature, scurrying around from one incompetent lawyer to the next. Rather than showing any independence, he sees independent intervention as the worst danger.

This again has affinities with anti-semitic stereotypes of the Jewish parasite with no independent identity. Weininger, for example, accuses the Jews of being the negation of all identity and in that respect like women. Block has the title of *Kaufmann*. He is, then, a man of commerce guiltily creeping about the household of a man whose name associates him with an ailing Christianity, though Huld briefly parodies Old Testament cadences when he insists, like a jealous Jehovah, that Block should have no other advocate but him: '"Wer ist denn Dein Advokat?" "Ihr seid es", sagte Block. "Und außer mir?" fragte der Advokat. "Niemand außer Euch", sagte Block' (K, 261). Block kneels before Huld, kissing his hand at Leni's command and addressing him as 'mein Advokat'. Like a supplicant before a lord bishop, he is presented by Leni in a parody of the Virgin's intercession with Christ in Judgement. Moreover Block has been reading a book given him by Huld, which perhaps transcends his understanding.

In all these ways Block is positioned as a convert to a faith whose representatives constantly humiliate him.[25] The racialist stereotyping is also imbued with gender and class elements. Thus a sign of the depths to which Block has sunk is the maid-servant's bedroom where he spends the night: for a business-man to sink to the status of a female servant is to fall low indeed. That the loss of male status is the ultimate humiliation comes out in K.'s horror at the sight of an elderly merchant, a man with a long white beard, pleading with a young girl. (Block seems to age rapidly through his appearances.) Thus the patriarchal order of age, gender and social status is obscenely reversed three times over, so compounding the racial humiliation of the would-be assimilant. The closing *tableau vivant* with K. as observer gives expression through thinly disguised sado-masochistic sexual symbolism to racial humiliation. An old, white-haired man, Block yet fails to represent the law. He lacks the bodily dignity of the patriarch. If the phallus is a sacred taboo set apart, forbidden to general use, prohibited to a particular class (especially to women), then Block's body, which as he kneels wriggles to and fro like a dog trying to wag its tail, is half-undressed, and is jerked about by a young man and then by a woman, signals his loss of all phal-lic power or legitimacy as patriarch. His Christian counterpart, the Advocate Huld, lies sick in bed, but his nakedness is at least covered by a quilt.

Read in the historical context of 1914, one meaning of K.'s refusal to follow Block's road is refusal of minority assimilation to a dominant community of a different, albeit dying faith. If Huld is an exponent of the pragmatic doctrine of adaptation and playing the system, Block represents the member of a minority trying to play the system of the majority. The horror of the scene suggests authorial repudiation of Block's path. However, the attack on assimilation, couched in images dangerously close to anti-Semitic stereotyping, is moderated through Block's angry questioning of K.'s right to feel contempt. In as far as Block is a mirror in which K. may observe a possible older self, the episode lucidly and painfully conveys the power of the hateful stereotypes to infiltrate and poison the imagination, turning the male subject into a demasculated object of hate-filled self-repudiation. And the fear of demasculation in turn demonises women. If the greatest humilia-tion which can befall the male member of a racial minority is loss of manhood, then women come to symbolise or indeed to embody the threat in a culture of binary oppositions: in the see-saw of the stereotypes, loss of dominant masculinity conjures up Leni as punishing dominatrix.

## THE END OF TABOOS?

In Block K. sees an *alter ego* who follows one of Titorelli's options: the path of postponement. K.'s death like a dog ends postponement and comes as the climax of a process of (self-)punishment for which the various *tableaux vivants* are a foretaste or foreplay. Indeed the final scene is like an accelerated replay of the whole novel. Thus K. is arrested at home as at the start, but this time he is ready, without having to be instructed, as he had to be first time round, on the proper dress to meet court officials. Where clothed K. was addressed as 'Herr' (K, 109) by plump Willem who had to take off his clothes, here two pale plump 'Herren' in frock-coats and top hats, conduct K. to the scene of his execution where they strip him naked to the waist, carefully folding his clothes as if they would be used again, though whether they are destined for one of his captors whom this time K. will not be able to denounce, or are the costume used by all cast in the role of the accused in this theatrical ritual is unclear. The executioners have prepared for their task by bodily cleansing. Such cleanliness may signify the law of purity to be enforced on Josef K.'s guilty flesh, but the excessive cleanliness paradoxically suggests an excessive interest in all the hidden dirt lurking in the body's crevices: the pure law excites interest in dirt; the sacred taboo produces the unclean taboo.

The execution is the culminating infusion of physical punishment with erotic meaning which is rendered the more perverse by a hint of religious iconography. As the two men manipulate K.'s body, one holding him down by the throat, the other thrusting the knife into his breast and twice turning it in his heart, they stand cheek to cheek observing. The blissful pose turns the low-class actors as K. saw them earlier into angels of death, but the stress on observation accompanied by a posture of mutual caressing also turns the killing into a pornographic presentation. That this moment comes as a long delayed, but long prepared outcome, gives the scene a perversely climactic effect. The hesitations – K. could have shouted to the policeman, he could have fought to escape, he could have followed Fräulein Bürstner – all this has the rhythm of an intercourse despairingly allowed to run its course, quickening in the thrusting sequence of brief questions, to the terrible orgasm suffered by the body into which the knife is thrust. The meaning of K.'s death has been much disputed. Should he have taken the proffered knife and killed himself, so salvaging a vestige of the autonomy, or does his refusal at least deny recognition to the henchmen of might cynically presented as right?[26] Yet is it even clear whether K. does refuse self-execution, for while he refuses to take the knife, his executioners can be seen a externalised aspects of the self which leaves the close ambiguous between execution and self-execution? If, however, the scene is read as the culmination of the series of sado-masochistic episodes beginning with the vampiric kissing of Fräulein Bürstner, through the pushing of Franz under the whip and finally the observation of Block's ritual humiliation, then a change is evident, for in the earlier episodes K. tended towards the sadistic role though flirting also with the masochistic position. At the end of the sequence, however, K.'s refusal to wield the knife himself becomes a refusal of the Janus-like position within the power structure which sado-masochism represents. The oscillation between power and powerlessness ceases when K. accepts the masochistic position of victim. That K. refuses to execute himself and that his last words suggest shame rather than guilt, constitute a minimal rebellion against the Court. To accept guilt or to seek acquittal from the Court would be to accept the Court's legitimacy; K.'s death like a dog does neither. While K. withholds recognition from the Court, he cannot break free because the Court externalises the logic of the world which he inhabits, a logic that is so ingrained within K. himself that he cannot simply pluck it out like an offending eye/I. It is the logic which has structured his desires; to excise our own desires is a kind of death of the self and would in any case not get rid of but merely fulfil the punitive logic.

The meaning of K.'s death depends on how the reader understands not just the Court but the whole legal metaphor. Most readers would no doubt agree that the Court is corrupt, but what of the law which it claims to administer? *Der Proceß* conveys a crisis of masculinity in an age when a posited traditional patriarchal order based on father-power within the family, on containment of women in marriage and on social hierarchy given by status at birth was perceived to be collapsing: the law of the fathers was dying even as the new market and the new nationalisms were about to unleash war on an unparalleled scale. If *Der Proceß* is in large measure a reflection upon modernity, then the legal metaphor implies the following choices: if the ugly world Josef K. inhabits is the effect of the crumbling of patriarchal law, then either that law must be restored, or it must be modified to suit modern conditions, or it must be overthrown in favour of a new, better law, or else the discourse of transcendent law must be abandoned altogether as but the veil hiding the punitive exercise of power. Kafka's novel is doubly transgressive in subverting the sacred taboos of patriarchal law by uncovering the taboo desires to which that law gives rise, but it is left to the readers to draw their own conclusions on life after the death of the law. Paradoxically, the sexual taboos are so blatantly displayed that, like the purloined letter in Poe's tale or the orgasmic deaths in *Buddenbrooks*, many readers fail to see them. More deeply disguised still, however, are the taboo fears and hatreds arising from a racist environment to which, once they are perceived, Kafka has given unforgettable expression.

## NOTES

**Abbreviations**
K = Franz Kafka, *Der Proceß. Kritische Ausgabe*, ed. M. Pasley, Frankfurt a.M., 1990

1. For a fuller version of this argument see my article 'Thomas Mann's *Buddenbrooks*: Bourgeois Patriarchy and *Fin-de-Siecle* Eros', in *Thomas Mann in Perspective*, ed. M. Minden, London, 1995, 125–42.
2. See S. Rimmon-Kenan, *Narrative Fiction: Contemporary Poetics*, London, 1983, on these narratological terms and on *mise en abyme* as a confusion of representational levels.
3. On the perverse sexual undertones in K.'s arrest and his wooing of Fräulein Bürstner see my article 'Blaubarts Braut und die Meduse. Weibliche Figuren in Kafkas Briefe an Felice Bauer und Milena Jesenká', in *Franz Kafka* (Text + Kritik Sonderband), ed. H.L. Arnold, Munich, 1994, 282ff.
4. Franz Kafka, *Sämtliche Erzählungen*, ed. P. Raabe, Frankfurt a.M., 1970, 124.
5. M. Anderson, *Kakfa's Clothes: Ornament and Aestheticism in the Habsburg Fin-de-Siècle*, Oxford, 1992; E. Pavel, *The Nightmare of Reason. A Life of Franz Kafka*, London, 1984. Sports and cycling tended to diminish the difference between male and female bodies by doing away with the womanly hour-glass silhouette in favour of a slim, boyish ideal and stigmatising the mature, fat or maternal female body as Kafka's letters all too graphically demonstrate.
6. Cf. S. Corngold, *Franz Kafka. The Necessity of Form*, Ithaca and London, 1988, 77ff., who sees Gregor's body, in its last dried out, flat stage just before death,

as translucently beautiful. The drying out and flattening of the body suggests growing abstraction or ascetic dis-embodiment.

7. A mixed category is the bourgeois adulteress: in crossing the line, she poses a particular threat to the phallic order. See T. Tanner, *Adultery in the Novel*, Baltimore and London, 1979.

8. Karl Kraus, *Schriften*, vol. 8, *Aphorismen: Sprüche und Widersprüche. Pro domo et mundo. Nachts*, ed. C. Wagenbach, Frankfurt a.M., 1986, 50.

9. *Facsimile Querschnitt durch die Jugend*, ed. E. Zahn, Berne and Munich, n.d.

10. It is available in facsimile reprint: *Geschlecht und Charakter. Eine prinzipielle Untersuchung*, Munich, 1980. The author committed suicide in 1903.

11. See for example W. Flex's bestselling novella of 1916, *Der Wanderer zwischen beiden Welten*, reprint, Freiburg, 1993, which offers images of mythically heightened male beauty: 'Feucht von den Wassern und von Sonne und Jugend über und über glänzend stand der Zwanzigjährige in seiner schlanken Reinheit da'(32); the youth has just recited Goethe's homoerotic poem 'Ganymed'.

12. See W. Daim, *Der Mann, der Hitler die Ideen gab. Die sektiererischen Grundlagen des Nationalsozialismus*, 2nd edn, Vienna, 1985, 119, on the racialist journal *Ostara* which printed a photograph of the French sculptor Fremiet's statue of a prototype King Kong seizing a Gretchen-like woman.

13. The drunken monster-father in Hauptmann's play *Vor Sonnenaufgang* is a notable exemplar.

14. On the Jews as anti-race see R. Chickering, *We Men Who Feel Most German: A cultural study of the Pan-German League 1886–1914*, London, 1984, 239.

15. W. Dodd, *Kafka: Der Prozeß* (Glasgow Introductory Guides to German Literature, 8), Glasgow, 1991, 5.

16. On clothes as homosexual markers see G. Deleuze and F. Guattari, *Kafka: Towards a Minor Literature*, Minneapolis, 1986, 68ff.

17. Wendla Bergmann's seemingly innocent questions about a father beating his daughter have a comparable prurience in Franz Wedekind's *Frühlings Erwachen*(1891). A closer parallel still is Törless's seemingly disengaged observation of the torture of the feminised and socially slightly inferior Basini with his Italianate name by his Germanically named companions, Beineberg and Reiting in Robert Musil's *Die Verwirrungen des Zöglings Törless* (1906).

18. Kafka elaborated and intensified such horrific eroticisation of power with the added elements of racism and colonialism in *In der Strafkolonie* which he wrote in October 1914 while working on *Der Proceß*.

19. D. Kremer, *Die Erotik des Schreibens*, Frankfurt a.M., 1989, 143–152.

20. On the complex and changing position of the Jewish community of Kafka's time see H.J. Kieval, *The Making of Czech Jewry: National Conflict and Jewish Society in Bohemia, 1870–1916*, Oxford, 1988, and C. Stölzl, *Kafkas böses Böhmen: Zur Sozialgeschichte eines Prager Juden*, Frankfurt a.M., 1975.

21. See R. Robertson, *Kafka: Judaism, Politics, and Literature*, Oxford, 1985, 165–171, on the metaphor of aping in racialist discourse and in Kafka's *Bericht für eine Akademie*. See also footnote 11.

22. Repeated scare stories about ritual murder, generally of young girls, set off pogroms and riots. Kafka refers in a letter to Milena Jesenská to the notorious Hilsner trial, for example. See Franz Kafka, *Briefe an Milena*, ed. J. Born and M. Müller, Frankfurt a.M., 1986, 68. See also Kieval, *The Making of Czech Jewry*, 73–79; Stötzl, *Kafkas Böhmen*, 67–71; W. Iggers (ed.), *Die Juden in Böhmen und Mähren. Ein historisches Lesebuch*, Munich, 1986, 292ff.

23. See Pavel, *The Nightmare of Reason*, 42f., on anti-Semitism among the Young Czechs.
24. See Kieval, *The Making of Czech Jewry*, chap. 2, on the Jews caught between German and Czech identificiation.
25. Robertson, *Kafka*, 114, reads the scene of Block's humiliation as a criticism of catholicism and the doctrine of intercession. I would agree with this but see the hermetic reference to assimilation as a key element.
26. Ibid., 127, exemplifies the first view; Dodd, *Kafka: Der Prozeß*, 43, who provides a useful summary of debate, concludes with the opposing view, while P.U. Beicken, *Franz Kafka. Eine kritische Einführung in die Forschung*, Frankfurt a.M., 1974, warns against either/or solutions of an irresolvable antinomy.

# 7

## THE FRUSTRATED POET: HOMOSEXUALITY
## AND TABOO IN *DER TOD IN VENEDIG*

——ᘛᘚ——

*T.J. Reed*

I meant to say no more about *Der Tod in Venedig*, having just finished a small book on it.[1] But a project on taboos plainly had to
have a text on homosexuality, and Mann's Venice novella is surely
*the* German text. Moreover 'taboo' offers a new angle on the story
– or rather it confirms what is now a necessary understanding of
both the writing and the reception of *Der Tod in Venedig*. Critics are
at last looking frankly at the homosexual element in Thomas
Mann's work. The concept of taboo helps to explain why it has
taken them so long to do that. And substantively it helps to
explain the genesis, the final form, and some of the crucial detail
of the novella itself.

To begin with some very obvious propositions and distinctions
about the phenomenon of sexual taboo in general: there are a)
taboo *subjects* and b) taboo *activities or relationships*. Heterosexuality has commonly been a taboo subject, even if always accompanied by the temptation and pleasure of breaking the taboo. Why
there was one at all on talking or writing publicly about an activity recognised as normal by society is a question for anthropologists. Was it feared that too much light might harm the mysterious
and necessary act of procreation? Or that open discussion might
turn what was already a prime preoccupation into an obsession (as
it since has)? Whatever the reason, society's principle was for a
long time: intercourse, yes; discourse, no. But by the late twentieth
century, European art, especially literature, has largely put paid to
that taboo. Homosexuality, in contrast, has been in most societies
and at most times a taboo *activity* – with the notable exception, in
some periods and at some social levels, of Ancient Greece. It was
thus necessarily a taboo subject as well, since b) almost necessarily

entails a), though not vice versa. The impulse to write – in an affirmative way, that is – about homosexuality consequently suffered, and to some extent still suffers, from two distinct kinds of taboo: a taboo imposed by society, which did not want to publicise and so risk encouraging what was widely held to be a deviation (hence recent British legislation); and a taboo self-imposed by the individual, to avoid publicly confessing to a deviation. That is, like any external social demand, this one too becomes internalised. Prohibition becomes inhibition. The potential conflict between individual and society is replicated as a conflict between two personal impulses, the one to truthful and self-liberating utterance, the other to conformity for the sake of safety. This can be summed up as the alternative: expression or discretion.

How far had literature gone in breaking down this taboo in Thomas Mann's early years? He was born in 1875. Oscar Wilde's trial and imprisonment came twenty years later, in 1895–97. André Gide published his novel *L'Immoraliste* in 1901, his dialogues on homosexuality *Corydon* in 1911, his autobiography *Si le grain ne meurt* in 1921. Proust's *A la recherche du temps perdu* appeared between 1913 and 1927. Gide is the franker. Proust, though he gives homosexuality extensive treatment, overtly condemns it; and he turns the central love-affair of his alter ego the narrator into a heterosexual one.

*Der Tod in Venedig* was written in 1911 and published in 1912. The earlier novella, *Tonio Kröger* of 1903, was in considerable measure inspired by Mann's feelings for the painter Paul Ehrenberg. To call that a homosexual relationship may give the wrong impression: it was all wistful adoration and intense lyrical feeling, which seems not to have been reciprocated except in the form of friendship. Yet it was not just friendship on Mann's side, and it confirmed what he knew about his sexuality from earlier episodes. Nevertheless, in 1905 he took what he was later to describe as the very deliberate step – not dependent, that is, on anything as random as 'falling in love' – of getting married.[2] His wife was the daughter of a rich and cultivated Munich academic family. By 1911, at thirty-six, Thomas Mann was a highly regarded writer, well off, with three children, a residence in Munich, a Bavarian country villa – to put it crudely, in a society still deeply hostile to homosexuality, he had a lot to lose.

There were meanwhile snags in his literary career. His first noted work, the family history *Buddenbrooks*, left him with an acute form of the 'successful first novel' problem. He desperately wanted to confirm his reputation with a second 'masterpiece', to prove he was the master his first novel had suggested. In letters to his brother Heinrich, he talks openly about the need for a masterpiece and about his ambition to achieve the status of a master.[3] What he had done since *Buddenbrooks* was either excellent but small-scale, like the novellas *Tristan* and *Tonio Kröger*, or large-scale but lightweight, like his second novel, *Königliche Hoheit*, an allegory of the artist's existence whose vehicle, the story of a lonely prince, is charming but far too long for its ha'porth of meaning. Mann had plans in plenty that were large in both scale and potential significance: a novel, *Maya*, which would do for Munich society what *Buddenbrooks* had done for Lübeck and also argue the metaphysical (Buddhistic or Schopenhauerian) theme that all human striving rests on illusion; a historical novel about the life of Frederick the Great; an exhaustive treatise on the relation of Intellect to Art in contemporary German culture. These were conceptions of a kind and a scope that a great writer might wish – might indeed be expected – to have written. The trouble was, Mann seemed unable actually to write them. They remained essentially pipe-dream works. Materials and notes accumulated, but composition would not begin. Meanwhile, gallingly, his brother was turning out one novel after another.

Entwined with these unfulfilled ambitions was the question what kind of writer he was, and what kind he needed to become if he was to retain public favour. He had a name as above all a cool ironist, a prober beneath the surface, a pessimistic modern marked by Nietzsche's radical psychology and the grim representations of Naturalism. But he could see new demands being made and new trends beginning. The German public, it seemed, was looking for beauty, for affirmation of life and moral certainties; it had become impatient of doubt, irony, and the uncovering of distasteful realities. Mann saw this realistically as a dilemma for his whole generation, requiring a conscious career choice: should they – and in particular should he – persist stubbornly with the old mode, or try to adapt gracefully to this new one?[4]

Much of this issue is summed up in the terms *Schriftsteller* versus *Dichter*. Dictionary equivalents do not explain it fully. Crucial is what the words connoted at this particular moment in German cultural history. *Schriftsteller* implied a writer by will and profession, hence already a conscious agent, which begins to suggest a preponderance of intellect, and that in turn points to the notion of an analyst of reality, which can easily be presented as a grubber in social fact and psychological motive, a jaundiced critic alienated from life itself. So *Schriftsteller* was itself virtually a criticism, certainly when contrasted with the term *Dichter*. This connoted not just – not even necessarily – a writer of verse, but a born and necessary creator, a maker of beautiful forms, a celebrator of life. It was thus itself virtually a celebration. Above all, it would be naturally applied to the great writer, the established master. Add to this some local associations, which Mann experienced as pressures. The characteristics demanded of a *Dichter* were analogous to the resolutely un-'spiritual' externality of the visual arts; and Munich, where Mann lived, was very much a city of the visual arts (he satirises its obsessions in the story *Gladius Dei* of 1902) and one which did not take serious literature seriously. In that, it was only the extreme case of a general and long-standing trend in German culture. Or so Thomas Mann felt.[5]

In 1911, he was beginning what would become (but not until nearly half a century later) the novel *Die Bekenntnisse des Hochstaplers Felix Krull*. But work was at a standstill and the writer physically and mentally at a low point. At the end of May he travels to Venice with his wife and his brother Heinrich, and there experiences, as the autobiographical *Lebensabriß* later reports, all the bizarre happenings and encounters he was to narrate in *Der Tod in Venedig* (XI, 123ff.). On his return, this new story supplants the *Krull* project, and is written over the next year.

My account now falls into four stages. First, a reminder of what is essential in the story for present purposes. Second, a sketch of the story's own story, that is its pre-publication history – what we know and can reasonably conjecture about how it was written, how its conception changed, and the probable reasons why. Third, its postpublication story – how it came to be read, by Mann himself as well as by critics, and how that too has changed. In all three stages, taboo can be seen at work, just how decisively is a matter for individual judgement. Finally, having looked at the effects of taboo on the story, I want to ask what effect the story has had on the taboo.

## THE STORY

Aschenbach is in his fifties, according to a work-note fifty-three, what the text calls (perhaps a little excessively – but then Mann was still only thirty-five) an 'ageing' artist. He is decidedly an established writer, he enjoys full social recognition, the text refers to him as a 'master'. Among other things, he has finished the major works Mann had only planned: the opening of chapter 2 lists them by name and gives a brief characterisation of each. He has moved away – explicitly moved *on* – from the psychological analysis he practised in younger years to a reborn confident morality; instead of peering into the depths, he is now devoted to the beauty of external form. It is easy to see how this very conscious development – the text speaks of the 'profound decision of the man who has become a master' – relates to Mann's preoccupations and temptations at the time. The story is in a very precise way his experiment with what it would be like if he were to make certain career choices himself.

Aschenbach is not consciously homosexual. He has been married, but his wife died young – one might say the fiction has conveniently disposed of her. He has since lived a life devoted wholly to his work. But this discipline is no longer enough, his work is at a standstill, and that, as with Mann, is what takes him to Venice. The impulse to travel comes from a violent vision, which is a first release of the dionysian energies Aschenbach has for so long been exploiting in the cause of art, but has left otherwise unsatisfied. In the Nietzschean terms Mann is consciously using, there are destructive forces under the beautiful surface of the master's mature work, Dionysos is latent in the world of Apolline appearance.

The Polish boy Tadzio embodies this Apolline beauty in what seems to Aschenbach perfection: 'Mit Erstaunen bemerkte Aschenbach, daß der Knabe vollkommen schön war'(VIII, 469). My argument involves giving their full force to the passages that describe it. This is Aschenbach's second sighting:

Er kam durch die Glastür und ging in der Stille schräg durch den Raum zum Tisch seiner Schwestern. Sein Gehen war sowohl in der Haltung des Oberkörpers wie in der Bewegung der Kniee, dem Aufsetzen des weißbeschuhten Fußes von außerordentlicher Anmut, sehr leicht, zugleich zart und stolz und verschönt noch durch die kindliche Verschämtheit, in welcher er zweimal unterwegs, mit einer Kopfwendung in den Saal, die Augen aufschlug und senkte. Lächelnd, mit einem halblauten Wort in seiner verschwommenen Sprache nahm er seinen Platz ein, und jetzt zumal, da er dem Schauenden sein genaues Profil zuwandte, erstaunte dieser aufs neue, ja erschrak über die wahrhaft gottähnliche Schönheit des Menschenkindes. Der Knabe trug heute einen leichten Blusenanzug aus blau und weiß gestreiftem Waschstoff mit rotseidener Masche auf der Brust und am Halse von einem einfachen weißen Stehkragen abgeschlossen. Auf diesem Kragen aber, der nicht einmal sonderlich elegant zum Charakter des Anzugs passen wollte, ruhte die Blüte des

Hauptes in unvergleichlichem Liebreiz, – das Haupt des Eros,
vom gelblichen Schmelz parischen Marmors, mit feinen und ern-
sten Brauen, Schläfen und Ohr vom rechtwinklig einspringenden
Geringel des Haares dunkel und weich bedeckt.
    Gut, gut! dachte Aschenbach mit jener fachmännisch kühlen Bil-
ligung, in welche Künstler zuweilen einem Meisterwerk gegenüber
ihr Entzücken, ihre Hingerissenheit kleiden. (VIII, 473f.)

Later, on the beach, he watches when Tadzio is called in from
swimming:

Er kehrte zurück, er lief, das widerstrebende Wasser mit den Beinen
zu Schaum schlagend, hintübergeworfenen Kopfes durch die Flut;
und zu sehen, wie die lebendige Gestalt, vormännlich hold und
herb, mit triefenden Locken und schön wie ein junger Gott, her-
kommend aus den Tiefen von Himmel und Meer, dem Elemente
entstieg und entrann: dieser Anblick gab mythische Vorstellungen
ein, er war wie Dichterkunde von anfänglichen Zeiten, vom
Ursprung der Form und von der Geburt der Götter. Aschenbach
lauschte mit geschlossenen Augen auf diesen in seinem Innern
antönenden Gesang; und abermals dachte er, daß es hier gut sei
und daß er bleiben wolle. (VIII, 478)

Oppressed by the scirocco, Aschenbach tries to leave Venice,
bungles it through staying to get a last glimpse of the boy, and finds
himself – to his delight – back at the hotel. From now on, he is free
to watch Tadzio all the time; and that means Thomas Mann is free
to go on describing young male beauty in a style that nothing else
in his normally cool detached prose can match for empathetic emotion. In the early stages links are ostentatiously made with aesthetic
reflection, art, literature. Tadzio's grace recalls the statue *Boy pulling
a thorn from his foot* which Mann must have been familiar with from
the Munich Glyptothek. Tadzio's statuesque form seems to Aschenbach analogous with the shapes his writing disengages from the
marble mass of language (VIII, 490). Beauty is also given a metaphysical grounding by allusions to the *Symposium* and *Phaedrus*,
where Plato argues that individual exemplars of beauty are only
pointers to the reality of the ultimate Forms: 'in aufschwärmendem
Entzücken glaubte er mit diesem Blick das Schöne selbst zu
begreifen, die Form als Gottesgedanken' (VIII, 490). Yet what follows these high-minded cultural references is always a warning
note. After the allusion to Plato's Ideas, the text reads: 'Das war der
Rausch; und unbedenklich, ja gierig hieß der alternde Künstler ihn
willkommen.' The warning note is louder, and more surprising,
when Aschenbach seems to be fulfilling the demands of Plato's

morality by using physical beauty as fuel for an act of spiritual creation: 'Er wünschte plötzlich, zu schreiben ... Und zwar ging sein Verlangen dahin, in Tadzios Gegenwart zu arbeiten, beim Schreiben den Wuchs des Knaben zum Muster zu nehmen, seinen Stil den Linien dieses Körpers folgen zu lassen, der ihm göttlich schien, und seine Schönheit ins Geistige zu tragen, wie der Adler einst den troischen Hirten zum Äther trug' (VIII, 492). It was Plato's ideal that erotic feeling should not spend itself on a single beautiful being but be sublimated into art, thought, noble action. And restoring his creativity, it must not be forgotten, was the point of Aschenbach's journey. In that process too the episode of writing on the beach would seem a desired consummation. Yet the passage ends with the thought that it is as well the world at large knows nothing of the origins of 'the beauty of the finished work'. There is a sudden switch to conventional moral, even moralistic, language: 'Sonderbare Stunden! Sonderbar entnervende Mühe! Seltsam zeugender Verkehr des Geistes mit einem Körper! Als Aschenbach seine Arbeit verwahrte und vom Strande aufbrach, fühlte er sich erschöpft, ja zerrüttet, und ihm war, als ob sein Gewissen wie nach einer Ausschweifung Klage führe' (VIII, 493). As if to match the judgement that implies, Aschenbach casts away all aesthetic analogies, pretexts and purposes and accepts the truth of his feelings in the closing words of chapter 4: 'Ich liebe dich.'

In the final chapter, he discovers there is cholera in the city which the authorities are hushing up, but stays on, too obsessed with Tadzio either to warn the family or to save himself. He pursues the boy more directly, eats infected fruit, and dies on the now deserted beach – the holiday-makers have got wind of the plague, the Polish family too is about to leave. At the end, Aschenbach has Tadzio in his gaze for one last time. The boy stands on a sandbank some way out from the shore and points out to sea. In the moment before Aschenbach collapses and dies: 'Ihm war, als ob der bleiche und liebliche Psychagog dort draußen ihm lächle, ihm winke; als ob er, die Hand aus der Hüfte lösend, hinausdeute, voranschwebe ins Verheißungsvoll-Ungeheure' (VIII, 525).

## THE GENESIS

So much for the story. Writing it gave Mann a lot of trouble. His letters speak of an 'impossible conception' or 'subject', he regrets having embarked on it, is desperate to finish it but can't see how.[6]

What was going on? The earliest public clue came seven years later, ironically enough in the preface to *Gesang vom Kindchen*, a long domestic poem celebrating the birth and christening of his sixth child. Here of all places, he looks back to an overwhelming emotion in Venice – though without specifying or locating it – and to the literary work it produced:

> Weißt du noch? Höherer Rausch, ein außerordentlich Fühlen
> Kam auch wohl über dich einmal und warf dich danieder,
> Daß du lagst, die Stirn in den Händen. Hymnisch erhob sich
> Da deine Seele, es drängte der ringende Geist zum Gesange
> Unter Tränen sich hin. Doch leider blieb alles beim Alten.
> Denn ein versachlichend Mühen begann da, ein kühlend
> Bemeistern, –
> Siehe, es ward dir das trunkene Lied zur sittlichen Fabel.
> War es nicht so? Und warum? Es scheint, du wagtest den Flug nicht?
> Was dir ziemte, was nicht, du wußtest's im innersten Herzen
> Und beschiedest dich still; doch schmerzte der tiefere Fehlschlag.
>
> (VIII, 1069)

The tone is one of disappointment at the way an impulse to write affirmatively, perhaps even in verse ('hymnisch', '...zum Gesange'), gave way to a less ecstatic mode. In context, significantly, Mann is ruminating on what makes a *Dichter* – natural enough in the preface to a work in verse by a habitual prose writer; but really it is the old issue that still rankles. Why can't people freely grant him the title of *Dichter*? The text implies that, if only he had followed his emotional impulse on that one occasion, it might have transformed his way of writing, and that in turn might have transformed his reputation. Not doing so made the eventual novella a 'secret defeat, a never-confessed failure' – an astounding repudiation of an acclaimed work. Incidentally, the hexameters in which he is saying all this recall the complete hexameters and hexameter fragments that were spotted by early readers of *Der Tod in Venedig*, especially in its most 'hymnic' section: the descriptions of Tadzio in chapter 4. We only need to join up the dots for a picture to emerge: long-standing aspirations to the accolade of *Dichter*, an emotional inspiration that seemed to be carrying him beyond analytic reflection to high style, a verse-form with classical antecedents ('loved by Germans and Greeks', albeit he now calls it a 'sober' metre) – all in the end frustrated by what he presents as an instinctive and involuntary return to his old cold mode.

What he was trying to do before that 'sobering' process took effect is plain enough from the descriptions of Tadzio. The cultural motifs too have a positive potential. The excerpts from Plato in Mann's work-notes along with other Greek materials might be read as a cumulative affirmation of homosexuality. They document the regard in which it was held by the ancients as a source of inspiration. Only the ignoble lover who knew nothing beyond physical passion failed both morally and metaphysically. Plato's ultimate ideal is stated in one of Mann's excerpts from the *Symposium*, in the 1903 translation by Rudolf Kassner:

> ... und so im Anblick dieser vielfachen Schönheit nicht mehr wie ein Sklave nach der Schönheit dieses einen Knaben verlange und dieses einen Menschen Schönheit wolle und gemein sei und kleinlich ... sondern, *an die Ufer des großen Meeres der Schönheit gebracht,* hier viele edle Worte und Gedanken mit dem *unerschöpflichen Triebe nach Weisheit* zeuge, bis er dann stark und reif jenes einzige Wissen, das da das Wissen des Schönen ist, erschaue ... Ja, Sokrates, wer immer von dort unten, weil er den Geliebten richtig zu lieben wußte, empor zu steigen und jenes ewige Schöne zu schauen beginnt, der ist am Ende und vollendet und geweiht. (work-notes fol.16; Mann's omissions and emphases)

The idea of initiation through and beyond the individual form, and of a sublimation in which the lover is inspired to noble things like poetry, could have made the writing episode something very different from the 'debauchery' of which Aschenbach's conscience accuses him. Similarly, when he thinks he sees in Tadzio Beauty itself as a divine idea, there was – in Platonic terms – no call to warn against 'intoxication'. In both passages, the chance of affirming Aschenbach's passion on culturally and philosophically strong grounds was offered to Thomas Mann – and finally refused. For Aschenbach to meet Plato's demands was somehow not enough.

All this looks like the taboo at work, and in a long self-interpretation of 1920 Mann explained just how it operated. He could afford to be and wanted to be frank because he was writing to a young homosexual poet, Carl Maria Weber, who had asked just what the tone of *Der Tod in Venedig* meant. In his reply,[7] Mann quotes the first seven lines of the passage from *Gesang vom Kindchen* discussed above. He then draws a distinction between two opposed principles, irresponsible dionysian lyrical self-expression and socially responsible apolline narrative – ('Unterschied zwischen dem dionysischen Geist unverantwortlich-individualistisch sich ausströmender Lyrik und dem apollinischen objektiv gebundener sittlich-gesellschaftlich verantwortlicher Lyrik'). Put simply, what these grand compounds with their Nietzschean core concepts mean is that it may be all very well to write lyrical effusions in private, but they will not do for the novelist's broad public. This is surely the external taboo I defined at the outset; and a phrase in the lines not quoted to Weber, that Mann knew 'somewhere inside him' ('im innersten Herzen') what kind of writing was his proper domain, catches the process of internalisation in literal terms. This is nearer still to completion when Mann goes on to confess his fundamentally bourgeois, puritanical temperament ('protestantisch-puritanische (bürgerliche) Grundverfassung') which mistrusts all passion as such and is committed to stable family life, even though his notion of unbourgeois erotic adventure is avowedly homosexual.

In addition to showing that in general a taboo was at work, the letter also helps to locate its effects on the text precisely. Mann calls the novella 'hymnic' in character and in origin. On and off since 1971, when I first offered a genetic interpretation based on Mann's letters and work-notes, scholars have argued about whether we should take any notice of Mann's account and specifically of the statement 'hymnic in origin'. Sometimes those words have been dismissed as if Mann's confession were my invention, or as if his words meant the opposite of their sense, or as if simply to reassert the novella's unity and quality were enough to rule out any other form of enquiry. Yet the account is Mann's, his words are unambiguous, and they deserve to be considered seriously.[8] But at least as important as the genetic statement, and neglected – I have to admit – by me as much as anyone in the debate, is the first half of the comment, namely that the story is at core hymnic in character. Mann almost passes over it as a mere stepping-stone to the genetic statement; yet it contains his view of what the story *is*, not merely of how it became what it is. A core is something still present, something that gives the story its inner substance, but it may have to be probed for because other elements have accreted round it. That, by implication, is why the statement goes on to its second half: the genesis explains both why the core is there at all, and why it is an inner core and not part of an open surface.

Mann's characterisation certainly fits the contrasts in the text: the lyrical evocations of Tadzio's beauty, framed by a moral commentary. Narratologically, the descriptions can be wholly attributed to the character's mental world, read as passages of Free Indirect Speech; while the moral judgements placed round them set him at arm's length – Aschenbach is infatuated, obstinate, gone astray ('der Betörte', 'der Starrsinnige', 'der Verirrte'). The effect is strongest in the final picture of his moral and physical nadir. He is identified and mocked as the writer who achieved all the things solemnly and triumphantly listed in chapter 2. 'Er saß dort, der Meister ...' – there he sits, the master, the artist who achieved dignity, the author of.... And so forth.

The tone is not just moral but moralising, and in his letter to Weber, Mann commented that the standpoint of the moralist could only be adopted ironically. Even without that hint, the text offers ground enough not to take the moral repudiation at face value. For it sounds, surely, very much as Aschenbach's narrative voice must have sounded when he returned in his maturity to simplified moral values and rejected what was depraved – 'verworfen' – rather than try to understand it. However, that moral confidence is something the story has now discredited, by showing that it was compatible with, even subtly conducive to, the master's self-abandonment. It can hardly, at this stage, be read straight. Which suggests that Mann's heavy judgements too, though in a very different way from those of Aschenbach in his moral heyday, are designed for public consumption. And we start to wonder whether, behind this overt conformity to public morality and its taboos, there is not a covert act of defiance? This is a tricky operation because the potential sympathiser – a homosexual like the young Weber, or a reader with socially liberal views – might take the moralising at face value. Yet the technique of undoing a moral judgement by overstating it – and this is not the only case where the text has to be read against its literal sense[9] – may be all the author can risk if his repute and social standing are to be safeguarded.

Or almost all. For even though, on Mann's own showing in the letter to Weber, both his temperament and the nature of prose writing itself pushed the pendulum in a moral direction, there are places where it obstinately stuck, or even swung back. Consider the close of chapter 4 and the climactic words 'Ich liebe dich.' Social taboo would require firm repudiation for a declaration of homosexual love, and the narrator duly finds hard words for it. But not the last word. The final sentence reads: 'Und zurückgelehnt, mit hängenden Armen, überwältigt und mehrfach von Schauern überlaufen, flüsterte er die stehende Formel der Sehnsucht – unmöglich hier, absurd, verworfen, lächerlich und heilig doch, ehrwürdig auch hier noch: "ich liebe dich"' (VIII, 498).

This first establishes feeling and its effects, then firmly repudiates it with massed pejoratives: the sequence matches what we know about the story's genetic sequence. There is then a reassertion, of the value of love generally and of the right of homosexual yearning to be recognised as one of its forms. The reassertion occurs in syntactically striking ways. First there is the surprise effect when a series of pejorative adjectives runs on into terms of affirmation without an adversative to separate the groups. Before we know where we are, we have linked the 'ludicrous and sacred'. The four pejoratives, which are all socially conventional, are then amply outbid by the claim to religious aura and intrinsic worth in the two positive ones 'sacred ... worthy of honour'. And the adversatives when they do come, reinforcing these adjectives, by trailing in the syntactically less orthodox position after them ('sacred yet', 'worthy of honour even here still') enact reassertion and its posture of defiance. The last words of the chapter are the 'standing formula' itself, disputed but left – precisely – standing.

Less straightforward is the closing scene. Aschenbach's death at the sea's edge recalls that excerpt from the *Symposium:* the lover who has passed beyond all mere individual forms comes to the shore of the 'sea of beauty' as an initiate. In a 'hymnic' conception, that might have been a celebration, a frank apotheosis. In the 'moral fable', Aschenbach has sunk too low for that. Yet the tone of the final page has left moralising behind and raises him to a level of tragic dignity: '"Dignity" is rescued only by death, by "tragedy", by the "sea"', reads the fourth of Mann's work-notes. Where the protagonist can be taken seriously and compassionately as a tragic character, the moraliser's writ no longer runs.

## READINGS

Mann was uneasy as he waited for the public's reactions to his novella, wondering whether he had produced, in a phrase from the text (VIII, 468), something 'absurd and forbidden' – note again the vocabulary of social convention. But his work was attacked for its negative, and not for any positive attitude to homosexuality. Mann mentions in the letter to Weber that the poet Stefan George, who practised his own neo-Grecian cult of a beautiful dead sixteen-year-old youth, had told his disciples that *Der Tod in Venedig* had 'drawn the highest things down into the sphere of decay'. And the leading homosexual propagandist of the day, Kurt Hiller, called the story 'an example of moral narrowness' unexpected from the author of *Buddenbrooks,* and accused Mann of putting love for a boy on a par with cholera. But there was no expression of moral outrage from the guardians of public decency; there were repudiations of homosexuality, but no suggestion that Mann had been defending it. It was clearly assumed that a specialist in decadence had treated another aspect of it. So the tone of the 'moral fable' had done its work. The elevated style appeared as a form of detachment, and the tragic ending seemed to put Mann on the *bien pensant* side – a Catholic critic even suggested that Aschenbach's death was a necessary punishment for his 'sinful thoughts'. Mann had not given himself away. That had been a definite risk, if only because so much of his work was avowedly autobiographical. But where critics made the equation between character and author, it was to scold Mann for implicitly claiming the status of an established 'master'.[10] This already diverted argument on to the story's manner and away from its sensitive matter. There were to be sporadic attacks for treating the homosexual theme at all – one belated moralist was still assailing Mann for his 'irresponsibility' in 1954[11] – but none for having his own emotional stake in it.

Over the years between and since, the discussion of style has been largely a displacement activity that allowed critics to pass over the taboo subject in silence and not probe the author's real relation to it, in effect a secondary taboo. Mann meantime kept his counsel. The confession in *Gesang vom Kindchen* went unnoticed. The account in *Lebensabriß* keeps passion at arm's length, merely noting that this questionable subject ('stoffliche Bedenklichkeit') paradoxically led to a moral rehabilitation – the 'morality', that is, of being a serious writer – after the lightweight *Königliche Hoheit* (XI, 124f.). In later self-interpretations Mann then concentrates on what is admittedly an important theme of the novella, namely the moral and social unreliability of art and the artist; and by linking this with a never-executed plan of 1906 for a story about the ageing Goethe's infatuation with a seventeen-year-old girl, he makes homosexual feeling seem a literary option, not a personal compulsion. Not until late in his life, in *Doktor Faustus*, did Mann make full literary use of his youthful passion for Paul Ehrenberg. But that now lay so far in the past, and there was so much else in a novel about Nazism's cultural roots to scandalise the German public (which it duly did) that the homosexuality was hardly noticed.

From the 1960s on, however, with the extensive publication of letters, and especially since 1975 when the *Tagebücher* became public, critics and biographers have had no excuse for not facing up to Mann's homosexuality. They have still commonly failed to do so.

The authorised biographer, Peter de Mendelssohn, is evasive to the point of the ludicrous about both Paul Ehrenberg and *Der Tod in Venedig*. The word 'homosexual' is not even used. The American biographer Richard Winston broaches the issues de Mendelssohn avoided, but then ludicrously trivialises them: Mann, he says, 'perhaps exaggerated' his homosexual feelings 'as he exaggerated all the little ailments, the colds and headaches that he recorded in his diary'.[12] So there is good reason for an avowed homosexual critic like Karl-Werner Böhm to attack critics for their squeamishness which, together with Mann's image-preserving tactics, meant that the story remained 'a provocation never understood'.[13] The concept of taboo carries us beyond the simple registering of that fact, and provides the social and cultural reasons for these failures and refusals. It is a history that does little credit to scholarship, with its theoretical claim to make value-free judgements. The claim – and consequently the failure – are greater when it is the scholarship of an art whose motto is 'homo sum: humani nil a me alienum puto', and whose students ought to be able to cope unfazed with matters of sexual orientation whether in a fiction or in its author. We ought not, in other words, to have had to wait for homosexual scholars to come along before taking seriously the evidence of homosexuality in Mann's work. Ironically, even homosexuals were liable to the taboo on such a reading. When I first used letters and work-notes to document the conflict in *Der Tod in Venedig* between homosexual feeling and an imposed morality, it was homosexual friends and colleagues above all who cried out against what they saw as a dismantling of their sacred text, even though it made plain how much more fully it was a homosexual work than people had allowed themselves to see till then.

## CONSEQUENCES

What then – the last question I undertook to look at – has been the effect of all this on the taboo itself? Karl-Werner Böhm attacks not just critics but Thomas Mann himself for what he sees as a policy of interpretative disinformation, and for a failure to go public about his sexual orientation lest it damage his career and fame. 'What is left of an artist's boldness', Böhm asks, 'if he is not prepared to stand by it with his social persona?'[14] – not prepared, that is, to 'come out'.

The answer, surely, is not as simple as the rhetorical question implies. 'Coming out' in 1912, whether in a version of *Der Tod in*

*Venedig* with a different emphasis or in franker public statements about the text as finally composed, could hardly have done much to change the social climate, and would certainly have done Mann massive damage, as witness the German scandals of 1902 and 1906 already mentioned, and the firm censorship provisions against homosexual writing. In contrast, the effects on culture and society of Mann's novella in the form it finally took, with all the caution of his statements about it, seem to me far from negligible. It is easy enough now to belittle the author for timidity about his sexual orientation, or even to ridicule the story's cultivated treatment of a taboo theme. Yet the case of Oscar Wilde shows that confrontation and revelation may not be the best tactic for changing the attitudes of society. In contrast, the cultivated formality and conventional moral elements of *Der Tod in Venedig* made it a difficult target to attack, and over the years its cultural presence and acceptance must have had consequences, no less real for being hard to measure exactly, for the way its subject is viewed. Add the prestige effect of the story's transformation into an art film and an opera, with Dirk Bogarde suffering in silence on Luchino Visconti's screen and Benjamin Britten underlining the story's latent drama with music, and the sarcastic comment of Mann's old enemy Alfred Kerr – that the novella had 'made pederasty acceptable to the cultivated middle classes' – comes close to being true in a straightforward sense.

Perhaps none of this would have quite removed Thomas Mann's bitterness at the 'secret defeat' he felt *Der Tod in Venedig* to be. The subject that briefly seemed to be carrying him beyond the limits of a *Schriftsteller* into the realm of the *Dichter* was one that the public of 1912 could not have tolerated in an affirmative treatment, however 'poetic'. Thus his only chance of ever giving them what they wanted was barred by the certainty that it would be unacceptable. The homosexual writer was denied both his emotional fulfilment and the ultimate literary recognition he craved. *Der Tod in Venedig* is in every sense the story of a frustrated poet.

# NOTES

1. T.J. Reed, *Death in Venice: Making and Unmaking a Master*, New York, 1994.
2. See the essay 'Über die Ehe'(1923) in Thomas Mann, *Gesammelte Werke in dreizehn Bänden*, Frankfurt a.M., 1974, vol. 10, 191–207. Further references in the text are to this edition.
3. See the letters to Heinrich Mann, 5.12.1905 and 11.6.1906, in *Thomas Mann–Heinrich Mann. Briefwechsel*, ed. H. Wysling, Frankfurt a.M., 1968, 44, 57.
4. See no. 103 of the notes for 'Geist und Kunst' published in P. Scherrer and H. Wysling, *Quellenkritische Studien zum Werk Thomas Manns* (Thomas-Mann-Studien, 1), Berne and Munich, 1967.
5. See the notes for 'Geist und Kunst'. nos 10, 12, 27, 35, 36.
6. See the letters to E. Bertram, 16.10.1911, to A. v. Bernus, 24.10.1911, and to W. Herzog, 8.12.1911, in H. Wysling (ed.), *Thomas Mann. Dichter über ihre Dichtungen*, Munich, 1975, vol. 1, 395; to H. Mann, 27.4.1912, in *Thomas Mann-Heinrich Mann. Briefwechsel*, 96; to A. Ehrenstein, 3.5.1912, in Thomas Mann, *Briefe 1889–1936*, ed. E. Mann, Frankfurt am Main, 1961, 96.
7. To C.M. Weber, 4.7.1920, in Mann, *Briefe*, 176–180.
8. For earlier discussions see Thomas Mann, *Der Tod in Venedig*, Oxford, 1971 and reprints; the chapter 'The Art of Ambivalence' in my *Thomas Mann: The Uses of Tradition*, Oxford, 1974, and my edition of *Der Tod in Venedig. Text, Materialien, Kommentar*, Munich, 1983. On the responses mentioned in my text see *Death in Venice: Making and Unmaking a Master* (note 1), p.121.
9. The repeated references to 'chance', each one plausible but cumulatively obtrusive, make the reader aware of Aschenbach's intentions and the not at all 'chance' nature of events.
10. See the passages quotes in the notes to Thomas Mann, *Briefe an Paul Amann*, ed. H. Wegener, Lübeck, 1959, 94f.
11. See the letter to J. Ernestus, 17.6.1954, in Wysling, *Thomas Mann. Dichter über ihre Dichtungen*, i, 448.
12. R. Winston, *Thomas Mann. The Making of an Artist*, London, 1982.
13. K.-W. Böhm, *Zwischen Selbstsucht und Verlangen: Thomas Mann und das Stigma Homsexualität*, Würzburg, 1991, 321.
14. Ibid., 321.

# 8

# DISCOVERING A TABOO: THE NAZI PAST IN LITERARY-POLITICAL DISCOURSE 1958–67

*Helmut Peitsch*

I n Günter Grass's novel *Die Blechtrommel*, published in 1959, the name of a club fashionable among the better off in Düsseldorf is Tabu.[1] Here they can do what they normally avoid doing both in public and in private; they can cry and remember. Grass's highly satirical description of a space reserved for mourning has been taken by later critics[2] as proof of the view put forward in 1967 by Alexander and Margarete Mitscherlich in their famous book *Die Unfähigkeit zu trauern* that West German memory in the 1950s 'derealised' the entire National-Socialist period.[3] Grass's characters can only enjoy their grief because in everyday life their private and political pasts have been forgotten. The problematic relationship between the West German present and the Nazi past also preoccupied the Italian writer Carlo Levi who travelled widely in West Germany in 1959. In the travelogue which he published three years later, a Munich bar with the name Tabu was given a similar symbolic significance.[4] In this paper I should like to question the assumption which led to the psychoanalytical term 'taboo' being applied to the ways in which German history of the years 1933–45 was remembered in the 1950s. At the same time I shall try to explain why the term came to be so widely used.

## 'DEREALISATION' OF THE NAZI PAST: FACT OR FICTION?

A reassessment of the different levels of memory at work in the FRG during the 1950s – the official, the public and the popular – casts doubt on the assumption of a silence about the past.[5] Factual evidence suggests a) that certain subjects were selected for remembering and b) that specific ways of remembering were favoured. Only when this particular memory was delegitimised in public debate, was it possible to recognise how by concentrating on the suffering German as the victim of the Second World War both the official and the popular mind had tabooed what became the central subject of at first public, and at a later stage, official remembrance of the Nazi past, namely the victims of racist and political-ideological persecution. From 1958 onwards writers, critics, journalists, and academics began to question the hitherto dominant memory of the Nazi past and to criticise both the official and the popular version of discussing the Nazi period. In speaking out about the previously unspeakable, they soon had to go beyond the limits of the institutionalized *Vergangenheitsbewälti-gung* or mastering of the past. They called for a break with specific German traditions.

This retrospective application of the term taboo might not seem something peculiar to the West German memory of fascism. A taboo probably can only be diagnosed as such when it no longer works. Calling something a taboo seems to be the first step towards breaking with it because the very act of naming challenges its working efficiency. What makes it necessary to retell the story of how the term taboo was introduced into the public discourse on the Nazi past in the FRG is the fact that the rather careless continuation of this way of speaking in the 1970s and particularly in the 1980s and 1990s – e.g., at the time of the screening of the television series 'Holocaust' and the film *Schindler's List*[6] – allowed right-wing revisionist historians and literary critics to pose as taboo-breakers when they tried to revitalise the official and popular memory of the 1950s.[7]

## Rediscovering the Discovery of the Taboo

One long-lasting problematic side-effect of the use of the term taboo has been the implication that prior to the taboo being broken nobody had spoken of the Nazi past at all. After the 1960s the way of speaking about it during the late 1940s and 1950s could thus be 'forgotten'. Revisionist historians, who are not the only ones to profit from this new kind of selective memory, blame the taboo-breakers of the 1960s (whom they wrongly identify with the so-called generation of 1968) for having forced new taboos on to the West Germans, for instance, taboos regarding the female victims of

Soviet rape or the male suffering among prisoners of war and in internment camps. The main protagonists of the right in the Historians' Debate of 1985 concentrated on the same figure as had symbolized the Cold War memory of the Federal Republic, i.e., the innocent German soldier on the Eastern Front who suffered in order to protect women and children against the threat of Asiatic barbarity. By linking two kinds of destruction,[8] the one of the German Reich and the other of European Jewry, the revisionist historians tried to do two things: a) to reconstruct the continuity which had been broken with in the 1960s and b) to take account of the changes in the official memory which had taken place since the late 1950s. The shift from Hermann Lübbe's cynical speech in the *Reichstag* in 1983 in which he declared the 'tactful silence' of the 1950s a necessity[9] to Manfred Kittel's attempt ten years later to prove that the Adenauer period was a 'work of mourning' because of the treaty with Israel[10] shows how the right became aware of the advantages to be gained from the obvious wrongness of the derealisation or silence hypothesis implied by the term taboo.

However, all the factual evidence that can be adduced from the 1950s to prove that the Nazi period was neither derealised or passed over in silence during the Cold War cannot undo the most important change of perspective on the Nazi years. That occurred between 1958 and 1967. The Mitscherlichs' book only summarised very effectively a public debate which changed the actual memory selected, as well as the way of remembering in public. This paper traces the pre-history of the canonized view in order to recall some of the circumstances surrounding the discovery. What is of particular interest here is the role of writers as intellectuals using the media to reshape the public memory of the Federal Republic.[11] The context in which this intervention took place, i.e., the seeming end of the Cold War in the first years of American-Soviet *détente*, has often been neglected in discussions both of the role of the intellectual as social critic and also of the function of literature in post-war Germany.

## INSTITUTIONALISING THE CRITICAL LITERARY-POLITICAL DISCOURSE IN THE EARLY 1960S

During the years 1958 to 1967 taboo was an element of the literary-political discourse that was institutionalized in cultural-political journals as well as in single- and multi-authored collections of essays. Never in the history of the FRG were so many literary anthologies published about political issues; nor were so many, at least temporarily successful, cultural-political journals founded.[12] A feature common to the titles of both journals and books was the stress they put on the need to bring literature closer to social reality. Thus one finds *Kursbuch*, *Bilanz*, and *Alternative*, the latter the title both of Martin Walser's famous collection of pro-SPD statements during the general election campaign of 1961 and also of a new literary journal brought out in the same year. The term *Bestandsaufnahme* or stocktaking, the title of one of the books which studied the political status quo in order to argue for change, was very soon transferred from the political to the literary domain by Hans Mayer, one of the emergent group of leading critics associated with Group 47. In 1965 Mayer saw taking stock as the dominant trend in truly contemporary literature.[13] The terminology of his then fellow critic, Marcel Reich-Ranicki, worked in a similar way. Reich-Ranicki used the political catchphrase *Politik der kleinen Schritte* to redefine realism as the 'literature of little steps'.[14] Enzensberger's journal, *Kursbuch*, opened with the pronouncement that Germans' literary consciousness was limited and that it ignored 'wide zones of contemporary civilisation '.[15] Realism in fiction and documentarism in drama also formed part of a discourse that was both based upon and also fostered what Jürgen Habermas later called the 'normalization of the role of the intellectual'.[16] The important part played in this discourse by the term taboo can be gauged from the fact that, regardless of their political standpoint, all those writing for the literary media, whether writers, journalistic critics, academics or even – at a later date – politicians, were impelled to use it.

In 1962, recognising that taboo was a word likely to catch readers' attention, Gerhard Zwerenz entitled his collection of newspaper articles *Wider die deutschen Tabus*.[17] In the same year Paul Schallück contributed a chapter, 'Vorurteile und Tabus', to Hans Werner Richter's *Bestandsaufnahme*.[18] Three years later the publisher Desch edited a follow-up to this successful anthology, updating the subtitle to *Eine deutsche Bilanz 1965*. The journalist Klaus Bölling contributed a piece entitled 'Tabus in diesem Land'.[19] The title pages of both books laid great stress on bringing together academics, writers and journalists. In his bestseller, *Wohin treibt die Bundesrepublik?* (1966), the philosopher Karl Jaspers saw literature, the media, and academic scholarship combining to promote 'a sense of facts' by challenging taboos.[20] Educating the public to a 'sense of facts' and to freedom was the task facing literature, journalism, and philosophy alike. Jaspers thus commended the writers belonging to Group 47 for 'saying how things are'[21] and praised the editors of the magazine *Der Spiegel* for 'uncovering facts'.[22]

Even before taboo appeared in the headlines however, the closeness to each other of literature, the media and knowledge in terms of engaging in social criticism was hinted at by two contributors to Walser's *Die Alternative*, Fritz J. Raddatz and Axel Eggebrecht. Like Zwerenz, Raddatz was a refugee from the GDR, while Eggebrecht belonged to a generation older than most of the members of Group 47. Whereas Eggebrecht stressed the taboo-breaking quality of literature,[23] Raddatz focused on the media, blaming them for creating taboos by using catchwords. He referred to *Bewältigung der Vergangenheit* as a recent instance of this.[24]

## THE CHALLENGE TO THE OFFICIAL MEMORY'S 'MASTERING OF THE PAST'

When the term *Bewältigung der Vergangenheit* entered public debate in the years 1958/59, writers like Heinrich Böll initially used it to mean breaking with all the German traditions which had led to fascism and with which the FRG had not as yet broken.[25] Once the oppositional sense contained in 'unmastered' had been jettisoned, the official language could take the term on board and ally it to the attempt being made to safeguard national continuity by 'mastering' the past. An example of this is the book *Regierung Adenauer 1949–1963*, edited by the Press and Information Office of the Federal Government. Here the official memory of the Nazi past was confined almost exclusively to the suffering of Germans. They were portrayed as the innocent victims of bombing, expulsion and captivity. Detailed documentation was provided. In contrast, victims of racist and political-ideological persecution were never mentioned. Special stress was laid on Adenauer's declaration on the subject of the honour of the German soldier. Adenauer's unqualified vindication of his role followed from the dominant legal view that the Federal Republic was identical with the German Reich, a claim which the book rehearsed at great length. The kind of national continuity postulated by the government and the judiciary was presented as the reason for the policy of restitution (*Wiedergutmachung*) and its restriction to payments to Israel. This legalistic view of the Federal Republic's relation to the Nazi past also allowed judicial 'atonement' to be seen as an adequate means of cleansing Germany of Nazism, indeed of liquidating Nazism for ever. Restitution payments and criminal justice were deemed to have succeeded in mastering this chapter in Germany's past.[26] This whole stress on the unchallenged continuity between the Reich as nation and the Federal Republic normalised Nazism by presenting it as a minor aberration from German history. Thus it is hardly surprising that leftist and left-liberal writers – if they had not already decided to polemicise explicitly against the term – started to put *Bewältigung* in inverted commas and often equated 'mastering' with tabooing.

Whereas very few of the professional journalists who took part in the debate either avoided the term completely or criticized it outright, many writers ironized the 'much-quoted',[27] 'much-talked about',[28] 'commonly confessed',[29] 'so readily quoted',[30] 'catchword', 'phrase', 'slogan' or even, as Enzensberger put it, 'highly specialised drivel about mastering'[31] in order to make clear that they wanted a clear break with nationalistic traditions, a break against which the government worked by congratulating itself on its success in mastering the past. Instead of this 'habitual ritual', Enzensberger called for the recognition that a compelling historical link existed between fascism and the division of Germany:'diese Vergangenheit hat direkte historische Folgen: statt seelischer Andachtsübungen legt sie politische Taten für die Zukunft nahe.'[32]

One of those who, like Enzensberger, criticized the term was Wolfdietrich Schnurre. Referring to the etymology of the word, he denounced *Bewältigung* as 'violent repression',[33] and his 1963 essays are important examples of how writers equated the 'mastering' sought by the official memory with both repression and taboo. Schnurre took issue with the glorification of the Second World War as well as with the 'ramparts of silence, the barricades of oblivion' which surrounded only the persecuted victims of fascism.[34] He criticised the official memory, not for derealising the Nazi past in general, but for selecting specific aspects of it. He explained this mode of selecting what was to be remembered and what forgotten in terms of the 'totems of tradition'.[35] In so far as he defined it as both one of the public media and a form of knowledge, literature played an important part in Schnurre's polemic against the nationalistic tradition and the gaps in its memory.[36] In recommending Gerhard Schoenberner's documentation *Der gelbe*

*Stern,*[37] a combination of photos and texts, Schnurre appealed to his readers, 'Glauben Sie nur der Realität. Es gibt Dokumente.'[38] Remembering what was left out of official and public memory became the main function he ascribed to literature. In his view it could usefully supplement the documents by providing a sense of links and connections[39] and by facilitating empathy.[40] The latter would facilitate the ability to mourn.[41] Narrative literature could not, however, he insisted, achieve these goals without documents.[42] Schnurre was not only very explicit about the function of literature with regard to the public memory; he also stressed the dangers of tabooing, 'Tabus verbauen den Blick auf wahre Erfahrungen, die uns heute weiterhelfen könnten.'[43]

## Recognising the Reality of Two German States as a Result of the Nazi Past

Schnurre was not the only writer to argue that one should recognise the two German states both as reality and as a result of Nazism. One of the most striking features of the emerging discourse in which the term taboo played such a central role is the link between the focusing of the public memory on Nazi crimes, particularly on their symbolisation in Auschwitz, and the 'relativisation of the Cold War' – as Gerhard Zwerenz put it in his book *Wider die deutschen Tabus. Kritik der reinen Unvernunft*(1962).[44] The main taboo attacked by Zwerenz was the aim of German reunification. He took 13 August 1961, i.e, the building of the Berlin Wall, as proof that this political goal had not only been questionable; it had been a pure fiction.[45] He called for the fictionalism enshrined in the political consensus of the parties represented in the Federal parliament[46] to be replaced by a policy of clinically naming these fictions in the public sphere.[47] Whereas he saw 'nauseating traditionalism' as safeguarding the taboo,[48] he presented criticism as the force which would enable Germans to face the reality both of the past and the present:

> Wir haben alles verloren, was unsern Altvordern lebenswichtig schien: das einheitliche Reich, die Größe und Herrlichkeit, das weltpolitische Mitspracherecht. Bitte, sehen Sie sich um, gewahren Sie die noch weinenden Gestalten: um Kolonien, um Schlesien, Ostpreußen, Sudetenland, Sachsen, Thüringen, Pommern, Mecklenburg wird geweint. Mit Recht oder Unrecht – wo aber weinen Deutsche um die gemordeten Polen, Juden, Russen?... Nennen wir

also die Dinge beim Namen. Unsere Väter haben Deutschland in zwei Kriegen verloren. Das deutsche Reich ist hinüber.'[49]

Zwerenz linked this recognition of the past reality of fascist-racist mass murder against Poles, Jews and Russians to the reality of the present and the future existence of two German states in presenting the end of the Reich on 8 May 1945 as the final judgement on German nationalism.

The image most frequently used to illustrate the causal relationship between the Nazi past and the existence of two German states was the Berlin Wall. Although Western Cold War propaganda relied heavily on the comparison between the Wall and the wire surrounding concentration camps, writers did not hesitate to suggest a rather different point of reference to which, in their view, the Wall had to be related. As early as in the anthology *Die Mauer oder Der 13.August* which Richter edited in the important series *rororo aktuell* in the late summer of 1961, Michael Mansfeld drew the line from the Berlin Wall to the wall around the Warsaw ghetto. It was less his criticism of 'a criminally short memory' than the rather paradoxical pronouncement, 'Niemand wagt es zu sagen'[50] which hinted at how Berlin Wall and Nazi past would in future be linked in the literary-political discourse on taboo. Schnurre initially reacted to the building of the Wall as a reborn cold warrior, attacking East German writers for not protesting against it. In his view this proved that they had not learnt the lesson of the Nazi past, namely that there is no such thing as 'inner emigration'.[51] Two years later, in contrast, he claimed that they were suffering, not from malicious chance events, but from fearful effects which had causes: 'Zum Beispiel hat es schon einmal eine Mauer gegeben, die Deutsche um Wehrlose errichteten, nämlich die Mördermauer, die den jüdischen Wohnbezirk Warschaus von der Außenwelt abschnitt, um die unglückseligen Menschen dahinter dem sicheren Verderben preiszugeben.'[52]

In the same year Hans Magnus Enzensberger, when defining the writer's role in a polemic against the traditional notion of 'the conscience of the nation', referred implicitly to taboo. The writer, he declared, had to speak up, 'weil von dem, was jeder weiß, niemand etwas wissen will, und keiner spricht es aus.'[53] The Wall was once again Enzensberger's evidence for a situation in which, because the media were politically controlled, what was obvious had become unthinkable. It symbolised the final end of all the illusions and fictions which had been based upon the core taboo, namely the identity of Reich and Federal Republic notwithstanding Auschwitz and Stalingrad.[54] He claimed that the Wall's foundation stone had been laid on 22 June 1941 and that both sides had constantly been building it up since 1946. He concluded, 'mit dem Bauwerk...ist eine Vergangenheit gewachsen, die sich so wenig bewältigen läßt wie jene andere, deren Erbe sie antritt.'[55] Enzensberger used the presentation of the Büchner prize to argue in favour of *détente*, insisting that the German nation, whether viewed as one state or as one culturally defined people, had ended. The only thing that Germans shared with each other was the division of Germany, 'Die Zerrissenheit ist unsere Identität.'[56] The notion that the realities brought about by the Nazi war in Europe were self-evident was also at the heart of Günter Grass's public commitment to the SPD. Like Enzensberger he did not refer to the traditional authority of the German poet as priest or prophet; instead he claimed that his political insights were obvious. Only taboos forced upon the populace by powerful institutions prevented people from recognizing the reality of the situation. In an election campaign speech in 1967 he singled out three taboos: the existence of the GDR, the definitive character of the Oder-Neisse border, and the honouring of Nazi medals like the *Ritterkreuz* by the *Bundeswehr*:

> Alle wissen es: Die DDR existiert. Alle wissen es: Schlesien, Ostpreußen, Pommern sind vertan und verloren. Alle wissen es: Das Ritterkreuz belohnte militärische Leistungen, deren Ziele ein verbrecherisches System gesteckt hatte. Aber trotz des umfassenden Wissens stehen die heiligen indischen Kühe in unserer politischen Landschaft herum; sie fressen kaum wachsender Erkenntnis die Triebe ab.[57]

The power of taboos was such that Heinrich Böll could regard explaining in public how the Wall came about as the ultimate proof of a writer's courage.[58]

An author who had only recently come to the West, Uwe Johnson, fell victim to those busy upholding the taboos aimed against the existence of the GDR, to say nothing of its legitimacy. His articles on the Berlin trams ridiculed the illusions of the boycotteers; he sought instead to promote a sober recognition of the present position.[59] In 1964 Johnson defined tabooing as not recognizing the consequences of the past in the present. For him reality was the opposite of what was tabooed:'Die Folgen des Krieges, den die vorigen Deutschen uns nach Hause geholt haben, schieben wir auf die Stadtbahn. Wir anerkennen sie nicht.'[60] Earlier, in August 1961, the exile Hermann Kesten was not alone in finding highly provocative Johnson's insistence that the Wall was the result of the Second World War.[61] Some writers even went further by not only insisting that the existence of two states was a consequence of the criminal attempt to dominate Europe by means of war and racist persecution, but also by criticising the problematic continuity produced by the official view of the Federal Republic as the legal successor to the Reich – whether Hitler's or somebody else's.

## THE BREAK WITH GERMAN CONTINUITIES

Schallück, in his contribution to Richter's *Bestandsaufnahme*, was one of the first writers to declare anti-Communism the continuation of Nazi anti-Semitism.[62] In the years which followed, such diverse writers as Peter Weiss, Martin Walser, and Erich Fried repeated this view. Weiss saw anti-Communism as the substitute for anti-Semitism when he argued for accepting that the GDR was the result of Auschwitz.[63] Martin Walser's essay 'Unser Auschwitz' stressed that re-education had amounted to replacing the nationalistic image of the Jew as the enemy with that of the Communist.[64] For his part, Erich Fried, while recognising remarkable parallels between the apparatuses of murder and oppression in the tyrannical systems of Hitler and Stalin found the widely favoured equating of Communism with National Socialism 'flachköpfig' und extremely unbefitting for Germans.[65] This view called into question the anti-totalitarian consensus underlying the Basic Law or, to be precise, the consensus among those parties who distanced themselves from so-called enemies of the constitution on the basis of the 'free democratic basic order'. Instead of equating red and brown, Schallück, Weiss, Walser and Fried now used the continuity claimed by the official memory to turn it against the FRG. They refuted the claim implied in the constitution's anti-totalitarianism that the FRG had broken with Nazism and pointed to an anti-democratic continuity linking, not only the personnel, but also the social-psychology of the present to those of the Nazi past.

Although the problem of continuity was not yet discussed in terms of political and economic structures, critics like Schallück did go beyond a personalizing polemic such as that against Adenauer's Secretary of State, Globke, who all too easily embodied the disputed continuity. However, Schallück was more concerned with the difference between the official and the popular memory. As he, like others, conceded that there had been some genuine distancing from Nazism in favour of parliamentary democracy and the rule of law, he was critical of the effect which the nationalistic stress on continuity could have on the populace. He criticised the official memory for providing a safe haven[66] for Nazi resentments and prejudices by upholding taboos about what was beyond discussion.[67] Schallück argued that because nationalism was not questioned in the official public sphere, ideological continuity could flourish in a semi-public, although not completely private area of West German society, namely in pubs and railway compartments. There opinions were to be heard which gave the lie to the official distancing from Nazism. The metaphors used by Schallück to support his claim that in socio-psychological terms taboos acted as a highly problematic guarantee of continuity are in themselves historically relevant to the issue of continuity or break between the Reich and the FRG. In asserting that taboos restored the thicket of prejudices,[68] Schallück went back to the metaphor of *Kahlschlag* or total, root-and-branch clearance.[69] He implicitly drew an unfavourable comparison between the 1960s in the FRG and the immediate post-war years in the Western Zones of Occupation. Whereas then an attempt had been made to chop down and clear out all Nazi wood from public opinion, the official memory of the restoration period had spared this thicket. Although Schallück did not explicitly advocate renewing the attempt to make a new beginning – the first having, in his view, failed in 1949 – most of the left-liberal contributors to the debate subscribed to this notion.

## THE REDISCOVERING OF THE IMMEDIATE POST-WAR YEARS

The renewed interest in the years prior to the founding of the two German states was closely related to the obvious delegitimisation of the two claims which the official memory of the Federal Republic had until then managed to combine, namely the notion of national continuity and that of a democratic break with Nazism. Once the Cold War had been relativised, it was possible to argue that both German states represented an attempt to learn from the Nazi experience. But in the early 1960s only a writer like Heiner Kipphardt would go this far. After leaving the German Democratic

Republic, he kept in contact with colleagues like Peter Hacks to whom he favourably compared the East German treatment of the past as a disease with the dangerous West German policy of leaving things alone.[70] Most writers on the liberal left, however, restricted their criticism to calling for the GDR to be recognised as a reality and refusing to continue anti-Communism in the Nazi style.

Both ways of relating GDR socialism to the Nazi past symbolised by Auschwitz – either by presenting it as the result of Nazism or by claiming that anti-Semitism had been replaced in the FRG by anti-Communism – can be found in Alexander Mitscherlich's writings. Interestingly enough, however, in *Die Unfähigkeit zu trauern* he and his co-author Margarete Mitscherlich confined their argument to the first one, whereas Mitscherlich's earlier contribution to Richter's *Bestandsaufnahme* drew a direct line from anti-Semitism to anti-Communism.[71] The first definition, or rather description, of taboo which occurs in the Mitscherlichs' book makes the same linkage between Nazi past and the existence of two German states that left-liberal writers and journalists had been arguing since the late 1950s, namely that if one denied what had happened in the Third Reich, one did not have to recognise the consequences of these events either.[72] Two descriptions, given *en passsant* by the Mitscherlichs of the socio-psychological consequences of taboos in politics and society, do, however, make clear that the discourse about taboo did more than link the Nazi past to the present of the two German states; it was also part of a wider process of modernising the Federal Republic: 'Tabu befördert Ressentiment, dieses blockiert ein freies Urteil und vermehrt die Rückständigkeit.'[73] Public criticism of taboos would, it was claimed, result in overcoming backwardness and gaining momentum with which to modernise West Germany. An unsparing critical reappraisal of the tabooed past would provide more 'mobility' for decisions in the present.[74] The main point, however, of the Mitscherlichs' reasoning on taboo – and in this it fitted in with previous literary and journalistic contributions to the discourse – was that they anchored it in the past. The term taboo served to explain all those patterns of behaviour which the Mitscherlichs saw as out of step with the reality of the present and which therefore made a truly modern future impossible.[75] For that reason they, like others, appealed for enlightenment, criticism, and a break with the traditionalism that had marked German backwardness.

They thus used taboo in 1967 as a term to explain and describe a principle governing the relation between past and present. The fact that certain aspects of the past were being ignored seemed the only possible explanation for the lasting influence of this past on the present. Whereas this suggested that the past blocked possible action in the present, one could argue that it was in fact the changed present which led to the past being reinterpreted. The notion that *détente* changed the perception of the past is supported by the fact that the Mitscherlichs used the term taboo in a sense which did not require substantiating from psychoanalysis proper and relied on the by then established way of talking about taboos.

The emergence of Karl Jaspers as a leading political critic in the years prior to the publication of *Die Unfähigkeit zu trauern* is another pointer in this direction. His hostility towards psycho-analysis underlines the fact that the discourse on taboo in which he participated was not a psychological one. Like Mitscherlich, he was also an academic author who had played a prominent intel-lectual role in the immediate post-war years, and the reemergence of both Mitscherlich and Jaspers shows that Schallück did not adopt the metaphorical language of *Kahlschlag* by accident. More open than Mitscherlich, Jaspers saw the 1960s as the chance to compensate for the missed opportunities of the late 1940s. His 1960 essay, *Freiheit und Wiedervereinigung*, abounds in metaphors like 'a thicket of vague notions' and anecdotes from the immedi-ate post-war years.[76] Jaspers explicitly urged his readers to give up the claim for reunification: it was the product of a vicious circle involving politicians and voters and depended on taboos which bred only a general untruthfulness, 'Die Wahrheit des politischen Lebens wäre es, diese Tabus zu durchbrechen.'[77] Reunification was seen as taboo, less because it was unachievable in practical terms, and more because of the refusal on the part of both the political parties and the populace to recognise the consequences of Nazism.[78] Jaspers went so far as to deny that the nation state was the norm in political life.[79] He argued against the supposed conti-nuity of the German state[80] and praised the rupturing of German political traditions as something essentially positive.[81] Because, in his view, the FRG had not completely broken with Nazism and the nation state, he called for the reinvigorating refounding of a Ger-man state, of the Federal Republic, based on public debate and the full participation of its citizens.[82] Jaspers argued that anyone for whom the *kleindeutsch* Wilhelminian state with its military power, its territorial boundaries, its economic prosperity, and its pseudo-constitutionalism were still the norm was being led astray by a ghost of the past.[83]

In 1963 Ulrich Sonnemann accorded Jaspers's essay the rather dubious merit of having created a perceptible silence around a taboo of which he had only scraped the surface.[84] Yet his own call for a new enlightenment,[85] even a revolution, in order to achieve self-purification from Nazism[86] remained quite close to the perspective which Jaspers sketched for the FRG. Thus he proposed that the state founded in 1949 should be re-established on a better base.[87] Public debate would replace the taboos and fictions of the 1950s and early 1960s.[88] The term *nachholen* captured the idea that something had to be done in the present which had not been done in the past, or had been done badly then. It became part of the discourse on *Vergangenheitsbewältigung* in the 1960s. Thus the exiled writer Jean Amery outlined the preconditions for at last carrying out the German revolution which had originally failed.[89] Harry Pross dwelt on the opportunities missed in 1945.[90] Such writers equated official West German taboos with the language regulations[91] imposed by Goebbels and accepted by a populace caught in authoritarian traditions of thought.[92] Gerhard Schoenberner argued that 'subaltern German overzealousness' meant that a Ministry of Propaganda was no longer needed.[93] The lack of cosmopolitan, liberal traditions provided Schoenberner with an explanation for the fact that in the FRG public taboos played a worse role than in other Western countries.[94] In his view, Bonn taboos and slogans of the day continued to dominate the largest section of public opinion.[95] At the same time the *Spiegel* affair encouraged him to generalise about the opportunities afforded public opinion by the impact of international *détente* on the domestic situation in the Federal Republic.[96] He challenged the alleged political-ideological and socio-psychological continuity between Nazi past and West German present. The Federal Republic was to be brought into line with American-Soviet *détente* by recognizing the results of the Second World War, i.e., the Oder-Neiße border as well as the German Democratic Republic. The same point was made by Walter Euchner, one of the young social scientists – mostly students of the Frankfurt School – who edited a rororo-aktuell anthology in 1965 which urged voters to vote against the irrational policy of the CDU/CSU and FDP. Euchner's argument in favour of *détente* was mirrored in the same volume by Rene Postius's polemic against the official 'mastering of the past'. Whereas Euchner described the consequences of failing to recognize post-war realities,[97] Postius found the reasons for this tabooing in the treatment of the Nazi past.[98]

## FROM BREAKING WITH TABOOS TO MARXIST CRITIQUE OF IDEOLOGY

In the preface to this anthology, however, the writer and university teacher Walter Jens, who as a member of the Group 47 was also one of the most influential literary critics at that time, detected a new current in the thinking of West German intellectuals. He traced it back to the authors' academic teachers, i.e., Adorno, Horkheimer, Mitscherlich, and – at a further remove – Bloch and Marcuse, all of whose methodology had been shaped by Marx's critique of ideology.[99] However, Jens's attempt to justify the version of socialism they recommended by equating it with that propagated in 1947 by the left-wing catholics of the *Frankfurter Hefte* does less to explain the increasing interest in Marxism than does the definition of taboo offered by another young social scientist and journalist, Harry Pross. Pross saw critique of ideology as a means of accounting for the existence of taboos within a society. Taking the painting of swastikas on synagogues and Jewish graves in the winter of 1959/60 as his point of departure, he defined the task of writing about contemporary history as being to challenge myths and penetrate the taboo-zone of national convention in order to discover whose interests taboos serve.[100] This came very close to the marxist definition of ideology. Critique of taboos was in his view the quintessential shared task of all those – poets, writers, journalists, and reporters – whom he subsumed under the term publicist.[101]

Pross juxtaposed apparatuses which utilise national taboos and publicists who bring negative aspects into public, open debate. Yet he was less interested in the specific interests served by taboos than in the general function of the public sphere as a means of democratising society in Germany.[102] Like Jaspers he brings together writers, those working in the media, and academics, all of whom he regards as critics and writers of contemporary history. Pross's position is close to the concept of literature as historiography[103] which Enzensberger presented to the very first international literary conference of writers from East and West in Leningrad in 1963. It is also part of a second emergent trend in the discourse on taboo. Pross commented on Enzensberger's 'Gratisangst und Gratismut' that what Enzensberger understood by gratuitous fear was, in sociological terms, the pressure of the social super-ego on the ego.[104] The subtitle of Pross's own work was *Zur deutschen Sozialpathologie*.

## FROM BREAKING WITH TABOOS TO THE SOCIO-PSYCHOLOGICAL CRITIQUE OF THE AUTHORITARIAN PERSONALITY

The application of Freudian terminology to the discourse on taboos increased over the years, and this can be seen in essays by Heißenbüttel, Kipphardt, and Geissler.[105] Enzensberger analysed how the reception of Freud was first delayed and then dominated by socio-psychological rather than clinical concerns. In his essay on the Eichmann trial he quoted extensively for the first time from Freud's writing on taboo. He argued that, whereas in the 1930s it was primarily sexual taboos which blocked reception of Freud's theories, it had long been their social and political consequences which now accounted for the resistance to psychoanalytical theory. The clearer these consequences became, the more thoroughly they were repressed.[106] In according priority to the socio-historical and political, Enzensberger followed the attempts made by his teachers in the Frankfurt School to bring together Marxism and psychoanalysis. There are echoes in Enzenberger's position of Adorno's writing on taboo. However, if one compares the definition of taboo in Adorno's speech 'Tabus über dem Lehrberuf'(1965) and his earlier 'Sexualtabus und Recht heute' (1963), a change can also be seen in Adorno's discussion of taboos. Whereas the later text dealt with them in accordance with the meaning dominant at the time, i.e., primarily as prejudices without any real foundation,[107] the earlier paper compared the relative strength of sexual and political taboos and concluded that sexual ones were at present stronger.[108] What seems to contradict Enzensberger's theory on the resistance to psychoanalysis, in the end actually supports it. Adorno stressed the strength of the sexual taboos only to point to the socio-psychological continuity between Nazi past and West German present, seeing the continuity of the authoritarian personality, even if this was politically only latent, as more dangerous than manifest neo-Nazism: 'Die deutschen Sexualtabus fallen in jenes ideologische und psychologische Syndrom des Vorurteils, das dem Nationalsozialismus die Massenbasis verschaffen half und das in einer dem manifesten Inhalt nach entpolitisierten Form fortlebt. Zu ihrer Stunde könnte sie auch politisch sich konkretisieren.'[109]

The emphasis which Adorno laid on the mass base distinguished his treatment of the taboos on Nazi racism and its consequences for the present from the thinking of those who went further in the direction of equating taboo and ideology. Whereas

Adorno's intervention in the discourse on *Vergangenheitsbewälti-gung* anticipated both the psychoanalytical concern with 'the subjective aspect' and also the Marxist foregrounding of the objective, socio-economic factor, the reception of Marxism led to some problematic consequences as far as German history was concerned.

## The Critique of the Private Ownership of the Means of Production

Although the initial reception was more aware of its shortcomings in terms of its accuracy about the factual memories of West German society, the Mitscherlichs' book began to become the seminal text on the relation between Nazi past and West German present in 1967.[110] In that same year Wolfgang Fritz Haug's *Der hilflose Antifaschismus* also appeared. The term taboo created some common ground between the two books which otherwise represented the differing directions of critique of ideology and psychoanalysis.[111] In his critique of recent lectures on National Socialism Haug concentrated on examining taboo words and phrases like 'jene Zeit', 'das, was geschehen', 'was möglich war'.[112] He demystified the prevailing generalisations about the past as a kind of repression both in terms of its nationalism and its 'hostility to sex'.[113] His study of the repressing vocabulary led him to conclude that the only genuine taboo was the economic continuity between Nazi and West Germany.[114] However, his insistence that naming individual Germanists who had been Nazis was the only real taboo-breaking, did not fit in with his preoccupation with structural, socio-economic continuity. There is a similar contradiction in the Mitscherlichs' book where, although private ownership of the means of production is called a central taboo,[115] it is never discussed again.

These contradictions were easily resolved by those critics, albeit very few in number, who, as Enzensberger put it, 'took their leave of the German question'[116] They reduced everything to monopoly capitalism, preferably US imperialism. Auschwitz was equated with Hiroshima. Enzensberger, for instance, claimed that the atomic strategies of both the US and the Soviet Union put both Auschwitz and Hiroshima in the shade.[117] In his series in *Kursbuch*, 'Die sprachlose Intelligenz', Karl Markus Michel warned intellectuals about reproducing the social conditions of their thinking in their thinking itself: 'Im heutigen Westdeutschland sind dies vorab der Monopolkapitalismus und die "deutsche Frage" – zwei Phänomene, von denen jedes den Blick auf das andere verstellt.'[118] Whereas Michel took this ideological reproduction of the conditions of critique as the real taboos,[119] shortly afterwards, in the cultural-political journal *Konkret*, all the issues which had been at the centre of the critical discourse of the early 1960s were ridiculed as a service done to West German industry. The German Democratic Republic, the Oder-Neiße border and, last but not least, the pill were dubbed innocuous taboos.[120] This cynical far-left postscript to the pre-1968 discourse on taboo totally omits the Nazi past! It mirrors the complex intertwining of issues observable in the reaction of right-wing intellectuals to the emerging hegemony of the left-liberal discourse on the taboos about past and present which had prevailed in the late 1950s and early 1960s.

## IN DEFENCE OF TABOOS: MORALS, THE NATION, AESTHETICS

This cluster of reactions can be seen most revealingly in the scandal surrounding the film version of Günter Grass's novella *Katz und Maus*. The scene in which the son of the Foreign Minister, Willy Brandt, masturbates on the *Ritterkreuz* caused an uproar. The Chairman of the Spitzenverband der Soldaten- und Traditionsverbände, Erwin Schönborn, claimed that his members (among whom were former members of the SS), members of the CDU/CSU and FDP and some Social Democrats were united in their rejection of this 'defiling of German decorations by this son of Brandt'.[121] Schönborn's apparently abstract claim that family morality and national morality were indivisible was aimed against Brandt, whose past and present politics contradicted the official, nationalist memory as well as the popular one. Having been in exile as a socialist and returned to Germany in a Norwegian uniform, Brandt accepted the existence of two German states as reality and as a consequence of the Second World War. Schönborn presented his son's masturbating as the result of Brandt's politics: 'Wer keine rechte Moral gegenüber seinem Volk und gegenüber dem Deutschen Reich gekannt hat, in dessen Familie kann eben auch die allgemeine Moral nicht in Ordnung sein.'[122] In a review of the novel the critic Jost Nolte had already commented: 'Der Angriff auf das Tabu wächst sich zu einer jede gebräuchliche Freizügigkeit übertreffenden Blasphemie aus.'[123] In suggesting that art had to stay within certain limits to preserve its autonomy,

Nolte added an important element to the conservative defence of morality and nationality against those who challenged taboos. In general, the argumentative strategy of the right-wing intellectuals who had dominated the literary life of the 1950s[124] was a kind of double-strategy. The self-contradictory nature of their undertaking showed them to be on the defensive. On the one hand they attempted to justify the existence of taboos on a) moral, b) national, and c) aesthetic grounds; on the other, they blamed the left and liberal intellectuals for erecting 'new' taboos. While they rejected the view that saw taboos as something negative, their own position nevertheless depended on regarding certain taboos in this light. But the taboos they criticised were confined to recently arrived concepts and images of critique, enlightenment and emancipation. They opposed these to venerable notions of long standing. Whereas right-wing intellectuals had to pose as critics when attacking the taboos of their opposite numbers, in their justification of taboos they called for emotions, not for reasoning. As far as morals were concerned, they opposed shame to sexual conformity.[125] With regard to the nation they preferred a sense of history to the 'seductive notion of zero hour'.[126] Finally, their aesthetics polarised good taste and the abuse of art for anti-aesthetic purposes.[127]

Initially their defence of taboos could rely on the hegemonic position conservative criticism had enjoyed in the 1950s. The key concept in the literary criticism of the editor of the *Frankfurter Allegemeine Zeitung*, Friedrich Sieburg, throughout the 1950s had been 'tact'. It became virtually impossible to distinguish between moral, national-political and aesthetic judgments. In a 1957 review of Erich Kuby's *Das ist des Deutschen Vaterland*[128] Sieburg rejected Kuby's questioning of the policy of reunification, asserting, 'nicht jede Hemmung ist eine "Tabu-Zone", nicht jede Scheu ist feiges Verschweigen, nicht jede Regung des Taktes ist Konformismus.'[129] The afterword to a volume of Rudolf Hagelstange's essays which appeared in 1958, as well as Hans Egon Holthusen's criticism of Hannah Arendt's *Eichmann in Jerusalem* (1964) show just how much tact was expected of writers if they were to unite morals and aesthetics for the sake of national solidarity. Hagelstange's editor justified the silence on Nazi crimes in the earlier 1950s in terms of 'shame', while at the same time stating that this silence had gradually ended because writers like Hagelstange had succeeded in balancing atonement and honour.[130] Upholding the honour of the German soldier and advocating reconciliation with the Jews – at least on the part of the German elite – were grounded less in the concept of collective liability elaborated by Jaspers in his 1946 lectures on the question of guilt, and more in the reformulation of this notion as 'collective shame'. The President of the Federal Republic had lent this term authority in two speeches delivered in Bergen-Belsen and Berlin-Bendlerstaße.[131] National pride and limited criticism of the German people's moral behaviour were thus reconciled. The same parallelising works in referring the imperative, 'Rühr mich nicht an',[132] both to the honour of the German soldier and to the feelings of the victim of racist persecution demanding atonement in the form of restitution. Seven years later Holthusen seemingly spoke on behalf of the sensibilities of former Jewish inmates of concentration camps and their need for taboos when he attacked Arendt's moralising for being inimical to any sense of solidarity.[133] Arendt's relentless criticism of the Jewish Councils typified for him the German left's moralising attempts to enlighten the public, which by their very tactlessness destroyed all national solidarity. Unless aesthetic considerations balanced moral criticism, the essential harmony required by the nation was, in his view, endangered.

Two popular catchwords – 'das eigene Nest beschmutzen' and 'auf den Gefühlen herumtrampeln' – served as means of casting doubts on the morals of any critics. Klaus Bölling and Hermann Schreiber, two journalists who on the whole supported the challenge to the tabooing of the Nazi past and its consequences in the present, could only maintain their middle-of-the-road position by seeking refuge with these catchphrases.[134] In his contribution to *Eine deutsche Bilanz 1965* Bölling, on the one hand, criticized the earlier promised title, *Tabus in unserem Land*, while, on the other, referring approvingly to the 'instinct to spare oneself'.[135] This term as well as the nest metaphor and the reference to sentiments made clear that what was at stake in the confrontation between those breaking taboos and those justifying them was the sense of a national self. The defenders of taboos appealed to the 'wholeness' of German history. Faced by an interpretation of German history which gave Auschwitz centrality and did not demand reunification as a future goal, they sought to build on the affirmation of historical continuity.[136] The Christian-Democratic Minister of Culture in Baden-Württemberg, Wilhelm Hahn, referring to the terms, collective liability and shame, rejected the left-liberal view of history in general for not having a positive relationship to the entirety of German history.[137] Similarly, Ernst Jünger's former secretary, Armin Mohler, condemned the left and the left-liberals for being attracted by the notions of 'zero hour' and 'tabula rasa'.[138] In overstating their actual influence in society for tactical reasons, Mohler went as far as to say that their history was for Germans no longer a tradition which gave them strength and support.[139] Conservatives saw 'experience' as the main guarantee of this endangered sense of continuity, wholeness and tradition. Thus the former Communist exile, William S. Schlamm, castigated the intellectual elite of the Federal Republic for their attempt to eradicate fifteen years of collective German experience from the collective memory.[140] This reference to one collective experience implied there was one single voice which alone could speak for the nation.

The criterion of 'experience' linked the question of authority, albeit in a contradictory way, to the concept of 'generation'. Conservatives' definition of the nation as a chain of generations lent the authority of experience to everyone who had lived in Nazi Germany, in particular those who had served their country as soldiers in the war. Age was irrelevant. The generation problem only arose when either those who had left Nazi Germany and gone into exile or those who did not share the accepted view of serving Germany by fighting Hitler's war spoke out. Even so, they could be delegitimised by referring to 'the war experience' as a collective experience in the singular. They could also be blamed, not only for being young, but for breaking with the tradition, the continuity, and the wholeness of German history. Political dissent was replaced – if only in its representation – by the conflict of the generations.[141] The national and the moral argument in favour of taboos was supported by the aesthetic one. Paul Noack, the editor from 1953 to 1958 of the *Frankfurter Allgemeine Zeitung*, under the heading 'Die Angst vor der Tradition', took issue with the notion that literature always had articulate opposition to power, to society. He spoke of ahistorical commitment, steeped in the present moment.[142] Instead he defended the supposed autonomy of poetry against catchwords which injected so many extraliterary arguments into the literary debate that it was almost impossible to talk simply of poetry or literature without any other qualifying adjective. He then mounted the kind of counterattack which was the other side of the conservatives' attempt to justify taboo; he declared that the literature of the left, while claiming to fight against taboos, had in fact created its own taboos and that it was dangerous to attack.[143]

## THE RIGHT'S ATTACK ON LEFT-LIBERAL 'TABOOS': FOUR EXAMPLES

Conservative intellectuals frequently cited four examples of tabooing by their left-liberal counterparts. In so far as the first concerned the intellectual's critical role, the second the nation, the third anti-Semitism, and the fourth socialism, or more specifically the German Democratic Republic, these 'taboos' mirror the attempts made by left-liberal critics to break the taboos about the consequences of the Nazi past for the present. The claim made by left-liberal intellectuals to be critical of power and to articulate dissent was now turned against them; they were presented as organised conspirators dominating the media by virtue of their conformist views. When those attacked defended themselves against polemics by CDU/CSU politicians and the Springer media, Rudolf Krämer-Badoni suggested that the 'free-floating left intellectuals' were demanding, 'Wir sind tabu!'[144] He congratulated himself on having violated, even destroyed the taboo which prevented a middle-class public with whom these trends found great favour from recognising the reasons behind a general European drift leftwards among literary publicists.[145] The domination of the left-liberal element was the result of a conspiracy and a 'fixated historical reflex.'[146]

Friedrich Sieburg, like Krämer-Badoni, targeted Group 47. Using terms carefully chosen to allude to the Nazi past, he declared that the success of 'these characters' proved that taboo-breakers were 'fellow travellers' marching in time with the general trend.[147] Both Sieburg's and Krämer-Badoni's polemical articles against the totalitarian rule of conformists from Group 47 over the literary life of the FRG constantly referred to the second taboo laid at the door of left-liberal intellectuals, namely the nation. In 1963, commenting on contemporary literature at the very moment when West German literature was beginning to enjoy international recognition, Sieburg named Bachmann, Böll, Grass, Johnson, and Walser and stated that this literature was meaningless since it tabooed the nation, 'Die Taue zur Vergangenheit sind gekappt'.[148] The writers of the FRG were people who knew about organisation and power and had taken over the cultural apparatus.[149] His conclusion was that the literature of the late 1950s and early 1960s added nothing to the cultural values which could turn Germans into a united whole. Only a literature which emerged from the kernel of the nation could form part of world literature, and therefore the path to world literature was blocked off for Germans.[150]

The break with the continuity, the tradition, and the wholeness of German history so deplored by the conservatives also had its point of reference in Auschwitz. In 1959 Schlamm asserted that the social taboo in Germany on all and every anti-Semitic cliché was stronger than all the social taboos he was acquainted with in Europe and the United States.[151] Schlamm himself did not explicitly say that some of the advice he had for the Germans if they wanted to develop a healthy nationalism was related to his diagnosis of the taboo on anti-Semitism. Six years later, however, Armin Mohler explicitly confronted the public reference to the six million victims of Auschwitz as 'das Groß-Tabu'.[152] The way in which Mohler appears to argue in favour of more objective research into contemporary history proves that the present is the main point of reference for his call for an end to the taboo on Auschwitz and anti-Semitism. He was anxious to end the causal connection between the moral guilt for those German crimes and all the political, economic, and financial payments in kind (!) demanded of the Germans after their defeat.[153] The prospect of a reunited, powerful Germany dominating Europe depended on Auschwitz being relativised and normalised. At this stage Mohler was in dispute with Ernst Nolte whose concept of fascism he attacked for abandoning the theory of totalitarianism and in particular for its tireless emphasis on the quite unique, incomparable nature of National Socialism.[154]

The fourth taboo projected onto left-liberal intellectuals by the conservative one was the reverse of the third in that the concept of totalitarianism made it possible to distance oneself from the course of German history and thus from both Auschwitz and the GDR. Auschwitz could be regarded as a product of a kind of totalitarianism similar to that in the GDR. At the same time, if Germany was to become a reunited, fully sovereign state, it was quite unacceptable for conservatives to recognise the GDR as reality and even less as a state legitimated by its anti-fascism. One simply could not put the FRG and the GDR on the same footing.

In much of the polemic revolving round Grass's and Schnurre's open letters to East German writers after 13 August 1961, writing or talking to communists was taken as proof that one had broken the anti-totalitarian consensus. Wolf Jobst Siedler, for instance, attacked Enzensberger precisely because of his 'scandalous' statement that one could compare the two German 'part-states',[155] even if for Enzensberger this comparability was damning for both sides.

—◆◆◆—

This survey of conservative counter-attacks makes two things clear: first, that they did not succeed in the 1960s, even if much of their thinking reemerged in the 1980s and took hold of the public debate after 1989/90; secondly, that the conservatives lost their hegemony as far as past and present were concerned long before 1968. When, in the aftermath of the official 'unification', the literary editors of the conservative *Frankfurter Allgemeine Zeitung* and the liberal *Die Zeit* joined forces to bring post-war literature to an end, the underlying assumption was clear: the re-erection of the sovereign nation state legitimised having forgotten a literature which had called into question the continuity of German history by remembering Nazi crimes. However, although it is possible to prove that Schirrmacher and Greiner are wrong in almost everything they write about the facts of literary life in West Germany during the 1950s and 1960s, it remains worrying that it was only acceptance of the fact that two German states existed which gave the horror of the past its centrality in public memory. One wonders what will happen after a 'normalisation' which has revitalised the spectre of the Reich and made a reality of a 'fiction' that had been attacked as *the* taboo by the critical writers, critics, and academics of the late 1950s and early 1960s.

## NOTES

1. G. Grass, *Die Blechtrommel*, Frankfurt a.M., 1971, 434.
2. D. Arker, *Nichts ist vorbei, alles kommt wieder. Untersuchungen zu Günter Grass' "Blechtrommel"*, Heidelberg, 1989, 138, 257–260.
3. A. and M. Mitscherlich, *Die Unfähigkeit zu trauern. Grundlagen kollektiven Verhaltens*, Munich, 1967, 43.
4. C. Levi, *Ich kam mit ein wenig Angst. Reisebilder aus Deutschland*, Frankfurt a.M., 1984, 27, 32.
5. See my article 'Towards a History of "Vergangenheitsbewältigung": East and West German War Novels of the 1950s', *Monatshefte* 87 (1995): 283–304.
6. P. Märthesheimer and I. Frenzel (eds), *Im Kreuzfeuer: Der Fernsehfilm Holocaust. Eine Nation ist betroffen*, Frankfurt a.M., 1979; *Der Spiegel*, 21.2.1994, 176.
7. Cf. H. Funke, *Der Verlust des Erinnerns im Gedenken*, in *Blätter für deutsche und internationale Politik*, 40 (1995): 37–45.

8. A. Hillgruber, 'Die Zerschlagung des Deutschen Reiches und das Ende der europäischen Juden', in R. Kühnl (ed.), *Vergangenheit, die nicht vergeht. Die "Historiker-Debatte", Darstellung Dokumentation Kritik*, Cologne, 1987, 23.

9. H. Lübbe, 'Es ist nichts vergessen, aber einiges ausgeheilt', in *Frankfurter Allgemeine Zeitung*, 24.1.1983.

10. M. Kittel, *Die Legende von der "Zweiten Schuld". Vergangenheitsbewältigung in der Ära Adenauer*, Berlin and Frankfurt a.M., 1993.

11. J. Habermas, 'Heinrich Heine und die Rolle des Intellektuellen in Deutschland', in *Merkur*, 40 (1986): 486.

12. G. Mattenklott, 'Kunst gegen das Künstliche', in H. Hoffmann and H. Klotz (eds), *Die Sechziger. Die Kultur unseres Jahrhunderts*, Düsseldorf, Vienna, New York, 1987, 75–93; W. Barner (ed.), *Geschichte der deutschen Literatur von 1945 bis zur Gegenwart*, Munich, 1994, 342–45.

13. H. Mayer, *Zur deutschen Literatur der Zeit. Zusammenhänge – Schriftsteller-Bücher*, Reinbek, 1967.

14. M. Reich-Ranicki, *Literatur der kleinen Schritte. Deutsche Schriftsteller heute*, Frankfurt a.M., Berlin, Vienna, 1971, 9 (first published in 1965).

15. I I.M. Enzensberger, 'Ankündigung einer neuen Zeitschrift', reprinted in *Kursbuch*, vol. 1, *Kursbuch 1–10 (1965–1967)*, Frankfurt a.M., n.d., 2.

16. Habermas, 'Heinrich Heine', 486.

17. G. Zwerenz, *Wider die deutschen Tabus. Kritik der reinen Unvernunft*, Munich, 1962. 18. P. Schallück, 'Vorurteile und Tabus', in H.W. Richter (ed.), *Bestandsaufnahme. Eine deutsche Bilanz 1962. Sechsunddreißig Beiträge deutscher Wissenschaftler, Schriftsteller und Publizisten*, Munich, Vienna, Basle, 1962, 432–43.

19. K. Bölling, 'Tabus in diesem Land', in H. Hammerschmidt (ed.), *Zwanzig Jahre danach. Eine deutsche Bilanz 1945–1965. Achtunddreißig Beiträge deutscher Wissenschaftler, Schriftsteller und Publizisten*, Munich, Vienna, Basle, 1965, 375–389.

20. K. Jaspers, *Wohin treibt die Bundesrepublik? Tatsachen. Gefahren. Chancen*, Munich, 1966, 182.

21. Ibid., 179.

22. Ibid., 181.

23. A. Eggebrecht, 'Soll die Ära der Heuchelei andauern?', in M. Walser (ed.), *Die Alternative oder Brauchen wir eine neue Regierung?*, Reinbek, 1961, 26–28.

24. F.J. Raddatz, 'Analyse, kaum Therapie', in Walser, *Die Alternative*, 82.

25. H. Böll, 'Zeichen an der Wand', in *Essayistische Schriften und Reden I: 1952–1963*, ed. B. Balzer, Cologne, 1978, 346.

26. *Regierung Adenauer 1949–1963*, ed. Presse- und Informationsamt der Bundesregierung, Wiesbaden, 1963, 301.

27. J. Amery, *Geburt der Gegenwart. Gestalten und Gestaltungen der westlichen Zivilisation seit Kriegsende*, Olten, Freiburg, 1961, 191.

28. H. Lindemann, 'Die neuen Lehren und Lehrer. Deutsche Mentalität im Wandel', in Hammerschmidt, *Zwanzig Jahre danach*, 134.

29. H. Schreiber, *Zwischenzeit. So leben wir*, Stuttgart, 1964, 109.

30. W. Schnurre, *Schreibtisch unter freiem Himmel. Polemik und Bekenntnis*, Olten, Freiburg, 1964, 243.

31. H.M. Enzensberger, 'Reflexionen vor einem Glaskasten', in H.H., *Im Gegenteil. Gedichte. Szenen. Essays. Vom Autor selbst zusammengetragen und mit einem Nachwort versehen*, Gütersloh, 1981, 96 (first published 1964).

32. H.M. Enzensberger, *Deutschland, Deutschland unter anderm. Äußerungen zur Politik*, Frankfurt a.M., 1967, 12.

33. Schnurre, *Schreibtisch*, p.243.
34. Ibid., 139.
35. Ibid., 234.
36. Ibid., 151.
37. G. Schoenberner, *Der gelbe Stern. Die Judenverfolgung in Europa 1933–1945*, 5th edn, Hamburg, 1961.
38. Schnurre, *Schreibtisch*, 138.
39. Ibid., 154.
40. Ibid., 169.
41. Ibid., 178.
42. Ibid., 169.
43. Ibid., 124.
44. Zwerenz, *Wider die deutschen Tabus*, 49.
45. Ibid., 171.
46. Ibid., 166.
47. Ibid., 49.
48. Ibid., 51.
49. Ibid., 52.
50. H.W. Richter (ed.), *Die Mauer oder Der 13. August*, Reinbek, 1961, 179.
51. Ibid., 65–66. See my analysis, 'Die Gruppe 47 und die Exilliteratur – ein Mißverständnis?', in J. Fetscher *et al.* (eds), *Die Gruppe 47 in der Geschichte der Bundesrepublik*, Würzburg, 1991, 108–34.
52. W. Schnurre, 'Mit der Mauer leben', in R. Hartung (ed.), *Hier schreibt Berlin heute. Eine Anthologie*, Munich, 1963, 44.
53. Enzensberger, *Deutschland*, 25.
54. 'Katechismus zur deutschen Frage', in *Kursbuch*, 4 (1966): 24, 49.
55. Enzensberger, *Deutschland*, 21.
56. Ibid., 22.
57. G. Grass, 'Rede von der Wut über den verlorenen Milchpfennig', in G.G., *Werkausgabe in zehn Bänden*, ed. V. Neuhaus, vol. 9, *Essays Reden Briefe Kommentare*, Darmstadt, Neuwied, 1987, 214.
58. H. Böll, 'Politik der Stärke als die schwächste aller möglichen', in K. Wagenbach *et al.* (eds), *Vaterland, Muttersprache. Deutsche Schriftsteller und ihr Staat seit 1945. Ein Nachlesebuch für die Oberstufe*, Berlin, 1979, 190.
59. U. Johnson, *Berliner Sachen. Aufsätze*, Frankfurt a.M., 1975, 41.
60. Ibid., 33.
61. Ibid., 14.
62. Schallück, *Vorurteile*, 440.
63. P. Weiss, *Rapporte 2*, Frankfurt a.M., 1971, 11 (first published in 1965).
64. M. Walser, *Heimatkunde. Aufsätze und Reden*, Frankfurt a.M., 1968, 16.
65. E. Fried, 'Warum ich nicht in der Bundesrepublik lebe', in Wagenbach, *Vaterland, Muttersprache*, 206 (first published in 1964).
66. Schallück, 'Vorurteile und Tabus', 443.
67. Ibid., 435.
68. Ibid, 435.
69. For an analysis of this metaphorics in the immediate post-war years see my article 'German Literature in 1945: Liberation for a New Beginning?', in N. Hewitt (ed.), *The Culture of Reconstruction. European Literature, Thought and Film, 1945–50*, Hounsmills, 1989, 172–90.

70. H. Kipphardt, *Schreibt die Wahrheit. Essays, Briefe, Entwürfe*, vol. 1, *1949–1964*, Reinbek, 1989, 275.
71. A. Mitscherlich, 'Humanismus heute in der Bundesrepublik', in Richter, *Bestandsaufnahme*, 151.
72. Mitscherlich, *Die Unfähigkeit zu trauern*, 14.
73. Ibid., 111.
74. Ibid., 135.
75. Ibid., 121.
76. K. Jaspers, *Lebensfragen der deutschen Politik*, Munich, 1963, 262.
77. Ibid., 249.
78. Ibid., 184.
79. Ibid., 182–3.
80. Ibid., 279–80.
81. Ibid., 216.
82. Ibid., 184.
83. Ibid., 184.
84. U. Sonnemann, *Das Land der unbegrenzten Zumutbarkeiten. Deutsche Reflexionen*, Reinbek, 1963, 146.
85. Ibid., 21.
86. Ibid., 25.
87. Ibid., 295.
88. Ibid., 12, 59.
89. J. Amery, *Jenseits von Schuld und Sühne. Bewältigungsversuche eines Überwältigten*, Munich, 1966, quoted from H. Glaser (ed.), *Bundesrepublikanisches Lesebuch. Drei Jahrzehnte geistiger Auseinandersetzung*, Munich, 1978, 259.
90. H. Pross, *Vor und nach Hitler. Zur deutschen Sozialpathologie*, Olten, Freiburg, 1962, 159.
91. C. Geissler, *Die Plage gegen den Stein*, Reinbek, 1978, 343.
92. Ibid., 414.
93. G. Schoenberner, 'Meinungslenkung contra Information', in P. Hübner (ed.), *Information oder Herrschen die Souffleure? 17 Untersuchungen*, Reinbek, 1964, 67.
94. Ibid., 69.
95. Ibid., 72.
96. Ibid., 71.
97. W. Euchner, 'Der permanente Selbstbetrug – Zur Deutschlandpolitik der Bundesregierung', in C. Nedelmann, Gert Schäfer (eds), *Politik ohne Vernunft oder Die Folgen sind absehbar. Zehn streitbare Thesen. Mit einem Vorwort von Walter Jens*, Reinbek, 1965, 40.
98. R. Postius, 'Die Bewältigung der Vergangenheit', in Nedelmann/Schäfer, *Politik*, 69, 71.
99. W. Jens, 'Vorwort', in Nedelmann/Schäfer: *Politik*, 9.
100. Pross, *Vor und nach Hitler*, 175.
101. Ibid., 20.
102. Ibid., 31.
103. Hans Magnus Enzensberger: 'Leningrader Gemeinplätze', in *alternative*, 1964, dokumente 1: *Leningrader Schriftsteller-Colloquium "Der zeitgenössische Roman"*, 26.
104. Pross, *Vor und nach Hitler*, p. 246.
105. Geissler, *Plage*, 412; H. Heißenbüttel, 'Schwierigkeiten beim Schreiben der Wahrheit 1964', in H.H., *Über Literatur. Aufsätze*, Munich, 1970, 219; Kipphardt, *Wahrheit*, 243–4.

106. Enzensberger, 'Reflexionen vor einem Glaskasten', 90.
107. T. W. Adorno, 'Tabus über dem Lehrberuf', in *Stichworte. Kritische Modelle 2*, Frankfurt a. M., 1969.
108. T.W. Adorno, 'Sexualtabus und Recht heute', in T.W.A, *Eingriffe. Neun kritische Modelle*, Frankfurt a. M., 1963, 107.
109. Ibid., 102.
110. See I. Frenzel, 'Der Wohlstand und die Schuld', in G. Rühle (ed.), *Bücher, die das Jahrhundert bewegten. Zeitanalysen – wiedergelesen*, Frankfurt a.M., 1980 (first published 1978), 216: 'Geblieben ist zweifellos das gebrochene Verhältnis zur eigenen Geschichte, das die Älteren den Jüngeren vererbt haben.'
111. W.F. Haug, *Der hilflose Antifaschismus. Zur Kritik der Vorlesungsreihen über Wissenschaft und NS an deutschen Universitäten*, 2nd edn, Frankfurt a.M., 1968, 26.
112. Ibid., 26.
113. Ibid., 18.
114. Ibid, 92.
115. Mitscherlich, *Die Unfähigkeit zu trauern*, 129.
116. H.M. Enzensberger, 'Versuch, von der deutschen Frage Urlaub zu nehmen', in Enzensberger, *Deutschland*, 37–48.
117. Idem., 'Reflexionen vor einem Glaskasten', 110.
118. K.M. Michel, 'Die sprachlose Intelligenz II', in *Kursbuch*, 4 (1966), 198.
119. Ibid., 170.
120. P. Neuhauser, 'Kehraus im Glashaus', in H.L. Gremliza (ed.), *30 Jahre KONKRET*, Hamburg, 1987, 152, (first published in *Konkret*, 21, 1971).
121. Quoted from A. Ritter (ed.), *Günter Grass: Katz und Maus* (Erläuterungen und Dokumente), Stuttgart, 1977, 177.
122. Ibid., 177f.
123. *Die Welt*, 19.10.1961.
124. The first critique of this hegemony, 'Literaturkritik und Restauration', was written by the same critic who published the first attack on the 'inner emigration', Franz Schonauer, and appeared in Richter, *Bestandsaufnahme*, 477–93.
125. W.S. Schlamm, *Vom Elend der Literatur. Pornographie und Gesinnung*, Stuttgart, 1966, 12.
126. A. Mohler, *Was die Deutschen fürchten. Angst vor der Politik. Angst vor der Geschichte. Angst vor der Macht*, Frankfurt a.M., 1966, 103.
127. H.E. Holthusen, *Plädoyer für den Einzelnen. Kritische Beiträge zur literarischen Diskussion*, Munich, 1967, 33.
128. For the significance of Kuby's book see my article 'Travellers' tales from Germany in the 1950s', in R.W. Williams *et al.* (eds), *German writers and the Cold War 1945–61*, Manchester, New York, 87–114.
129. Friedrich Sieburg, *Verloren ist kein Wort. Disputationen mit fortgeschrittenen Lesern*, Munich, 1969, 57.
130. R. Hagelstange, *Offen gesagt – Aufsätze und Reden. Mit einem Nachwort von Ernst Johann*, Frankfurt a.M., 1958, 136.
131. See Peitsch, 'Towards a History of 'Vergangenheitsbewältigung'.
132. Hagelstange, *Offen gesagt*, 172.
133. Holthusen, *Plädoyer*, 102.
134. Bölling, 'Tabus in diesem Land', 385; Schreiber, *Zwischenzeit*, 88.
135. Bölling, 'Tabus in diesem Land', 380.

136. W. Hahn, 'Die Bewältigung unserer Vergangenheit als politisches und theologisches Problem', in W.H., *Kurt Georg Kiesinger: Bewältigte Vergangenheit und Zukunft*, Constance, 1966, 19.

137. Ibid., 18.

138. Mohler, *Was die Deutschen fürchten*, 103.

139. Ibid., 183.

140. W.S. Schlamm, *Die Grenzen des Wunders. Ein Bericht über Deutschland*, Zürich, 1959, 110.

141. Hahn, 'Die Bewältigung unserer Vergangenheit', 24.

142. P. Noack, 'Die Angst vor der Tradition', in H. Krüger *et al.*, *Literatur zwischen links und rechts. Deutschland – Frankreich – USA*, Munich, 1962, 55.

143. Ibid.

144. R. Krämer-Badoni, *Vorsicht, gute Menschen von links. Aufsätze und Essays*, Gütersloh, 1962, 23.

145. Ibid., 40.

146. Ibid., 41.

147. Sieburg, *Verloren*, 198.

148. Ibid., 212.

149. Ibid.

150. Ibid., 211.

151. Schlamm, *Die Grenzen des Wunders*, 64.

152. Mohler, *Was die Deutschen fürchten*, 125.

153. Ibid., 126.

154. Ibid., 106.

155. W.J. Siedler, 'Die Linke stirbt, doch sie ergibt sich nicht', in Richter, *Die Mauer*, 112.

# 9

## INARTICULACY: LESBIANISM AND LANGUAGE IN POST-1945 GERMAN LITERATURE

—◆◆◆—

### Georgina Paul

'What are the words you do not yet have? What do you need to say?'

Audre Lorde[1]

The public history of lesbianism – and of lesbians – in Germany has, during this century at least, been peculiarly bound up with the question of women's emancipation. It is not by chance that it was precisely in those periods when women were most active in challenging the roles prescribed for them within a social order shaped by the interests of male power – broadly speaking the 1920s and the 1970s – that lesbians and the issue of lesbianism made the most significant inroads into the public sphere, nor that it was in the periods of greatest ideological prescription with regard to the social role of women – in Nazi Germany, Adenauer's Federal Republic, and the GDR – that they were most effectively banished from it.

To some extent, then, the taboo that surrounded (and partially still surrounds) the lesbian has its correlation in the taboo that surrounded (and partially still surrounds) the woman who does not fit in with historically defined cultural expectations of womanhood, who rebels against the structures of a male-oriented society, who is active and articulate in her own interest and ultimately uncontrollably unfeminine. Being an extreme case, the lesbian perhaps offers a particularly sensitive measure of the degree to which the emancipatory process has progressed. For the lesbian striving to attain the position of articulate subject *as a lesbian* is also confronted with the larger taboo that surrounds her sexuality in a society quick to condemn any aberration from its heterosexual norms.

For her the path to articulacy – and with it to cultural agency – is particularly full of obstacles, both external and internalised.

My first concern here is to examine the slow emergence of the lesbian voice in post-war German literature, to offer an analysis of the shifting social parameters which permitted that emergence, and to describe the difficult passage to literary subjecthood to which lesbian writing in this period bears witness. However, while working on this topic, I increasingly became interested in a wider problem, namely the extent to which pre-existent language (and thus patterns of thought) may determine what it is possible to experience, or at any rate what it is possible to communicate of experience. For the lesbian, propelled by the vision of a world which will no longer indict her, learning to speak in already existing terms is not enough. She must wrest new meanings, new perspectives from that preexisting language. In this, of course, she has common cause with all who strive for true emancipation.

In recent years much work has been done in North America, and to a lesser extent in Britain, on homosexuality in English-language literature, and 'gay theory' has established something of a niche for itself in the English-language academy. In Germany, in contrast, work on homosexual themes has tended to remain the preserve of separatist interest groups. The little that has come from within the academy has largely been smuggled in under the guise of historical studies (work on homosexual culture in the period of the Weimar Republic, for example) or feminist analysis of individual lesbian writers. The conservative nature of university structures in Germany has largely maintained the taboo on homosexuality, which for some years now gay and lesbian writers have been attempting to combat within the literary and publishing spheres. In 1991, however, Madeleine Marti completed a doctoral dissertation at the University of Marburg which appeared the following year in the prestigious Metzler Studienausgaben series under the title *Hinterlegte Botschaften. Die Darstellung lesbischer Frauen in der deutschsprachigen Literatur seit 1945*.[2] Marti examines the efforts of lesbian writers from Germany, Austria, Switzerland, and the GDR to emerge from the cultural shadowlands, locating these efforts in the context of a changing sociopolitical and publishing landscape. She devotes a chapter in the book to analysing in detail the literary career of Christa Reinig who, since the publication in 1976 of her novel *Entmannung*, has enjoyed prominence as one of the chief exponents of radical lesbian-feminism on the German literary scene. Reinig's progression from widely respected mainstream author to controversial feminist radical is shown as typifying the strategies first for self-concealment, later for self-revelation which Marti identifies in the works of other writers.

———*∽∽∽*———

Born in 1926, Reinig began writing in her early twenties in the newly founded GDR. Her first published works, the short stories 'Eine Ruine' (1949) and 'Ein Fischerdorf' (1951) demonstrate her early fascination with communities of women apart from the company of men. The subject of 'Eine Ruine', which is based on her own experience, is the solidarity and community amongst the *Trümmerfrauen* of the post-war years, while 'Ein Fischerdorf' tells the story of a village inhabited only by women following the arrest or death of their men. Already in this second text Marti finds evidence of Reinig's hesitation about associating herself with an exclusively female view of the world. While the brief narrative frame features a female first-person narrator, the main narrative switches to a third-person authorial narrator whose primary interest is not the community of women so attractive to the first-person narrator of the frame, but the fate of the men now absent from the village. The gender-neutral or male perspective was to dominate Reinig's work for the next twenty years. Marti offers the following explanation: 'Im ersten publizierten Prosatext hatte Christa Reinig Frauen ins Zentrum gestellt und, nachdem sie auf diese Weise erstmals einen Fuss [sic] in die literarische Öffentlichkeit gesetzt hatte, die Notwendigkeit zur Anpassung erfahren und sich in den nächsten zwanzig Jahren männlicher Maskierungen bedient'(HB, 319). The question of 'die Notwendigkeit zur Anpassung' offers a lead into the discussion of those institutional pressures which are so significant a factor in self-censorship. For of course the writer is under no obligation as such to conform to the conditions of the literary market, or to avoid topics of interest to her. It is the ambition to succeed, even if only in order to make a living by writing, and to gain public recognition on terms already established which imposes restraints. Marti does not explicitly address ambition as a factor leading to internalisation of existing literary standards, but it should in my view be added to the motives behind Reinig's relative conformity early in her career. Already as a young woman she expressed the desire to be a writer, and, having studied art history and archaeology at the Humboldt-Universität in Berlin from 1953 to 1957, she published her first volume of poetry, *Die Steine von Finisterre*, in the West in 1960. This was followed by the prose text *Der Traum meiner Verkommenheit* in 1961 and a further volume of poetry in 1963. In 1964, having been awarded the Bremen Prize for Literature, she stayed in the West. From then until 1971 she relied on her literary publications and journalistic writing to earn a living. Prior to the impact of the women's movement there was little context for the exploration of specifically female experience or what subsequently became defined as the feminine tradition, let alone lesbian experience and lesbian tradition. Therefore it is not altogether surprising to find these thematic areas absent from her early work. Among the established women writers of this period, many others also chose to focus on male or gender-neutral experience and to work extensively with male or gender-neutral narrators. Perhaps the most renowned case is Ingeborg Bachmann who famously wrote her novel *Malina* (1972) in order to trace what had happened to the absent female 'Ich'. The answer she came up with was that 'Ich' had been immured, silenced, murdered.

The difficulty of saying 'I' was, as Marti shows, a problem for Reinig, too. In a 1983 interview with Marti, she recalled: 'Wenn ich *ich* dachte, hab ichs immer als *er* gemacht. *Der Lächler* [a persona in her early poetry] oder so – und ich hatte Schwierigkeiten, Frauengestalten darzustellen. Das war ja immer nicht *ich*, *ich* als Frau war ja irgendwie nicht in die Literatur reinzukriegen' (HB, 321). She had attempted to write lesbian poetry as early as the 1950s but had been actively discouraged from doing so by a friend: 'Ich habe ja schon vor langen Jahren versucht, Lesbengedichte zu machen. Das hat mir ein Freund geradezu verboten, weil er auch gesehen hat, dass [sic] es schlecht war'(HB, 321). In a later interview with Marie Luise Gansberg, she added: 'Es ging nicht allein darum, dass [sic] sie schlecht waren. Es ging um das Thema. Es war nicht die Zeit für diese Dinge'(HB, 322). This interview also affords a further insight into the strategies of self-concealment. Asked about 'camouflage texts', Reinig provided an autobiographical key to the prose text 'Drei Schiffe', composed in 1959 and published as the title story of a volume in 1965.[3] The subject of the story is a man in flight from some indeterminate danger who is picked up by three ships in turn, but secretly escapes from each of them. The story tells of his suffering and despair, his vain appeals to divine authority, and his attempts at survival. At the end he goes into the wilderness. The style of the text is that of the adventure story featuring a male protagonist pitted against a hostile world. Reinig commented:

Das ist die Darstellung von Unterwelt als Oberwelt. Was die Frauen heute ihre Beziehungskisten nennen, das hatte ich damals auf dem Hals und gleich dreifach. Ich hatte drei Beziehungen. Ein ganz modernes Problem: Die Mehrfachbeziehung. Ich habs nicht verkraftet. Ich bin daran fast kaputt gegangen. Und dieses Kaputtgehen wollte ich darstellen. Ursprüngliche Entwürfe gab es, in denen ich versuchte, die Beziehungen zu drei Frauen darzustellen. Es gab einfach nicht die Formeln dazu. (HB, 329f.)

As Marti indicates, without this gloss the autobiographical impulse behind the writing of the story could not be deciphered, for the process of writing has involved a threefold displacement: the female subject has been transformed into a male subject, the psychological suffering into physical suffering, and authentic experience into an adventure fiction.

How and why did parameters shift? Two factors can be identified in Reinig's development, one private, one public. In 1971 a fall left her disabled. A disability pension relieved her of the need to write for economic survival, and the two years of subsequent seclusion provided her with the opportunity to rethink her life and goals. In 1975 she published her first novel, *Die himmlische und die irdische Geometrie*, a kaleidoscopic text which combines autobiography with critical reflections on religion, cultural history, and philosophy. By the time it appeared – and this is the second, public factor relevant to the shift of parameters – the emergent women's movement of the 1970s had provided a context for the satirical critique of the traditions of male thought contained in the text's philosophical *intermezzi*. However, despite the autobiographical impetus of the text as a whole and despite the fact that Reinig is far from shy of breaking taboos concerning, for example, religion or death, the novel does not thematise lesbian experience. In fact Reinig revealed a decade later that she had written an entire chapter on lesbianism, but, as with her lesbian poetry of the 1950s, had again been advised against publishing it by a friend, this time a female one, on the grounds that it was badly written (HB, 337).

Not until her next novel, *Entmannung* (1976), which was, as she put it, her 'Weg in die Frauenbewegung',[4] was the theme of lesbianism included. However, it is still not a central theme. Subtitled *Die Geschichte Ottos und seiner vier Frauen*, the text follows the involvements of Professor Dr Otto Kyra and four women who represent stereotypical female experience: the unmarried career woman, Doris, the housewife Menni (short for Klytemnestra!), the whore, Thea, whom Otto marries, and the housemaid, Xenia. It also features a fifth woman, the lesbian Wölfi, a refugee from the GDR who briefly resides in Kyra's household. The iniquitous position of the lesbian in a male-dominated and heterosexually oriented society is addressed through Wölfi:

> Es bleiben unausgekehrte Ecken. Wölfis Ohnmacht, Kyras All-macht. Kyra kann Thea heiraten, Wölfi nicht. Kyra kann Menni ein Kind machen, Wölfi nicht. Kyra darf sich nach einer wohlgeschaf-fenen Frau öffentlich umdrehen. Er darf sie ansprechen, er darf sie zum Tanz auffordern. Er darf ihr Komplimente machen. Er darf auf ein Zeitungsbild zeigen und öffentlich sagen: "Wackerer Busen, das!" Kyra darf alles, Wölfi nichts. In der Folge bekommt Wölfi ihren manisch-depressiven Charakter. (CR, 139)

With the exception of Wölfi all the women are in one way or another destroyed by their association with the patriarchal Kyra. She makes a timely departure from his house, leaving the walls papered with satirical commentaries on well-known plots from the Western cultural tradition, for example the following:

> *Romeo & Julia*
> Das handelsübliche Hetero-Stück. Shakespeare gelingt es, das deli-kate Thema, die Liebe zwischen einem Mädchen und einem Mann, frei von Peinlichkeiten glaubhaft zu machen. (CR, 158)

The novel also includes a sequence on the Ihns trial of 1974, in which a lesbian couple were given life sentences for instigating the murder of the husband of one of them. Two pages of authentic newspaper headlines document sensationalist attitudes to lesbians in the press.

*Die himmlische und die irdische Geometrie* and *Entmannung* rep-resent stages in a process of liberation from internalised fears of self-revelation which is completed in Reinig's volume of poetry, *Müßiggang ist aller Liebe Anfang* (1979), a calendar of poems for every day of a year in the life of a lesbian couple which attracted a number of aggressive reviews from male critics (HB, 328), and in her prose work of the 1980s. This comprised feminist essays, col-lections of short prose, and the novel *Die Frau im Brunnen* (1984) which depicts a lesbian relationship between two older women, one of whom is specifically identified as Reinig herself. By this time she had changed her regular publishing house from the Eremitenpresse to the feminist press Frauenoffensive. Such small feminist presses which sprang up across the Federal Republic in the 1970s provided an outlet for feminist and lesbian writing and ultimately influenced the criteria of the larger established publishing houses, thereby shifting parameters.

Reinig's career may, then, serve as paradigmatic for the postwar lesbian writer. Ambitious to succeed, she internalised the standards of the literary market. Unable as an active and intellectually independent subject to identify with the culturally produced images of woman as passive object dominant in the prefeminist era, she adopted the mask of gender-neutrality or masculinity. Where she did explicitly attempt to articulate her lesbian identity, she was discouraged by friends and associates who labelled such attempts 'bad writing'. When, despite all the obstacles, an autobiographical impulse aroused in her a desire to work through personal experience in her writing, she transposed that experience until it became unrecognisable and simulated conformity with established literary conventions. Personal economic independence and the economic independence of a publishing house sympathetic to her political programme alone liberated her from the constraints of convention. At the same time a significant shift in, or perhaps rather addition to, public discourse brought about by the women's movement provided a larger context in which to articulate experience and beliefs hitherto deemed taboo.

It would have been relatively easy, having once established these categories, to apply them to other writers such as Johanna Moosdorf (b.1911) or Marlene Stenten (b.1935). However, in the second half of this paper, I want to consider another, more complex issue, that of cultural attitudes to lesbianism and how these related to the difficulty of saying 'I' experienced by the lesbian writer before the women's movement in the 1970s and the establishment of a feminist publishing environment created new possibilities of public discourse.

In a patriarchal culture which privileges the male as cultural subject and subordinates the female to his interests, the lesbian represents a potential threat to the cultural order. Already in 1949 in *The Second Sex*, Simone de Beauvoir read lesbianism as a revolt against the submissive sexual role allotted to women in patriarchal culture. Yet patriarchy has always been ambiguous in its attitudes to lesbianism. On the one hand, the sexual subjecthood of women has held a certain fascination for the male imagination. As with the rampant sexuality of the whore, the resistant sexuality of the lesbian may offer a greater challenge to the domineering sexual instinct of the heterosexual male than the easy prey of the naturally passive woman; the lesbian is more his equal, her submission a greater tribute to his power. Then again, there is the erotic fascination of self-absorbed female sexuality in relation to which the male subject positions himself not as sexual agent, but as *voyeur*. One only has to think of the representation of lesbianism in art: the numerous portraits euphemistically entitled 'Friends', or the erotically charged depictions of sisters, or – at the other end of the aesthetic scale – the peepshow photographs of the turn of the century showing naked female couples in sexually suggestive positions. Yet where this exclusively female sexuality threatens to evade male control, perversion attractive becomes perversion abhorrent, and the lesbian is demonised as sick monster or – and this is perhaps the most pervasive strategy for social control – subject to ridicule. She does, after all, lack the signifier of subjecthood and the means of bestowing sexual satisfaction: the penis. She is exposed as a poor imitation, laughable, inadequate, a castrate. It is, incidentally, one of the many treacheries of de Beauvoir that she reinscribes this patriarchal commonplace in *The Second Sex*.[5]

The culture that privileges the male as sexual subject privileges him also as linguistic subject: he is the originator and perpetuator of language, and it is through his language that culture is transmitted. Moreover, he appears in this language, not only as the male subject, but also as the generic norm. In German a gathering of ninety-nine *Dichterinnen* and one *Dichter* becomes a gathering of *Dichter*! To articulate specifically as a *Dichterin*, then, is to articulate as a deviation from the norm. Traditionally, woman has been permitted to articulate specifically as a woman as long as what she says conforms to culturally produced expectations of femininity. Thus she may describe the domestic sphere, or praise her children, or write poetry that bears witness to her naive, as opposed to intellectual, relationship to the natural world. But woe betide her if she aspires, for example, to sexual subjecthood, if she objectifies the male, or if she competes with him for the love of woman. To do so invites the censure or the ridicule of the men who occupy with more ease than she does the position of cultural subject. It is far easier for her not to make an issue of her gender and instead either to camouflage herself in the language of masculine normality or to masquerade as male subject – hence the widespread use by lesbian writers of the male perspective when aspiring to intellectual status.

The terms that I have been using in this brief account of attitudes to lesbianism before the women's movement of the 1970s are, of course, drawn from the discourse of feminism which over the past twenty years or so has provided women with a language to criticise the construction of a culture that diminishes and objectifies them. But when it is a question of going beyond criticism and evolving a language which will make it possible to articulate hitherto uncommunicated experience or which will create new perspectives, new models of human relations, and new ways of living, feminism in general and lesbianism in particular seem all too often to encounter a barrier. To use Reinig's words, 'Es gab einfach nicht die Formeln dazu.' So how does one evolve new formulae and communicate new ideas when the language at one's disposal comes weighed down with the baggage of centuries? How does one break with a tradition which has denied one the position of articulating subject?

Precisely this question lies at the heart of the first post-war prose text in German to focus specifically on a lesbian encounter: Ingeborg Bachmann's 'Ein Schritt nach Gomorrha'. It is one of two texts in the 1961 collection *Das dreißigste Jahr* to adopt the female perspective, and, like other stories in the collection, shows its central character in a borderline situation, a moment of danger which threatens to destroy her world but which also contains within it the potential for change and renewal. Charlotte is a successful concert pianist, married to fellow-musician Franz to whom she has remained essentially subordinate. One night after a party, a young woman, Mara, stays behind when all the other guests have gone. She entices Charlotte to accompany her into the twilight world of a dance club. Later, back in the apartment, she challenges Charlotte to throw over her marriage to Franz and enter into a relationship with her, Mara. Charlotte sees in Mara's manipulative submissiveness a distasteful reflection of her own behaviour towards men:

> So also waren ihre eigenen Lippen, so ähnlich begegneten sie einem Mann, schmal, fast widerstandslos, fast ohne Muskel – eine kleine Schnauze, nicht ernst zu nehmen. (IB, 155) ... Sie selber hatte oft so dahingeredet, besonders in der ersten Zeit mit Franz, auch vor Milan war sie in diesen Ton verfallen, hatte die Stimme zu Rüschen gezogen; diesen Singsang voll Unverstand hatte er sich anhören müssen, angeplappert hatte sie ihn, mit verzogenem Mund, ein Schwacher den Starken, eine Hilflose, Unverständige, ihn, den Verständigen. Sie hatte die gleichen Schwachheiten ausgespielt, die Mara ihr jetzt

gegenüber ausspielte, und hatte den Mann dann plötzlich im Arm gehalten, hatte Zärtlichkeiten erpreßt, wenn er an etwas anderes denken wollte, so wie sie jetzt von Mara erpreßt wurde, sie streicheln mußte, gut sein mußte, klug sein mußte. (IB, 159)

However, as the night progresses, Charlotte begins to overcome her inhibitions and sees in this different relationship a utopian chance to escape from the narrow limitations which have so far kept her from herself:

Könnte dieses Geschlecht doch noch einmal nach einer Frucht greifen, noch einmal Zorn erregen, sich einmal noch entscheiden für seine Erde! Ein anderes Erwachen, eine andere Scham erleben! Dieses Geschlecht war niemals festgelegt. Es gab Möglichkeiten. (IB, 166) ... In früher Zeit mußten Schwan und Goldregen noch die Ahnung gehabt haben von dem größeren Spielraum, und ganz vergessen konnte in der Welt nicht sein, daß der Spielraum größer war, daß das kleine System von Zärtlichkeiten, das man ausgebildet hatte und überlieferte, nicht alles war an Möglichkeit. (IB, 168)

Yet she misses her chance because ultimately both she and Mara, like all the other characters in *Das dreißigste Jahr* who aspire to overstep their limits, are unable to step outside the language and the images that circumscribe them. Mara has only the language of passive femininity, while Charlotte, in seeking to redefine herself, simply adopts an already existing role, the one that Franz has occupied in relation to her. With a stroke of genius, Bachmann shows us Charlotte's failure in a single sentence: 'Ich will bestimmen, wer ich bin,' Charlotte says – and here is the break – 'und ich will mir auch mein Geschöpf machen, meinen duldenden, schuldigen, schattenhaften Teilhaber'(IB, 166). Here she reestablishes the hierarchical order of the old world, adopts the language of the domineering male subject in relation to the objectified, passive Mara. 'Sie waren beide tot und hatten etwas getötet'(IB, 177). The utopian potential has been lost.

It seems to me far from coincidental that this text which was the first to break significantly the taboo on lesbianism after 1945 came from a writer who, at the very least because of her highly publicised affair with Max Frisch, was known to be heterosexual. Here there was no danger of author and text being identified in the way so many lesbian writers would have feared; the thematisation of lesbianism in 'Ein Schritt nach Gomorrha' can be seen to serve an abstract purpose which coincides with that of the collection as a whole. Yet Bachmann's text prefigures quite remarkably the political idealisation of the lesbian relationship as a potential location of resistance to the patriarchal construction of society which was typical of lesbian feminism in the 1970s when the women's movement began to make its impact. Indeed, it is tempting to see Bachmann's influence in one of the major founding texts of feminist literature in Germany, Verena Stefan's *Häutungen* (1975).[6]

In keeping with the slogan of the 1970s women's movement 'Das Private ist politisch', *Häutungen* is unashamedly autobiographical: its sub-title is *Autobiographische Aufzeichnungen Gedichte Träume Analysen*. Yet it still has the quality of creative literature. The transformation of life into text allows symbolic values to emerge and creates resonances in a way in which the unpoetical autobiography does not. *Häutungen* has the structure of an *Entwicklungsroman*. It shows the first-person narrator progressing from dependence on a relationship with a man in order to attain worth in the eyes of society, traces her early involvement in the women's movement which gradually enables her to develop an independent sense of self-worth and to liberate herself from the relationships with men that have so belittled her, and finally depicts a new phase in which she enters into a relationship with a woman, Fenna. Central to Stefan's text, as to Bachmann's, is the theme of language which must be destroyed in order to be renewed:

> ich zerstöre vertraute zusammenhänge. ich stelle begriffe, mit denen nichts mehr geklärt werden kann in frage oder sortiere sie aus. – beziehung, beziehungsschwierigkeiten, mechanismen, sozialisation, orgasmus, lust, leidenschaft – bedeutungslos. sie müssen durch neue beschreibung ersetzt werden, wenn ein neues denken eingeleitet werden soll. (VS, 3f.)

Here again, while Stefan is eloquent and forceful in her critique of male-female relations, she finds herself up against the barrier of inadequate language when it comes to describing her relations with women. In her foreword Stefan had written: 'Als ich über empfindungen, erlebnisse, erotik unter frauen schreiben wollte, wurde ich vollends sprachlos'(VS, 4). In order to combat this inarticulacy, she reverts once again to preexisting language and images, not, this time, the language of the male subject, but the old equivalence, so prominent in the Western cultural tradition since the eighteenth century and so often employed to exclude women from cultural and intellectual agency, of woman and nature: 'deshalb entfernte ich mich zuerst so weit wie möglich von der alltagssprache und versuchte, über lyrik neue wege zu finden. naturvergleiche sind naheliegend' (VS, 4). It is, as she admits herself, a cliché – 'frau – natur scheint ein abgedroschenes thema zu sein' – and one which her efforts at justification do not fully resolve: 'die natur selber scheint ein abgedroschenes thema zu sein; sie ist vom patriarchat zerstört worden. unser verhältnis dazu ist ein gebrochenes, wir müssen es neu untersuchen (VS, 4). Perhaps in the painfulness of the narrator's poetic attempts (VS, 91f., 95, 109) and her awkward descriptions of herself and her lover in terms of roots, leaves, moss, and pools, we find an indication of the particular difficulty of articulating emotions in an age in which sentimentality and obscenity have, as it were, exchanged places. Obscenity now enjoys a greater degree of cultural acceptance than sentimentality which is well on the way to becoming a new taboo, at least in so-called 'high culture'. For Stefan, although articulating the emotional and physical relationship with a woman is new, the vocabulary she has at her disposal belongs to a tradition of romanticising emotion which appears anachronistic and ineffectual in the time in which she writes.

The limitations of language are not just a problem for the narrator seeking to describe her relationship with Fenna, but for the relationship itself. 'Wir wollten nicht nachahmen,' the narrator says of herself and Fenna – and here the echoes of Bachmann are particularly strong – 'sondern aus uns heraus, aus dem erotischen rohstoff zwischen uns neue wege und handlungen formen'(VS, 81). And yet: 'die männergesellschaft sitzt uns allen unter der haut. es erfordert eine ungeheure kraft, sie nicht jeden tag neu herzustellen mit vertrauten handgriffen, wünschen, tätigkeiten und reaktionen'(VS, 88). Ultimately the relationship between the two women fails because they cannot reconcile their desire for symbiotic unity with the need to establish themselves as independent subjects which has been engendered above all by their work in the feminist movement. Thus the trajectory of the *Entwicklungsroman* is also denied its structural resolution; at the end the narrator presents a vision of herself as at one with her body in a way that was impossible in her alienated state at the beginning. Yet the problem of non-hierarchical intersubjective relationship is left unsolved. Perhaps, quite simply, the lesbian relationship has here become overburdened by the utopian expectations levelled against it.

As the huge success of *Häutungen* showed – the first edition of 3,000 sold out within a month of publication and by May 1977 it had sold 125,000 copies – the articulation of one woman's personal experience had considerable political value in that it acted as a catalyst, enabling others to review their own experience and to begin to formulate their own desires. The linguistics professor Luise F. Pusch had this political value in mind when in 1976 she began to write an account of her own long-term lesbian relationship which had ended in the suicide of her partner. It took her three years to complete. *Sonja. Eine Melancholie für Fortgeschrittene* was published under the pseudonym Judith Offenbach in 1981, ironically enough by Suhrkamp which had, as already mentioned, turned down Johanna Moosdorf's lesbian novel *Die Freundinnen* eleven years before. *Sonja* became a cult book in lesbian circles in Germany in the 1980s. Whereas in *Häutungen* Stefan effected a literary transformation of personal experience, Pusch/Offenbach's aim is authenticity: she even takes up using a dictation machine at one stage in order to evade the seductions of literary language:

> Ich liege jetzt im Bett, und hier bewährt sich mein neues Diktiergerät prächtig. Ich kann völlig entspannt und warm und geschützt durch meine Bettdecke, ohne die Anspannung des Am-Schreibtisch-Sitzens, mich meinen Erinnerungen, Gedanken und Assoziationen hingeben. Ich hab das Licht ausgeschaltet und spreche wie im Traum, betätige nur noch diese beiden Hebel – Record und Stop. Das ganze Buch wird dadurch sicher immer weniger kunstvoll und immer echter. (JO, 152)

The book is structured as a series of diary entries over the three-year writing period, often with long intervals between entries as the narrator attends to the demands of her academic career. It begins with an account of Sonja's suicide, and goes on to reconstruct chronologically the progress of their ten-year relationship up to her death. At the same time, it recounts aspects of the narrator's life – her career progress and her various attempts at forming new relationships – during the course of the writing. While the political value of publication is often reiterated in the text, the writing of it also clearly serves a therapeutic purpose, and this is affirmed by a psychotherapist with whom the narrator is in treatment during the period reproduced in the book. The account often makes for painful reading, not only because the relationship between the narrator Judith and her dependent partner Sonja, who is disabled from an earlier suicide attempt, is often profoundly claustrophobic and unhappy, but because of the excruciating detail with which every aspect of their relationship is recounted. Of particular interest for my theme here is the relation the text bears to the public life of the narrator as depicted in the book. As an ambitious young academic she fears above everything the discovery of the nature of her relationship with Sonja. That could, she thinks, jeopardise her career chances. As a result she casts herself outwardly in the role of self-sacrificing friend, a role which has disastrous repercussions for their closeted private life together. The diary entries that are often written at night offer a woman suffering from bereavement the chance to articulate the publicly suppressed private self, which remains for the course of the writing process strictly separated from the daytime public persona of the successful academic. The division of public and private lives is still evident in Pusch's decision to publish under a pseudonym. Following its publication, however, she increasingly dedicated herself to feminist politics. She achieved a *succès de scandale* in the mid-1980s with her work on feminist linguistics which, according to her own account, prematurely ended her university career.[7] She then continued her work outside the academy as an independent writer and archivist, 'coming out' in the meantime as the author of *Sonja*. In that sense, the writing process seems to have offered an effective therapy. The real problem with the book, though, is not only, as Madeleine Marti points out in her commentary, that it reproduces a great many prejudices about lesbians which the author had evidently internalised (HB, 222ff.), but that it falls in with the literary mode traceable back to Radclyffe Hall's *Well of Loneliness* of representing the lesbian as martyr and victim of society.[8] The aspiration to authenticity is not sufficient to resist the force of preexisting images of lesbianism. Indeed, by its very authenticity the text shows the extent to which stereotypical assumptions from without shape even the lesbian's private view of herself.

How can the problem be solved? Is there a course to be navigated between the Scylla of the idealisation of lesbianism as the locus of resistance to patriarchy and the Charybdis of the representation of the lesbian as the victim of heterosexist society? Above all, is there a language or a literary strategy which can circumvent the apparently inevitable reproduction of the traditional identification of homosexuality as 'other' with the norm of heterosexuality?[9] In short, can lesbians ever speak a language of their own?

Although not the work of a lesbian-identified writer, Helga Königsdorf's novel *Gleich neben Afrika* (1992) offers one possible solution. In the first place, the novel is not about lesbianism, but about the effect of German unification on the life of an East German woman writer. Thus Königsdorf is able to approach the narrator's lesbian relationship in the way that in *A Room of One's Own* Virginia Woolf suggested her fictional modern writer Mary Carmichael should generally approach the unlit areas of women's lives: 'The only way for you to do it, I thought, addressing Mary Carmichael as if she were there, would be to talk of something else.'[10] Königsdorf introduces the lesbian relationship as if it were not an issue:

> Ich saß zwischen allen Stühlen und dachte über den Weltuntergang nach, um nicht an die ganzen Peinlichkeiten denken zu müssen, die mir passiert waren. Aber nicht einmal die Sintflut interessierte noch jemanden. Die Leute hatten andere Sorgen. Meine Freunde zogen sich zurück ... Der einzige Lichtpunkt war Maria, und Maria sagte, daß sie mich liebe. Ich liebte alles an ihr. Ihre Haut. Ihre Stimme. Ihre Logik. Ihre Wutanfälle. Maria war der erste Mensch, den ich liebte, ohne ihn mir umerfinden zu müssen. Maria war weich und warm. Sie war anwesend. Maria durchschaute zwar, daß ich eine Hochstaplerin war. Aber wo der Mensch glauben will, ist er unbeirrbar, selbst wenn ihm ständig das Gegenteil vorgeführt wird. Diese historische Lektion lag gerade hinter uns. (HK, 20)

This tactic is interesting because, for a writer coming from a GDR background, lesbianism was far from not being an issue. Homosexuality was, after all, a far greater taboo in the GDR than it was in the West, and this text takes its place among a very small number of works by GDR writers to address the issue at all.[11] Seen in this context, Königsdorf's aim seems primarily to be to disarm her reader. Maria's fiery temperament is a great source of energy in the novel, and an element in the strong characterisation of the relationship between the two women which thus takes centre stage. It is not juxtaposed with heterosexual relationships although there are indications that the narrator has had these, nor does the manner of its representation invite abstractions as to the nature of homosexuality or the relation between heterosexuality and homosexuality. Rather it is portrayed as an eminently natural relationship between two individuals, and this gives the novel a strikingly utopian dimension. To some extent, Königsdorf reproduces stereotypical assumptions about lesbian relations, but she does so with an irony which conveys sovereignty rather than suffering:

> Die Liebe zwischen Frauen besteht im wesentlichen aus Zärtlichkeit und Eifersucht ... Ich hatte nie zuvor einen Menschen getroffen, der zu solcher Eifersucht fähig war. Sie war auf alles eifersüchtig. Auf die Partei, auf Dick Hach aus Colorado, auf Alexander, auf den

Computer, auf den besonders, und auf die Zeitung. Nun also noch
auf den Tod. Ich war gerührt und versprach, mit ihr im Herbst nach
Indien zu fahren. Woraufhin sie sich sofort beruhigte und in
meinen Armen einschlief. (HK, 20)

Does she avoid the objectification of the lover? Maybe not entirely.
Does she fall into the trap of being too light? Perhaps. Although
taken in isolation the one love scene between the two women is as
hackneyed as Stefan's poems in *Häutungen*, it takes on an extraordinary force against the foil of the self-irony which dominated the
tone of the narration. In it the mask of irony for a moment falls and
reveals a simple passion which commands respect:

> Maria schlief mit dem Kopf in meinem Schoß. Als der Mond auf-
> ging, mußte ich immerzu ihr Gesicht ansehen. Sie sah jung und
> wunderschön aus. 'Zigeunerin.' Sagte ich leise. Da lächelte sie,
> richtete sich auf und herzte mich. Ich fühlte, wie die Lust in mir bis
> in die Schläfen aufloderte. Ihr Körper wurde mein Körper, und
> alles, was ich ihr tat, geschah mir. Ich flog in gewaltigen Wellen
> über das Land. Und den Absturz von Terrasse zu Terrasse beglei-
> tete eine Folge von allerletzten Seufzern. Bis ich mich auf der Erde
> wiederfand.
> Gegen Morgen wurde es kühl. (HK, 119)

—◦◦◦—

Looking back over the development of lesbian writing from the
1960s to the 1990s, it can be seen that considerable progress has
been made in the overcoming of inarticulacy after all. It is
undoubtedly easier for the lesbian writer today to write of her
experiences and her desires than it was three decades ago. My
discussion has focused on a limited number of texts which are in
some ways paradigmatic for this progress. I have not considered
other kinds of writing. The popular genre of lesbian detective fiction has, for example, made an impact on the German market in
recent years as it has in the United States and Britain. However
questions remain about the extent to which the literary representation of lesbians and lesbianism is still limited by cultural
attitudes to gender and gender roles, to sexuality and to inter-
personal relations, and by the language which we use to discuss
these issues. Questions also remain about the potential role of
literature in illuminating hitherto unlit experience and, in the
process, extending the possibilities and scope of our experience as
social and sexual beings.

I will end where I began: with Christa Reinig, herself a great self-ironist. In the calendar *Müßiggang ist aller Liebe Anfang* the poem for 23 June runs:

> 23 Freitag
>
> Die einzig weibliche vokabel
> ein liebender summton
> mit dem frauen auf frauen antworten
> auf frauen allein.[12]

Where language ends, there are always other signals.

## NOTES

**Abbreviations**

HB   M. Marti, *Hinterlegte Botschaften. Die Darstellung lesbischer Frauen in der deutsch-sprachigen Literatur seit 1945*, Stuttgart, 1992.
CR   Christa Reinig, *Entmannung. Die Geschichte Ottos und seiner vier Frauen*, Frankfurt a.M., 1977.
IB   Ingeborg Bachmann, *Das dreißigste Jahr. Erzählungen*, Munich, Zürich, 1961.
VS   Verena Stefan, *Häutungen. Autobiographische Aufzeichnungen Gedichte Träume Analysen*, Munich, 1975.
JO   Judith Offenbach (= Luise F. Pusch), *Sonja. Eine Melancholie für Fortgeschrittene*, Frankfurt a.M., 1981.

1. A. Lorde, *Sister Outsider. Essays and Speeches*, Trumansburg, New York, 1984, 41.
2. I am indebted to Charlotte Dittmer for bringing this volume to my attention and for her advice on primary texts relating to my theme.
3. C. Reinig, *Drei Schiffe. Erzählungen, Dialoge, Berichte*, Frankfurt a.M., 1965.
4. *Mein Herz ist eine gelbe Blume. Christa Reinig im Gespräch mit Ekkehard Rudolph*, Düsseldorf, 1978.
5. See S. de Beauvoir, *The Second Sex*, trans. H.M. Parshley, Harmondsworth, 1983, 432: 'The lesbian could readily accept the loss of her feminitiy, if in doing so she gained a successful virility; though she can employ artificial means for deflowering and possessing her loved one, she is nonetheless a castrate and may suffer acutely from the realisation of that fact. She is unfulfilled as a woman, impotent as a man, and her disorder may lead to psychosis.'
6. An illuminating parallel reading of Bachmann's 'Ein Schritt nach Gomorrha' and Stefan's *Häutungen* is offered by R. Schmidt in her *Westdeutsche Frauenliteratur in den 70er Jahren*, Frankfurt a.M., 1982.
7. See L. F. Pusch, 'Ladies First – Ein Gespräch über Feminismus, Sprache und Sexulatität, Bamberg, 1993, 79–82.

8. See L. Faderman, *Surpassing the Love of Men. Romantic Friendship and Love between Women from the Renaissance to the Present*, London, 1991 (first published 1981), 392: 'Before the rise of the lesbian-feminist movement, lesbian writers of popular literature generally depicted one of two types in their works: the lesbian as martyr ( for which Clare of *Regiment of Women* was a prototype) and the lesbian as martyr ( for which Stephen of *The Well of Loneliness* was a prototype). It is not surprising that those authors who internalized society's views of them … should write of the lesbian as sickie. Nor should it be surprising that those writers who felt society's homophobia should have latched on to Radclyffe Hall's trick of presenting the lesbian as a poor suffering creature …' Arguably, *Sonja* includes both stereotypes, with Sonja cast as sickie and Judith as martyr.

9. To think in any other terms than an opposition of heterosexuality-homosexuality is an extraordinarily difficult imaginative entreprise, for traditions of Western thought are so structured by oppositions. In her 1980 essay 'The Straight Mind', Monique Wittig proposed the strategy of doing away entirely with oppositional differences, above all that of man-woman, for 'straight society is based on the necessity of the different'other at every level', and she concludes her essay with the provocative statement: 'Lesbians are not women'. In M.W., *The Straight Mind and Other Essays*, Hemel Hempstead, 1992, 28, 32. But as Judith Butler counters in her commentary on this essay:' Whereas Wittig clearly envisions lesbianism to be a full-scale refusal of heterosexuality, I would argue that even such a refusal constitutes an engagement and, ultimately, a radical dependence on the very terms that lesbvianism purports to transcend.' In: J.B., *Gender Trouble: Feminism and the Subversion of Identity*, London, 1990, 124. Ultimately any generalisation about lesbianism (or homosexuality) automatically suggests the implied opposite term, heterosexuality.

10. V. Woolf, *A Room of One's Own*, Panther Books, London, 1977, 81.

11. See Marti's chapter 'Lesbische Frauen in der DDR-Literatur', in HB, 244–78, and my own article '"Über Verschwiegenes sprechen": Female Homosexuality and the Public Sphere in the GDR before and after the *Wende*', in *Women and the Wende: Social Effects and Cultural Reflections of the German Unification Process*, ed. E. Boa and J. Wharton, Amsterdam, 199 226–37.

12. C. Reinig, *Müßiggang ist aller Liebe Anfang. Gedichte*, Düsseldorf, 1979, 23. Juni.

# 10

## SEX AND POLITICS: THE CASE OF THE GDR

—⁓⁓—

### *J.H. Reid*

On 9 November 1993 BBC television broadcast a documentary programme on the 'sexual liberation' of Russia. Extraordinary footage was shown of striptease schools and what appeared to be stage orgies of the kind that Kenneth Tynan was propagating in England in the 1960s. Comparable developments took place in Spain following the death of Franco. Totalitarian regimes, whether of the left or of the right, have tended to be prudish in sexual matters; their collapse has generally been followed by a pendulum swing in the other direction.

As it happens, the programme on Russia was shown on the fourth anniversary of the opening of the Berlin Wall. The GDR, however, was always different from the Soviet Union, largely because of the omnipresence of the West German media, which broadcast liberal programmes into East German homes; even printed material from West Germany was relatively easy to smuggle in, especially before 1961 and later in the 1980s, when the number of visits from and to the West escalated. The difference is alluded to in Irmtraud Morgner's story 'Gute Botschaft der Valeska in 73 Strophen'. On a visit to the Soviet Union the title figure finds Moscow 'eine deutliche Stadt'; Berlin was 'verschwommener'. When she and her Russian friend Shenja attempt to go to the 'Peking' restaurant, they are turned back at the door: 'Weil Peking ein anständiges Lokal wäre.'[1] Whether they are, not unjustifiably, suspected of being lesbians or, quite unjustifiably, prostitutes looking for customers is not made clear. At any rate, one of the many provocations of Morgner's story is the implication that the GDR might be, however slightly, ahead of its Big Brother in terms of the emancipation of women, 'verschwommener' in the sense that the traditional gender roles were being gradually eroded. Nevertheless, when the Berlin Wall was opened, it was widely reported that the first destination of many East German males was Hamburg's Reeperbahn, and that the West Berlin peepshows, some of which offered free entry to Easterners, did a roaring trade. The GDR's first porn shop opened on 15 June 1990, and for those of us who can remember East Berlin before 1990, one of the most startling contemporary scenes is the nightly parade of prostitutes on the Oranienburger Straße. Clearly the sexual demands of some had not been met under the SED regime. Whether peepshows and prostitution are progress is another matter, although the post-*Wende* mass media have tended to suggest that they represent a return to normality.[2]

It is a cliché to suggest that Freud's model of the self is couched in terms borrowed from the political sciences. The term 'repression' has connotations primarily in the political domain, but is used in psychology as well; more generally, the model of a superego 'controlling' the impulses of the id reflects the enlightened despot of the eighteenth century wisely keeping his unruly subjects in order. This is more than a metaphor, however. Authoritarian societies tend to be prudish out of fear, fear of what they cannot control. The private sphere is especially suspect, and sexuality is potentially a disruptive force. Conversely, erotic literature has often been linked with attacks on authoritarian social structures. Reviewing Lynn Hunt's *The Invention of Pornography, 1500–1800*, Elizabeth Wilson suggests that the emergence of pornography in the sixteenth and seventeenth centuries was closely bound up with the democratisation of society.

> Such a society increasingly rebelled against the traditional sources of authority, and, right up until the French Revolution, pornography played an important political role. Licentious writing was almost always bound up with political satire and general attacks on authority, especially that of the church and the aristocracy. Until the 18th century, attempts at censorship were more concerned to suppress the political than the sexual aspects of pornographic writings. It is only later that purely commercial and apolitical pornography takes over.[3]

Frank Wedekind's late nineteenth-century play *Frühlings Erwachen* shows just how terrified of youthful sexuality repressive societies can be. In Horkheimer and Adorno's *Dialektik der Aufklärung* the Marquis de Sade is a key witness: his work fulfils Kant's definition of an enlightenment society in which the bourgeois individual is freed from tutelage.[4] Peter Weiss's play *Die Verfolgung und Ermordung Jean Paul Marats dargestellt durch die Schauspielgruppe des Hospizes zu Charenton unter Anleitung des Herrn de Sade* (1964) with its numerous references to copulation, masochism and other aspects of human sexuality, places particular stress on the nature of Charenton as a political prison and on the view of Sade as a disillusioned revolutionary. One of the early productions of Weiss's play was, perhaps surprisingly, in Rostock. This production played down the role of the individualist Sade in favour of the revolutionary Marat. As Weiss himself recognised, it was only possible to put his play on in the GDR if Marat appeared as the 'positive hero'.[5] It is my contention that it remained as true of the GDR as of earlier centuries and societies that political taboos were stronger than sexual ones.

How prudish was the GDR? It certainly had the reputation of small-minded repressiveness. As with the other communist-run states it was as if, having had to combat the early accusations levelled against Marx and his friends that they were propagating free love and wife-sharing,[6] its rulers had to present themselves as puritanical Victorians. Initially, however, it was not much more prudish than the UK, where the stifling and well-documented role of the Lord Chamberlain in theatre censorship was not abolished until 1968; originally appointed to protect the Prime Minister of the day against political lampooning, he latterly was preoccupied with his own narrow conception of public decency. D.H. Lawrence's *Lady Chatterley's Lover* was not published in England in full until 1961, accompanied by the famous trial of its publishers Penguin Books. West Germany was possibly more liberal in the 1950s, although it is worth remembering the fate of Günter Grass's *Die Blechtrommel*, awarded the Bremen Prize for Literature in 1960, only to have it withdrawn again when the so-called obscenities were pointed out to the jurors. *Die Blechtrommel* was not published in the GDR until the end of the 1980s; the delay, however, had much more to do with politics than with prudishness, its author's known hostility to the GDR, documented at least since his play *Die Plebejer proben den Aufstand* put the GDR's Bertolt Brecht in the dock for his failure to support the workers' uprising of 1953. The beginning of the 1960s saw the beginning of a decade of debates on pornography and literature in England and West Germany. Ludwig Marcuse's *Obszön* appeared in 1962 in West Germany, documenting some of the absurdities of historical judgements on what was claimed to be pornographic. By 1965 the editors of *Akzente* were alarmed enough by developments such as the pressure group 'Aktion Saubere Leinwand' and demands that the laws on what should be deemed obscene be tightened up to devote a whole issue to the theme 'Pornographie?' – one of the texts they published was Goethe's poem 'Das Tagebuch', which the standard post-war edition of Goethe's works throughout the 1950s, the Hamburg edition, had omitted. The GDR was never entirely impervious to cultural developments on its western borders and the 1960s were key years there, too. Although debates took place behind the scenes, the sometimes vehement public utterances of politicians and cultural bureaucrats give some indication of what was happening.

The general drabness of the GDR produced an impression of prudishness. However, from 1954 the journal *Das Magazin* was printing monthly pinups; more surprisingly, perhaps, the *Armee Rundschau* ('Magazin des Soldaten') always seems to have included pinups on its back cover, mostly well-covered up, occasionally bikini-clad but always sexy and invariably young women, and also numerous photographs of young women on its inside pages. The earliest number I have seen (February 1965) included a reader's letter requesting 'wahre Kurvenköniginnen' and not ones who were 'bis obenhin zugeknöpft'. By 1974 nudes were to be found inside, and by 1990 these were hardly distinguishable from West German products. There is an implicit contradiction here between the GDR's claim to represent the interests of women and the exploitation of women's bodies for male gazes – but when it comes to boosting the morale of the troops even ideology goes by the board. The February 1965 issue included a survey of soldiers' premarital sexual experience: 69 per cent of those questioned were sexually experienced before marriage; the comments by the 'expert' were not altogether different from what one might have expected in the West: respect your partner, frequent changes of partner are not compatible with a socialist individual – and do use contraceptives!

In fact GDR literature in the 1960s was not all that prudish either, depending on one's definition of prudishness. Relations between the sexes were certainly not those of Abélard and Héloise. Joachim Wohlgemuth's *Egon und das achte Weltwunder* (1962) is a conventional portrayal of the development of a young hooligan into a properly integrated member of socialist society and went through countless editions. Towards the end of the

novel Egon and his girlfriend Christine go off by themselves on a
boat trip overnight. And they do not just practice navigation! The
knots which Egon encounters are those on Christine's bikini:

> Der Bikini hat überall Schnüre und Knoten. Egon kommt mit den
> Knoten und Schnüren nicht klar. 'Wart mal', sagt sie und zieht an
> einer ganz bestimmten Schleife. 'Und hier auch noch.'
> Egon zieht auf, entknotet, und auf einmal hat Christine gar
> nichts mehr an. 'Hab ich wirklich krumme Beine?'[7]

At which point we are left, quite properly, listening to the
sounds of the night. In Christa Wolf's *Der geteilte Himmel* (1963)
Rita and Manfred are lovers, not just 'good friends'; Manfred's
'Mansarde' is their 'gondola', with all the undertones of sexuality that metaphor has. There are no explicit descriptions of sexual
relations: but the trip in Manfred's car to the town in the Harz is
overtly symbolic:

> 'Kannst du nicht schneller?' fragte sie.
> Manfred gab Gas.
> 'Mehr!' forderte sie. Sie wischten in eine Kurve, dann lag eine
> gerade Strecke vor ihnen, eine Apfelbaumallee.
> 'Mehr!'
> Manfred war ein ungeübter Fahrer. Er saß verkrampft am
> Steuer, mißtrauisch gegen sich selbst, er schwitzte, regte sich auf
> und horchte gespannt auf die Geräusche des Motors.
> 'Mehr!' rief Rita.[8]

They arrive at a bridge over a river beyond which is the town gate:

> Ein schmales, steinernes Tor, hinter dem sich die Weite der Welt auf-
> tat, und neue Sehnsucht und neue Weite. Sie rasten durch die Brücke.
> 'Genug', sagte Rita. Der Wagen rollte aus. Sie schloß die Augen
> und lehnte sich in den Sitz. Sie war erschöpft und glücklich.
> Manfred saß locker am Steuer. Er zündete sich eine Zigarette an
> und blies den Rauch aus dem Fenster.[9]

Everything in this passage points to sex, down to the post-coital
cigarette. Manfred is 'verkrampft' – sexually as well as politically.
Rita is the more spontaneous, relaxed, liberated individual. Interestingly, one of the criticisms levelled at the novel when it first
appeared was of Wolf's presentation of personal relationships. In
their review for the newspaper *Freiheit* entitled 'Die große Liebe?',
Dietrich Allert and Hubert Wetzelt regarded *Der geteilte Himmel* as
outdated and bourgeois because of the private nature of Manfred
and Rita's love affair.[10] Rita's love for Manfred was doomed from

the outset; her despair when he leaves her ought to have been because of her failure to convert him to socialism. Implicit in this criticism is the fear that the uncontrolled private sphere is potentially subversive. In the end, however, Allert and Wetzelt's criticism did not prevail. Extra-marital sexual relations are a problem only when there is a political dimension as well. In Erik Neutsch's *Spur der Steine* (1964), for example, Werner Horrath has an affair with Katrin Klee, as a result of which she becomes pregnant. The problem was not so much that Horrath was a married man, but that he was the local Party secretary and as such was supposed to be like Caesar's wife and beyond suspicion; the scandal is that he tries to conceal the affair to the extent of allowing Klee to go through a horrific 'Parteiverfahren', at the same time damaging the reputation of the Party when his rival Balla finds out what he is up to. Although Neutsch's novel was to become one of the standard novels of the GDR, its initial reception was not entirely unproblematical; the film of the book, which contains a scene in which Balla's men strip off to go swimming in a duck pond, was banned – not, however, because of the naked male bottoms on show, but because the men proceed to drag a policeman, the embodiment of the SED state, into the pond.[11]

Conventional GDR sources were taciturn on the subject of the erotic. The *Kulturpolitisches Wörterbuch* (1978 edition) has no entry between 'Serenade' ('freies, meist mehrsätziges Instrumentalwerk') and 'Show-Geschäft' ('Teilbereich des imperialistischen Kultur- und Kunstbetriebes'), nor between 'Geschichtsbild, marxistisch-leninistisches' and 'Geschmack, ästhetischer'. Nor is there any entry under 'Erotik', 'Pornographie' or 'Obszön'. However, under 'Massenkultur im Imperialismus' we read:

> Mit der Darstellung von Gewalt und Grausamkeit, Brutalität und Verbrechen, Mord und Totschlag reflektieren die verschiedenen Formen der Massenkultur auf spezifische Weise den vom Konkurrenzkampf geprägten Alltag der kapitalistischen Gesellschaft. In den meisten Fällen werden diese ahumanen Erscheinungen jedoch fetischisiert, von ihren sozialen Ursachen abgetrennt und zu kreatürlichen Eigenschaften der 'unveränderlichen Natur des Menschen' erhoben. Als Pendant zu dieser Reduzierung des Menschen auf den angeblich alles bestimmenden Aggressionstrieb fungieren jene Erscheinungen der Massenkultur, die den Sexualtrieb zum bestimmenden Moment eines biologischen Bildes vom Menschen erklären und Sexualität mit Pornographie gleichsetzen.[12]

Much of this analysis would be subscribed to by liberals any-where. Pornography, however, is firmly placed in the culture of capitalist societies. By implication, socialist societies are free of exploitation and therefore free of pornography.

Elimar Schubbe's *Dokumente zur Kunst-, Literatur- und Kultur-politik der SED,* which covers the period 1946-1970, is a West German publication, which is no doubt why it is more helpful. Under 'Sex (Sexkult, Sexpropaganda, Sexualismus, Sexualität)' there are eleven entries, under 'Pornographie' ten, and under 'Obszöni-täten' a further three. The second volume, edited by Gisela Rüß, and covering the years 1971-1974, by contrast has only two entries under 'Sex', none under 'Pornographie' and none under 'Obszöni-täten', while the third and last volume (1975-1980) has no relevant entries at all. This in itself suggests that by the 1970s sexual themes were no longer tabooed by the SED. In the early years pornogra-phy is associated with 'formalism': Wilhelm Girnus's 'Bemerkun-gen zur Frage des Formalismus und des Kosmopolitismus' (1951) describes 'Gangstermoral und Pornographie' as 'nur die Kehrseite des Formalismus und nicht von ihm zu trennen, denn Gangster-Mentalität und Pornographie können nur dort die Massen ver-giften, wo eine echte volkstümliche Kunst fehlt'(Dok 1, 172). Similar ideas were expressed by the SED in its document 'Der Kampf gegen den Formalismus in Kunst und Literatur' of 1951 (Dok 1, 180, 182). In the 1960s the attempt to class the whole of West European literature under the heading 'formalism' is dropped, while pornography remains an exclusively Western phe-nomenon, associated with the 'Sex-Kult des Westens' (1960) (Dok 1, 653), the 'Sex-Rummel im Westen' (1969) (Dok 1, 1277). The term 'Dekadenz' is more frequently used, in 1966, for example, to describe phenomena ranging from the James Bond films to the Theatre of the Absurd and the Theatre of Cruelty, a 'Mischmasch von Entfremdung, Seelenschmerz, Hoffnungslosigkeit und Sex' (Dok 1, 1191).

1965 was, as ever, a key year. By that time the liberalisation of West Germany's regulations on pornography was beginning, and the GDR may have felt it had to set an example. More likely is that from 1965 onwards the SED found itself on the political defensive: events in Czechoslovakia were already pointing for-ward to 1968, and the beginnings of a new *Ostpolitik* in West Ger-many, especially from 1966 onwards, were a potential threat to the SED's position. At any rate, accusations of pornography were a welcome addition to the critics' armoury when controversial writers were to be attacked. At the infamous December plenum of 1965 Walter Ulbricht warned that 'die große schöpferische Freiheit, die in unserer Gesellschaftsordnung für die Schriftsteller und Künstler besteht' must not be misunderstood as 'Freiheit für Nihilismus, Halbanarchismus, Pornographie oder andere Methoden der amerikanischen Lebensweise' (Dok 1, 1087). He repeated the warning in his letter to the film-director Kurt Maetzig, three weeks later (Dok 1, 1143) in words which in turn were quoted by Erwin Pracht and Werner Neubert in their article 'Zu aktuellen Grundfragen des sozialistischen Realismus' in March 1966 (Dok 1, 1156). Much the same words were repeated by Ulbricht in November 1969 (Dok 1, 1585). At the December plenum of the SED in 1965, texts by Wolf Biermann, Werner Bräunig and Peter Hacks, and films such as *Das Kaninchen bin ich* and *Spur der Steine* were targetted specifically as pornographic. The 'Heiße Eisen' slot on the GDR radio programme DT64, which broached questions of youth sexuality, was also singled out. If, however, one looks at these texts in detail, it becomes apparent that it was the political, rather than the sexual dimension which was the stumbling block.

Earlier in 1965, Klaus Wagenbach had published Biermann's *Die Drahtharfe* in West Berlin, whereupon Biermann had been attacked by Alexander Abusch: 'Hätte er…nur die 'Leistung' vollbracht, naturalistisch-buchstäblich Worte aus dem Bereich der Kloake in die Lyrik einzuführen und sie durch sexuelle Primitivitäten und Obszönitäten 'anzureichern', so hätte gewiß sein in Westberlin finanziertes dünnes Bändchen nicht den schlagartig organisierten Beifall von einem dreiviertel Dutzend Konzernblättern gefunden' (Dok 1, 1075). The attack was repeated by Erich Honecker at the December plenum: 'Biermann verrät heute mit seinen Liedern und Gedichten sozialistische Grundpositionen.' His poems were 'Machwerke, die zugleich auch stark pornographische Züge aufweisen'(Dok 1, 1078). The latter accusation was presumably a reference to one or two poems such as 'Meine Miets- kasernenbraut', which ends with the (ambiguous) lines:

> Meine Mietskasernenbraut
> braucht ein' Ehemann.
> Doch kommt wieder nur ein Mann,
> dann kommt's ihr nicht
> dann kommt's ihr nicht
> dann kommt's ihr nicht darauf an.[13]

Another example is the 'Ballade von den alten Weibern von Buckow', in which Fiete Kohn, 'ein Fischer, jung und stark', who is responsible for the supply of fish to Buckow, oversleeps regularly with 'ein junges Weib': 'Das hat die Weiber von Buckow / so bös und naß gemacht.'[14] The problem, however, was in reality not the promiscuity but the fact that Fiete Kohn represents 'den Staat'. Biermann's poems were unacceptable because their author was adopting a critical stance with regard to 'actually existing socialism'. Poems such as 'Antrittsrede des Sängers' and 'An die alten Genossen' directly express the poet's mock puzzlement at the Party's 'fear of his guitar' and their inability to understand his refusal to be content with the 'achievements' of the present. Nor did his mocking of the director of the Politbüro's Commission for Cultural Affairs, Alfred Kurella, in his 'Ballade auf den Dichter François Villon' go down well. Abusch's words can be reversed: if the West German publishers and media were attracted by the obscenities, one wonders conversely whether the SED would have been much concerned with the obscenities if the political criticism – including publishing the collection in the enemy West – had been lacking.

A second example is that of Werner Bräunig, attacked by Erich Honecker at the December plenum for the 'obszöne Details' but also the 'falsche, verzerrte Darstellung des schweren Anfangs in der Wismut'(Dok 1, 1079) in the novel he was working on, a chapter from which had been published in *Neue deutsche Literatur* earlier that year under the title 'Rummelplatz'. The novel was an ambitious 'Bildungsroman' focusing on a number of representative characters and set in the early years of the GDR. Bräunig never really recovered from the attacks, and died in 1976 of alcoholism. In 1981 an anthology of his writings was brought out, containing substantial passages from the incomplete novel and including a revised version of the 'Rummelplatz' chapter. Two changes are particularly interesting, one comic, the other less so. The original did indeed contain an obscene anecdote, the one which Honecker found objectionable. The men are discussing how to avoid contracting VD; one of them declares: 'Das ist ganz einfach. Zuerst gehe ich immer mit dem Tabakfinger ran. Wenn sie da zuckt, ist die Fregatte leck.'[15] In the revised version the passage has become 'eine Zote…, die war jenseits aller Kritik, die kann nicht zugemutet werden erwachsenen Frauen und Töchtern etwa, die lassen wir also aus.'[16] The 'grown-up women and daughters' were, of course, in reality the men of the Politbüro; this was Bräunig's revenge. The other major change, however, relates to the presentation of the

Soviet Union. All pejorative references to Russian soldiers have been excised, including the sentence: 'Die Wismut ist ein Staat im Staate, und der Wodka ist ihr Nationalgetränk.'[17] The GDR's one major asset as far as raw materials were concerned was uranium; but the entire uranium output, mined by East German workers for the Wismut company, went to the Soviet Union. Bräunig's ironic reference to the Soviet Union as controlling a 'state within the state' was provocative and had to be removed. One can be fairly certain that the 'obszönes Detail' would have been ignored had it not been for the political elements.

A third example of a work attacked for pornographic features at this time is Peter Hacks's play *Moritz Tassow*. At the same December plenum Helmut Sakowski referred to this play and declared: 'Bräunigs Pornographie ist harmlos gegen die rüpelhafte Obszönität, die in der 'Volksbühne' über die Rampe gelassen wird und die Spießbürger begeistert'(Dok 1, 1109). *Moritz Tassow* was premiered at the Berlin theatre festival in 1965, but dropped shortly after the December plenum. The title figure of the play is an intellectual, a book worm, who has survived the twelve years of Nazi rule by pretending to be dumb. With the arrival of socialism he finds his voice again, embarrassingly for the young couple Jochen and Jette, who are making love in the rye. Moritz's first words are obscene: 'In einem Ort wohnen heißt alle Weiber / Vögeln und mit den Männern allen saufen.'[18] His conception of socialism is one in which, in Marx's words, 'die freie Entwicklung eines jeden die Bedingung ist für die freie Entwicklung aller',[19] in Moritz's words one in which

> ...nur der sei noch als Mensch gezählt,
> Der tut, wonach ihm ist, und dem nach viel ist,
> Und kratzt sich, was ihn juckt, und nicht aus lauter
> Verlegenheit woanders, und wenns mitten
> Im Beinkleid ist.[20]

Towards the end of the play Jette's father catches sight of his naked daughter silhouetted against the light and realises that she and Moritz have an amorous rendezvous. Moritz appears at the window in his dressing gown and is called indignantly to question. He defends himself with a fine erotic description of Jette's charms:

> Den schlanken Leib umspann ich mit den Händen,
> Aber die Hüfte mit den beiden Armen.
> Sie wiegt nicht schwer, und doch erdrückt sie mich,
> Die kleine Schurkin.

· · ·

Die Brüste sind fest, doch an den Kuppen schmelzend,
Und zwischen ihnen liegt das Himmelreich.
Die Lippen sind benetzt, die Augen offen.
Die Zunge ist ein spitzer Fisch. Die Haare
Sind wie zwei Felle, ein glattes und ein rauhes.
Des Hinterns flinker Kreisel macht
Das Bett krachen. Er ist wie heller Honig,
Aber die Füße sind wie dunkler und vom Sommer verbrannt.

· · ·

Die Beine sind von schönem Ebenmaß,
Die Schenkel üppig. Und unter der Haut,
Die, wie bekannt, der Seele Wohnung ist,
Spür ich, wohin ich fühl, genügend Fett
Und zartsten Drucks empfindende Erwidrung.
Sie ist, daß kurz ichs sag und ohne Ihnen
Weiter zu schmeicheln, denn ich weiß, ich red
Von Ihrer Tochter, eine Herrlichkeit
Und von den Freuden dieser Erde eine.[21]

The play was taken off very quickly and not revived for a number of years. However, in spite of Sakowski's criticisms, the erotic elements were not the point at issue. *Moritz Tassow* is a socialist version of Goethe's *Torquato Tasso*. The poet Moritz is a libertarian socialist; his antagonist is the Party functionary Mattukat, the Antonio of the play. Although, as Heinz Klunker puts it, 'die prüde sozialistische Moral wird mit der Mittelbauernideologie identifiziert',[22] the play is as much a debate about socialism, in particular about the Party's early tactics with regard to the collectivisation of agriculture, as it is about petty bourgeois morality. Moritz's polemical 'Oh, ein Mann von Partei ist nie ein Mann von Redlichkeit'[23] could not go down well with an insecure Party leadership in 1965.

That there was also prudishness at work cannot be denied. One entertaining example of censorship, which, however, might equally have occurred anywhere outside the GDR, relates to the German equivalent of the four-letter words which so disturb the British television viewer. It was recalled by Adolf Endler in 1993.[24] In 1966 in Karl Mickel's collection *Vita nova mea* one word in the poem 'Odysseus in Ithaka' had been reduced to its initial 'v' and completed with three dots... Kurt Bartsch thereupon wrote a comically indignant letter to the publishers:

Sehr geehrte Herren, ich muß Sie leider auf einen Fehler hinweisen, der bei der Lektorierung oder Drucklegung des Gedichtbandes von

Karl Mickel unterlaufen ist: Ficken, meine Herren, wird nicht mit V wie Vater, sondern mit F wie Fasan geschrieben … Sie werden den Fehler in der zweiten Auflage gern korrigieren wollen!

In the 1990 edition of Mickel's works, however, the relevant lines read:

> Dreihundert Stück! Penelope, entweder
> Mit jedem macht sie's, keinen will sie dauernd
> Dreihundert Mann ersetz nicht einmal ich!
> Oder mit Keinem? da wär sie zu langweilig
> Und Kirke fällt mir ein, wenn ich sie vögle
> Die Sau.[25]

Endler went on to wonder to what extent the new freedoms of 1990 really represented progress over the old 'Sauberkeit'. Even here, the censorship was not consistent: the word 'vögeln' appears in full in the *Sinn und Form* version of *Moritz Tassow* (1965).

In 1971 Erich Honecker replaced Walter Ulbricht as First Party Secretary. His most widely quoted speech came in December of the same year, although it had been adumbrated six months previously at the Eighth Party Congress. In it he said, in words directed at writers and artists and immediately related to our topic: 'Wenn man von der festen Position des Sozialismus ausgeht, kann es meines Erachtens auf dem Gebiet von Kunst und Literatur keine Tabus geben. Das betrifft sowohl die Fragen der inhaltlichen Gestaltung als auch des Stils' (Dok 2, 287). Honecker probably did not have in mind the sexual area when he spoke of there being 'no taboos'. However, it is certainly the case that in the 1970s and 1980s there was an increasing frankness in writers' presentation of the erotic. Among other things, the 'Protokolliteratur' which became so fashionable during these years, beginning with Maxie Wander's interviews with women from all walks of life, *Guten Morgen, du Schöne* (1977), and continuing through Christine Müller's *Männerprotokolle* (1985) and Christine Lambrecht's *Männerbekanntschaften* (1986), documented in increasing detail the sexual proclivities of anonymous individuals, male and female, straight and gay. Society became more liberal in the sexual sphere. Georgina Paul has described the development of attitudes to homosexuality, for example.[26] Although it had actually been decriminalised in 1968, a year earlier than in the Federal Republic, it stayed very much under ground into the 1980s. However, in 1979 an interdisciplinary research group on homosexuality was set up at the Humboldt University in Berlin, which led to a number of attempts to end discrimination. It was probably not fortuitous that in the same year one of the GDR's establishment writers, Dieter Noll, published a novel, *Kippenberg*, in which one of the minor characters, Harras, is a homosexual, who is treated with a great deal of sympathy. Paul points out the difference in emphasis in the GDR's approach to discrimination against homosexuals as compared to that in the West, 'the consistency with which the problems of homosexual citizens are put forward as problems affecting GDR society as a whole, since they served to prevent the full social integration of a substantial proportion of citizens in a society expressly understood as a collective.'[27] This political, rather than moral, emphasis always held sway in the GDR.

At the same time, sex education began to take account of the psychology of children and adolescents, instead of confining itself to biology and 'sozialistisch-puritanische Verhaltensregeln', and questions of sexuality were answered frankly and without prejudice in the encyclopaedia *Jugend zu zweit* (1982).[28] The first exhibition of photographic nudes in the GDR took place in 1979, while by 1981 nude scenes in films had become so prevalent that protests were registered,[29] a sure sign that the Party was becoming alarmed. However, a translation of Henry Miller's *Tropic of Cancer* appeared in 1986 and had reached its third printing by 1989, while by 1987 the publishers Kiepenheuer in Weimar even had a 'Bibliotheca erotica' in their programme, including such classics as John Cleland's *Memoirs of a Lady of Pleasure*.

Not all of this liberalisation could be termed progressive. The pinups in *Das Magazin* and the *Armee Rundschau* were redolent of just the kind of fetishised sexuality excoriated by the editors of the *Kulturpolitisches Wörterbuch*. The grand opening of the Friedrichstadtpalast vaudeville theatre in 1984 in the presence of Erich Honecker himself, with its tasteful lineup of long-legged female dancers and the occasional, but invariably female, nudes suggested that the new socialist society was in this area not altogether different from bourgeois society after all. The boundary between libertarianism and exploitation is very hard to define: one wo/man's liberation may be another's exploitation. The Friedrichstadtpalast was explicitly to be 'ein Ort der Erholung und Entspannung, der Heiterkeit und der Schönheit, der Sinnenfreude und Besinnung'.[30] But was 'Sinnenfreude' to be exclusively for the male gaze? In fact the first male pinup was printed in *Das Magazin* in 1974.[31]

The overtly erotic did still occasionally lead to controversy. Irmtraud Morgner's story 'Die gute Botschaft Valeskas', referred to at the beginning of my paper, had originally been written as a contribution to an anthology edited by Edith Anderson and published in 1975 under the title *Blitz aus heiterm Himmel*, in which a number of writers, both male and female, were invited to imagine a situation in which somebody suddenly was transformed into a member of the opposite sex. Sarah Kirsch, Christa Wolf and Günter de Bruyn were among the contributors. Morgner's story was turned down: was her presentation of a woman who was equally at home sexually with a woman as with a man regarded as too daring? Was the rejection evidence of continuing taboos in the sexual area? Or was it the unfavourable presentation of the position of women in the Soviet Union which was regarded as delicate? In fact 'Die gute Botschaft Valeskas' had been published a year previously in Morgner's novel *Trobadora Beatriz*. Was it regarded as less inflammatory to allow it to be published in a 700-page novel which was unlikely to find a wide readership rather than in a collection of short pieces with an overtly daring theme: the sex change?

A more public example of sexual puritanism came from the pen of Wolfgang Harig in his tirade against Heiner Müller's adaptation of Shakespeare's *Macbeth* in 1973: among other things Harig objected, in elegant language, to the scene in which Müller's Lady Macbeth bares her breasts to her husband.

> Die Gelegenheit ist, von der Logik der Fabel her gesehen, denkbar ausgefallen. Denn Ehepaar Macbeth bereitet gerade ein für denselben Abend angesetztes Diner vor und hat außerdem alle Hände voll damit zu tun, dafür zu sorgen, daß einer der erwarteten Gäste, Banquo, vorher unterwegs ermordet wird. Ich möchte die Hausfrau sehen, die in dieser Situation, mit dem Braten im Herd, die Nerven hat, ihren Gemahl durch den Anblick ihrer Brüste zur Liebe zu ermuntern. (Dok 2, 672)

Müller was accused of following Western fashions: 'Befangen in der Mentalität des außengeleiteten Intellektuellen, hat er nur daran gedacht, der westlichen Pornowelle, die sich auf seinem interiorisierten Radarschirm abzeichnete, Tribut zu zollen, um 'in' zu sein. Irgendwo wollte er in den 'Macbeth' einen nackten Busen hineinstopfen, alles andere interessierte ihn nicht' (Dok 2, 673). But this was a minor element in Harig's polemic. He was much more concerned about Müller's revisionist political position, the historical pessimism which presented even the Scottish peasantry of Shakespeare's play as hopelessly backward. For better or for worse, Harig's position did not prevail, although the GDR's theatres were never comfortable with Müller.

The changing climate is documented in Günter de Bruyn's novel *Preisverleihung* (1972). Theo Overbeck's literature seminar springs into life when one of the students suggests that the GDR's literature deals with love as if they were still living in the Middle Ages. People's political development has been frequently described, she says, never their emotional development. The discussion that follows runs on for an hour over the normal time. It includes questions such as whether private emotions are a luxury in view of the American presence in Vietnam, whether socialist morality is no more than that of the Protestant petty bourgeoisie, and whether there should be a socialist 'sex wave' like the one currently enveloping the Federal Republic. Overbeck's student is not primarily concerned with explicit descriptions of the physical act of love, but with the motives and causes of falling in love, and de Bruyn's tale of emotional entanglements with its old-fashioned ironic narrator would hardly satisfy the prurient. Nevertheless, in the years that followed the publication of *Preisverleihung* human sexuality in many of its forms was not only a theme but was treated with increasing explicitness.

It is not my purpose here to anthologise erotic passages in GDR literature of the 1970s and 1980s. Some, however, may be mentioned to indicate that any 1950s prudishness had disappeared. In Christoph Hein's *Der fremde Freund* (1982) Claudia's nude sunbathing pleases the local teenagers; when her lover Henry comes back from a swim she rubs him dry with her pullover and they laugh at his 'Geschlechtsteil, das vor Kälte zusammengeschrumpft war'.[32] Joachim Walther's *Bewerbung bei Hofe* (1984) opens with the detailed description of a scene in which the aging roué poet Besser has engaged three courtesans to pleasure him, but in spite of erotic engravings and readings from the writings of the Earl of Rochester 'Priap' denies him his favour. In Bernd Ulbrich's *Abends im Park* (1983) the title story is an explicit account of an old man's encounter with a young prostitute in a public park, while 'Fang die Sonne auf' describes the masturbatory fantasies of a teenager. Uwe Saeger was possibly the most adventurous GDR writer in the sexual sphere: homosexuality is a central motif of his novel *Nöhr* (1979), transsexuality of his novel *Sinon* (1983). His *Warten im Schnee* (1981), the story of an aging libertine teacher and part-time rock musician, contains numerous erotic details and refers to such traditionally taboo subjects as menstruation and temporary impotence. It also depicts a side of GDR life which tended to be ignored. In socialism prostitution was supposed to have been abolished.

Saeger's Berlin contains pubs where men go to pick up women, and homosexuals have their known haunts, too.

Perhaps the most remarkable example of erotic literature, however, is to be found in Irmtraud Morgner's *Leben und Abenteuer der Trobadora Beatriz*. The title figure is a twelfth-century French lady. Her husband's disregard of her sexual needs contributes to her decision to sleep for over eight hundred years; to her great disappointment she finds on awakening that, even at the height of the 1968 movement, French men are as sexually selfish as ever. Inspired by an official account of the GDR's 'realisation' of equality between man and woman, she moves to East Berlin, where, however, she is once more disappointed. However, things are moving in the right direction. Laura, her assistant in the novel, hopes that the GDR's liberalisation of the abortion laws in 1972 will unleash the 'Produktivkraft Sexualität'[33] by placing men and women on an equal footing, removing the fear of unwanted children. Beatriz, like Moritz Tassow before her, is a poet. As a counterpiece to Tassow's enthusiastic description of the female body, her erotic poem inspired by the body of her lover is worth quoting:

> Dach
> Bevor Gahmuret einschläft,
> legt er meine Hand
> auf sein Geschlecht.
> Ich krümme sie,
> die Haut verliert Wärme,
> Spannung,
> sinkt weg.
> Druck gegen Hüfte und Knie.
> Der nimmt zu
> mit abnehmender Atemfrequenz:
> Ruhe breitet sich aus.
> Ich weiche vorsichtig.
> Er folgt.
> Flutet die Matratze.
> Strandet mich auf die Dielen.
> Ihr Holz prägt meinen Rücken.
> Ich beobachte die Dünung des Leibs. Lausche.
> Sammle Strandgut:
> Schnarchen, ein 'Du'.
> Mein Arm schläft ein.
> Meine Hand ist leer.
> Frieden.[34]

This can hardly be described as 'prudish'. However, the novel in which it appears is unambiguously socialist. Morgner makes it quite clear that, however imperfect, the GDR's socialism is the only hope for women in the future. Nor is her novel unique in its presentation of women's sexuality. Katherine Vanovitch concluded her 1982 survey of female roles in East German drama with the assertion that 'from the late sixties and throughout the seventies...the taboos which traditionally inhibited dramatic expression of sexuality, and above all female sexuality, were cast aside'. Singling out the female protagonists of plays by Heiner Müller, Volker Braun and others, she went on to suggest that 'the self-assertive desires' of these protagonists 'were in themselves a stimulation for the eradication of oppressive psychology in personal and political life.'[35]

With hindsight this analysis may appear hopelessly optimistic. A state in which the *Stasi* was omnipresent cannot be said to have eradicated oppressive psychology. Reality was always more complicated. The GDR's literature contained both a utopian and a realistic element, the latter of which tested the reality of the GDR against the former. It may have been illegal to set up meeting places for homosexuals,[36] but such places did exist, as Saeger's *Warten auf Schnee* makes clear. And when Christa Wolf's *Kassandra* propagates an alternative community to the officially sanctioned one, one in which free, non-exploitative sensuality has its place, it implies that such sensuality has no official outlet in the actually existing GDR. The increasing frankness in dealing with sexual matters had to do with both realism and utopia. It was related to the privatisation of GDR culture. This too had various implications: on the one hand a turning away from explicit political and social themes, on the other the recognition that the private *is* the political, and as with the classical erotic fiction of earlier centuries, this could even be subversive. Joachim Walther's *Bewerbung bei Hofe* is the pastiche of an early eighteenth-century erotic novel: and like its models it is the hypocrisy of the rulers – in sexual, but not only in sexual matters – which is the major target of the satire. In terms of cultural politics, however, sexual liberalisation came at the expense of blurring the difference between the GDR and its western neighbour, although there never was anything like the officially tolerated pornography of the FRG in the GDR. However, what started as a kind of safety valve, giving the population certain 'cultural' freedoms to make up for the lack of political freedoms, probably awakened even more yearnings for the real thing.

As I suggested earlier, the realm of the senses is difficult to rule. Authoritarian regimes cannot last forever. The first production of Wedekind's *Lulu* in the GDR had to wait until 1984. The West German reviewer for *Deutschland Archiv* declared that even with this production, in which the title figure briefly appeared naked, the GDR still found it difficult to show eroticism on stage.[37] The GDR, however, showed a considerable amount of latitude in sexual matters, as I hope to have shown. To what extent the events of 1989 and after can be seen as a sexual liberation seems dubious. Former East German Daniela Dahn comments bitterly:

> Zur kulturellen Vereinheitlichung rechne ich auch die Intoleranz im scheinbar Nebensächlichen: In den CDU-regierten neuen Ländern verschwinden immer mehr FKK-Strände. (Die aus der Arbeiterbewegung der 20er Jahre stammende Freikörperkultur war in der DDR auch ohne besondere staatliche Förderung eine sehr verbreitete Gewohnheit.) Gleichzeitig hat sich im Beitrittsgebiet ein flächendeckendes Netz von Pornokinos, Sexshops und Prostitution ausgebreitet.[38]

Fewer (free) nudist beaches – more (commercial) sex shops. What was it the *Kulturpolitisches Wörterbuch* said about fetishised sexuality under capitalism?

# NOTES

### Abbreviations

Dok 1   *Dokumente zur Kunst-, Literatur- und Kulturpolitik der SED*, ed. E. Schubbe, Stuttgart, 1972, 172.

Dok 2   *Dokumente zur Kunst-, Literatur- und Kulturpolitik der SED 1971–1974*, ed. G. Rüß, Stuttgart, 1976, 287.

1.  I. Morgner, *Leben und Abenteuer der Trobadora Beatriz nach Zeugnisssen ihrer Spielfrau Laura. Roman in dreizehn Büchern und sieben Intermezzos*, 5th edn, Berlin, 1980, 669.
2.  I. Sharp, 'To the Victor the Spoils: Sleeping Beauty's Sexual Awakening', in *Women and the Wende: Social Effects and Cultural Reflections of the German Unification Process*, ed. E. Boa and J. Wharton, Amsterdam and Atlanta, 1994, 177–88, 183.
3.  E. Wilson, 'Erogenous Tomes', *The Guardian*, 19.7.1994, G2, 11.

4. M. Horkheimer and T. W. Adorno, *Dialektik der Aufklärung*, in M.H., *Gesammelte Schriften*, vol. 5, ed. G. Schmid Noerr, Frankfurt a.M., 1987, 109.

5. *Materialien zu Peter Weiss' 'Marat / Sade'*, ed. K.-H. Braun, Frankfurt a.M., 1967, 112f.

6. K. Marx and F. Engels, *Ausgewählte Werke*, vol. 1, 11th edn, Berlin, 1985, 434–5.

7. J. Wohlgemuth, *Egon und das achte Weltwunder*, 17th edn, Berlin, 1977, 341.

8. C. Wolf, *Der geteilte Himmel. Erzählung*, 15th edn, Halle, 1969, 81.

9. Ibid., 82.

10. *Literaturpolitik und Literaturkritik in der DDR. Eine Dokumentation*, ed. H. Fischbeck, 2nd edn, Frankfurt a.M., 1979, 62f.

11. See J.H. Reid, 'Erik Neutsch's Spur der Steine: The Book, the Play, the Film', in *Geist und Macht: Writers and the State in the GDR*, ed. A. Goodbody and D. Tate, Amsterdam and Atlanta, 1992, 58–67.

12. *Kulturpolitisches Wörterbuch*, ed. M. Berger *et al.*, 2nd edn, Berlin, 1978, 478.

13. W. Biermann, *Die Drahtharfe. Balladen Gedichte Lieder*, West Berlin, 1965, 42.

14. Ibid., 19.

15. W. Bräunig, 'Rummelplatz', in *Neue Deutsche Literatur*, 13(1965), no. 10., 7–29.

16. Idem., *Ein Kranich am Himmel. Unbekanntes und Bekanntes*, ed. H. Sachs, Halle, 1981, 60.

17. Bräunig, 'Rummelplatz', 8.

18. P. Hacks, *Stücke*, 3rd edn, Berlin, 1978, 250.

19. Marx and Engels, *Ausgewählte Werke*, vol. 1, 438.

20. Hacks, *Stücke*, 295.

21. Ibid., 332f.

22. *Zeitstücke und Zeitgenossen. Gegenwartstheater in der DDR*, 2nd ed., Munich, 1975, 47.

23. Hacks, *Stücke*, 295.

24. A. Endler, 'Sehnsucht nach der DDR', *Die Zeit*, 4.6.1993, supplement 'LITERATUR', 5.

25. K. Mickel, *Schriften I: Gedichte 1957–1974*, Halle and Leipzig, 1990, 77.

26. G. Paul, '"Über Verschwiegenes sprechen": Female Homosexuality and the Public Sphere in the GDR before and after the Wende', in Boa and Wharton, *Women and the Wende*, 226–37.

27. Ibid., 234f.

28. *DDR Handbuch*, 3rd ed., ed. H. Zimmermann, Cologne, 1985.

29. H. Kersten, 'Nackedeis in "wilden Betten". Das Filmjahr 1981 in der DDR', *Deutschland Archiv*, 14(1981), 232.

30. See *Durch Berlin zu Fuß. Wanderungen in Geschichte und Gegenwart*, ed. H. Prang and H.G. Kleinschmidt, 2nd edn, Berlin and Leizpig, 1986, 140.

31. See the teevision documentary 'Der nackte Osten', directed by Uta Kolano, broadcast by ARD on 11 August 1994.

32. C. Hein, *Der fremde Freund*, 6th edn, Berlin and Weimar, 1989, 84.

33. Morgner, *Trobadora Beatriz*, 336.

34. Ibid., 96.

35. K. Vanovitch, *Female Roles in East German drama 1949–1977. A selective history of drama in the G.D.R.*, Frankfurt a.M., 1982, 153.

36. Paul, 'Über Verschwiegenes sprechen', 228.

37. A. Roßmann, 'Zwei problematische Klassiker – rehabilitiert? Wedekinds "Lulu" and Hebbels "Nibelungen" am Staatsschauspiel Dresden', *Deutschland Archiv*, 18(1985), 7f.

38. D. Dahn, 'Über kulturlose Versuche kultureller Vereinheitlichung – Anpassungszwänge im Beitrittsgebiet', in *Understanding the Past – Managing the Future: The Integration of the Five New Länder into the Federal Republic of Germany. Selected Papers from the Eighteenth New Hampshire Symposium*, ed. M. Gerber and R. Woods, Lanham, New York, and London, 137. The television programme 'Der nackte Osten' (note 31) made similar points about the threat to the GDR's nudist beaches.

# NOTES ON CONTRIBUTORS

**Elizabeth Boa**

Professor of German, University of Nottingham. Publications include *Critical Strategies: German Fiction in the Twentieth Century* (1972) (with J.H. Reid), *The Sexual Circus: Wedekind's Theatre of Subversion* (1987), and *Women and the Wende: Social Effects and Cultural Reflections of the German Unification Process* (1994), (joint editor with J. Wharton).

**David Constantine**

Fellow in German, The Queen's College, Oxford. Publications include *Early Greek Travellers and the Hellenic Ideal* (1984), *Hölderlin* (1988), and *Friedrich Hölderlin* (1992).

**David Jackson**

Senior Lecturer, School of European Studies, University of Wales Cardiff. Publications include *C.F. Meyer in Selbstzeugnissen und Bilddokumenten* (1975), Theodor Storm, *The Life and Works of a Democratic Humanitarian* (1992), *Gottfried Keller. "Kleider machen Leute"* (1993).

**Edward McInnes**

Professor of German, University of Hull. Publications include *German Social Drama 1840–1900. From Hebbel to Hauptmann* (1976), *J.M.R. Lenz: "Die Soldaten"* (1977), *Ein ungeheures Theater*(1987), *Georg Büchner. "Woyzeck* (1991), *J.M.R. Lenz: "Der Hofmeister"* (1992)

**Georgina Paul**

Lecturer in German, University of Warwick. Publications include *Subjective Authenticity – Contemporaneity and Commitment in the Works of Christa Wolff* (1990) and '"Über Verschwiegenes sprechen": Female homosexuality and the public sphere in the GDR before and after the *Wende*' (1994).

## Helmut Peitsch

Professor of European Studies, School of European Studies, University of Wales Cardiff. Publications include *Eine Kulturmetropole wird geteilt. Literarisches Leben in Berlin (West) 1945–1961* (1987) and *"Deutschlandsgedächtnis an seine dunkelste Zeit". Zur Funktion der Autobiographik in den Westzonen Deutschlands und den Westsektoren von Berlin 1945 bis 1949* (1990).

## Terence James Reed

Taylor Professor of German and Fellow of The Queen's College, Oxford. Publications include *Thomas Mann, the Uses of Tradition* (1974), *The Classical Centre, Goethe and Weimar 1775–1832* (1980), *Goethe* (1984), and *Schiller* (1990).

## James Henderson Reid

Professor of German, University of Nottingham. Publications include *Critical Strategies. German Fiction in the Twentieth Century* (1972) (together with E. Boa), *Heinrich Böll. Withdrawal and Re-emergence* (1973), *Heinrich Böll: A German for His Time* (1987), and *Writing Without Taboos. The New East German Literature* (1990).

## Martin Swales

Professor of German, University College London. Publications include *Arthur Schnitzler* (1971), *The German Novelle* (1977), *The German Bildungsroman from Wieland to Hesse* (1978), *Adalbert Stifter* (1984) (with E.M. Swales), *"Buddenbrooks". Family Life as the Mirror of Social Change* (1991).

## Chris Weedon

Reader, Centre for Critical and Cultural Theory, University of Wales Cardiff. Publications include *Feminist Practice and Poststructuralist Theory* (1987), *Die Frau in der DDR* (1988) and *Cultural Politics* (1994) (with G. Jordan).

# BIBLIOGRAPHY

Adorno, T.W. 'Sexualtabus und Recht heute', in T.W.A., *Eingriffe. Neun kritische Modelle*, Frankfurt a.M., 1963, 99–124.
——. 'Tabus über dem Lehrberuf', in T.W.A., *Stichworte. Kritische Modelle 2*, Frankfurt a.M., 1969, 68–84.

Alt, P.A. *Tragödie der Aufklärung*, Tübingen, 1994.

Amery, J. 'Jenseits von Schuld und Sühne. Bewältigungsversuche eines Überwältigten', in H.Glaser (ed.), *Bundesrepublikanisches Lesebuch. Drei Jahrzehnte geistiger Auseinandersetzung*, Munich, 1978, 255–62.
——. *Geburt der Gegenwart. Gestalten und Gestaltungen der westlichen Zivilisation seit Kriegsende*, Olten and Freiburg, 1961.

Anderson, E., (ed.) *Blitz aus heiterm Himmel*, Rostock, 1975.

Anderson, M. *Kafka's Clothes: Ornament and Aestheticism in the Habsburg Finde-Siècle*, Oxford, 1992.

Andreas-Salomé, L. *Fenitschka. Eine Ausschweifung*, Stuttgart, 1898, reprinted Frankfurt a.M., 1982.
——. *Die Erotik*, Frankfurt a.M., 1992.

Arker, D. *Nichts ist vorbei, alles kommt wieder. Untersuchungen zu Günter Grass' "Blechtrommel"*, Heidelberg, 1989.

Axton, W. 'The trouble with Esther', *Modern Languages Quarterly*, 26(1965): 545–57.

Bachmann, I. *Das dreißigste Jahr. Erzählungen*, Munich and Zürich, 1961.

Barner, W., (ed.) *Geschichte der deutschen Literatur von 1945 bis zur Gegenwart*, Munich, 1994.

Beauvoir S. de. *The Second Sex*, trans. H.M. Parshley, Harmondsworth, 1983.

Beicken, P.U. *Franz Kafka. Eine kritische Einführung in die Forschung*, Frankfurt a.M., 1974.

Berg, J. *Hochhuths Stellvertreter und die Stellvertreter-Debatte. Vergangenheitsbewältigung in Theater und Presse der sechziger Jahre*, Kronberg, 1977.

Berger, M., et al., (eds) *Kulturpolitisches Wörterbuch*, 2nd edn, East Berlin, 1978.

Bernd, C.A., (ed.) *Theodor Storm – Paul Heyse*, 3 vols, Berlin, 1969–74.

Bettelheim, A. *Louise von François und Conrad Ferdinand Meyer. Ein Briefwechsel*, 2nd edn, Berlin, 1920.

Biermann, W. *Die Drahtharfe. Balladen Gedichte Lieder*, West Berlin, 1965.

Bleibtreu-Ehrenberg, G. *Tabu Homosexualität. Die Geschichte eines Vorurteils*, Frankfurt a.M., 1978.

Boa, E. 'Thomas Mann's *Buddenbrooks*: Bourgeois Patriarchy and *Fin-de-Siècle* Eros', in M. Minden (ed.), *Thomas Mann in Perspective*, London, 1995, 125–42.

——. 'Blaubarts Braut und die Meduse. Weibliche Figuren in Kafkas Briefe an Felice Bauer und Milena Jesenka', in H.L. Arnold (ed.), *Franz Kafka* (Text + Kritik. Sonderband), Munich, 1994, 272–93.

Boa, E. and Wharton, J., (eds) *Women and the Wende: Social Effects and Cultural Reflections of the German Unification Process*, Amsterdam and Atlanta, 1994.

Böhlau, H. *Halbtier*, Berlin, 1899.

Böll, H. 'Zeichen an der Wand', in H.B., *Aufsätze – Kritiken – Reden*, vol. 1, Munich, 1969, 39–42.

——. 'Politik der Stärke als die schwächste aller möglichen', in Wagenbach, *Vaterland, Muttersprache*, 190.

Bölling, K. 'Tabus in diesem Land', in Hammerschmidt, *Zwanzig Jahre danach*, 375–89.

Borscheid, P. and Teuteberg, H.J. *Ehe, Liebe, Tod*, Münster, 1983.

Bowie, M. *Freud, Proust, and Lacan: theory as fiction*, Cambridge, 1987.

Boyle, N. *Goethe. The Poet and the Age*, vol. 1, *The Poetry of Desire*, Oxford, 1992.

Braun, K.-D., (ed.) *Materialien zu Peter Weiss 'Marat / Sade'*, Frankfurt a.M., 1967.

Bräunig, W. *Ein Kranich am Himmel. Unbekanntes und Bekanntes*, ed. H. Sachs, Halle, 1981.

——. 'Rummelplatz', *Neue Deutsche Literatur*, 13(1965): no. 10, 7–29.

Breuer, D. *Geschichte der literarischen Zensur in Deutschland*, Heidelberg, 1982.

Brinkmann, R., (ed.) *Begriffsbestimmung des literarischen Realismus* (Wege der Forschung, 212), Darmstadt, 1969.

Brunner, O. *et al. Geschichtliche Grundbegriffe*, vol. 2, Stuttgart, 1975.

Bucher, M. *et al. Realismus und Gründerzeit. Manifeste und Dokumente zur deutschen Literatur (1848–1880)*, 2 vols, Stuttgart, 1975–76.

Butler, J. *Gender Trouble: Feminism and the Subversion of Identity*, London, 1990.

Campe. J., (ed.) *Andere Lieben. Homosexualität in der deutschsprachigen Literatur. Ein Lesebuch*, Frankfurt a.M., 1988.

Chickering, R. *We Men Who Feel Most German: A Cultural Study of the Pan-German League 1886–1914*, London, 1984.

Constantine, D. 'Translation and Exegesis in Hölderlin', *Modern Language Review*, 81(1986): 388–97.

Corngold, S. *Franz Kafka. The Necessity of Form*, Ithaca and London, 1988.

Dahn, D, 'Über kulturlose Versuche kultureller Veeinheitlichung – Anpassungszwänge im Beitrittsgebiet', in M. Gerber and R. Woods, *Understanding the Past – Managing the Future: The Integration of the Five New Länder into the Federal Republic of Germany. Selected Papers from the Eighteenth New Hampshire Symposium*, Lanham, New York, London, 1994, 129–138.

Daim, W. *Der Mann, der Hitler die Ideen gab. Die sektiererischen Grundlagen des Nationalsozialismus*, 2nd edn, Vienna, 1985.

Dankert, B. and Zechlin, L., (eds) *Literatur vor dem Richter*, Baden, 1988.

Dannhauer, M. *et al. Wörterbuch zu Friedrich Hölderlin*, I: *Die Gedichte*, Tübingen, 1983.

De Bruyn, G. *Preisverleihung*, Halle, 1972.

Deleuze, G. and Guattari, F. *Kafka: Towards a Minor Literature*, Minneapolis, 1986.

Derks, P. *Die Schande der heiligen Päderastie. Homosexualität und Öffentlichkeit in der deutschen Literatur 1750–1850*, Berlin, 1990.

Dodd, W. *Kafka: Der Prozeß* (Glasgow Introductory Guides to German Literature, 8), Glasgow, 1991.

Dohm, H. *Werde, die Du bist*, Breslau, 1894, reprinted Zürich, 1988.

Durkheim, E. *Les formes élémentaires de la vie religieuse*, Paris, 1912.

Eggebrecht, A. 'Soll die Ära der Heuchelei andauern', in Walser, *Die Alternative*, 26–8.

Eibl, K. *Miß Sara Sampson*, Frankfurt a.M., 1971.

Eisele, U. *Realismus und Ideologie. Zur Kritik der literarischen Theorie nach 1848 am Beispiel des Deutschen Museums*, Stuttgart, 1976.

Endler, A. 'Sehnsucht nach der DDR?', *Die Zeit*, 4.6.1993, supplement 'LITERATUR', 5.

Enzensberger, H.M. 'Ankündigung einer neuen Zeitschrift', *Kursbuch. Bd.1: Kursbuch 1–10 1965–1967*, Reprint, Frankfurt a.M., n.d., 1–2.

———. 'Reflexionen vor einem Glaskasten', in H.M.E., *Im Gegenteil. Gedichte. Szenen. Essays. Vom Autor selbst zusammengetragen und mit einem Nachwort versehen*, Gütersloh, 1981, 86–115, first published 1964.

———. *Deutschland, Deutschland unter anderm. Äußerungen zur Politik*, Frankfurt a.M., 1967.

———. 'Leningrader Gemeinplätze', *alternative*, 1964, dokumente 1: *Leningrader Schriftsteller-Colloquium "Der zeitgenössische Roman"*, 25–26.

Euchner, W. 'Der permanente Selbstbetrug – Zur Deutschlandpolitik der Bundesregierung', in Nedelmann and Schäfer, *Politik ohne Vernunft*, 28–47.

Faber, K.-G. 'Realpolitk als Ideologie', *Historische Zeitschrift*, 203(1966), 1–45.

Faderman, L. *Surpassing the Love of Men. Romantic Friendship and Love between Women from the Renaissance to the Present*, London, 1991, first published 1981.

Fischbeck, H., (ed.) *Literaturpolitik und Literaturkritik in der DDR. Eine Dokumentation*, 2nd edn, Frankfurt a.M., 1979.

Flex, W. *Der Wanderer zwischen beiden Welten*, 1916, reprinted Freiburg, 1993.

Fontane, T. *Sämtliche Werke* (Hanser Ausgabe), *Romane, Erzählungen, Gedichte*, vol. 4, ed. W. Keitel, Munich, 1963.

———. *Werke Schriften und Briefe* (Hanser Ausgabe), Section 4, *Briefe*, vol. 3, *1879–1889*, 1982.

Frazer, J.G. *The Golden Bough*, 2 vols, London, 1907–15.

———. 'Taboo', in *Encyclopaedia Britannica*, vol. XIII, 9th edn, London, 1888.

Frenzel, I. 'Der Wohlstand und die Schuld', in G. Rühle (ed.), *Bücher, die das Jahrhundert bewegten. Zeitanalysen – wiedergelesen*, Frankfurt a.M., 1980, 212–7, first published 1978.

Freud, S. *Totem und Tabu*, Leipzig and Vienna, 1913.

——. *Totem and Taboo*, London, 1950.

Freytag, G, *Soll und Haben*, 2 vols, Leipzig, 1858.

Fried, E. 'Warum ich nicht in der Bundesrepublik lebe', in Wagenbach, *Vaterland, Muttersprache*, 206, first published in 1964.

Funke, H. 'Der Verlust des Erinnerns im Gedenken', *Blätter für deutsche und internationale Politik*, 40(1995): 37–45.

Geissler, C. *Die Plage gegen den Stein*, Reinbek, 1978.

Girard, R. *Violence and the Sacred*, Baltimore, 1977.

——. *'To double business bound': Essays on literature, mimesis, and anthropology*, Baltimore, 1978.

Gittings, R., (ed.) *Letters of John Keats*, Oxford, 1970.

Glaser, H.A., (ed.) *Vom Nachmärz zur Gründerzeit* (Deutsche Literatur. Eine Sozialgeschichte, 7), Reinbek, 1982.

Goethe. J.W.v. *Werke* (Hamburger Ausgabe), vol. 6, *Romane und Novellen I*, ed. E. Trunz and B.v. Wiese, Munich, 1977.

——. *Roman Elegies and The Diary*, trans. F.D. Luke, introd. H.-R. Vaget, London, 1988.

Goldstein, R.J. *Political Censorship of the Arts and the Press in Nineteenth-Century Europe*, London, 1989.

Good, C.F. *Domination and Despair. Father-daughter relationships in Grillparzer, Hebbel and Hauptman*, Berne, 1993.

Graham, I. 'Passions and Possessions in *Kabale und Liebe'*, *German Life and Letters*, 6(1952/3): 12–20.

Grass, G. *Die Blechtrommel*, Frankfurt a.M., 1971.

——. 'Rede von der Wut über den verlorenen Milchpfennig', in G.G., *Werkausgabe in zehn Bänden*, (ed.) V. Neuhaus, vol. 9, *Essays Reden Briefe Kommentare*, Darmstadt and Neuwied, 1987, 213–17.

Greis, J. *Drama Liebe. Zur Entwicklungsgeschichte der modernen Liebe im Drama des 18. Jahrhunderts*, Stuttgart, 1991.

Gronewold, H. '"Die geistige Amazone". Autobiographische Mitteilungen in den literaturwissenschaftlichen und philosophiekritischen Texten von Helene von Druskowitz', in Härle *et al.*, *Erkenntniswunsch und Diskretion*.

Guthke, K.S. *Das deutsche Trauerspiel*, 3rd edn, Stuttgart, 1980.

Habermas, J. 'Heinrich Heine und die Rolle des Intellektuellen in Deutschland', *Merkur*, 40 (1986): 453–68.

Hacks, P. *Stücke*, 3rd edn, Berlin, 1978.

Häerle G. *et al.*, (eds) *Erkenntniswunsch und Diskretion. Erotik in biographischer und autobiographischer Literatur*, Berlin, 1992.

Hagelstange, R. *Offen gesagt – Aufsätze und Reden. Mit einem Nachwort von Ernst Johann*, Frankfurt a.M., 1958.

Hahl, W. *Reflexion und Erzählung. Ein Problem der Romantheorie von der Spätaufklärung bis zum programmatischen Realismus*, Munich, 1971.

Hahn, W. 'Die Bewältigung unserer Vergangenheit als politisches und theologisches Problem', in W. Hahn, K.G. Kiesinger, *Bewältigte Vergangenheit und Zukunft*, Constance, 1966, 7–29.

Hammerschmidt, H., (ed.) *Zwanzig Jahre danach. Eine deutsche Bilanz 1945–1965. Achtunddreißig Beiträge deutscher Wissenschaftler, Schriftsteller und Publizisten*, Munich, Vienna, Basle, 1965.

Haug, W.F. *Der hilflose Antifaschismus. Zur Kritik der Vorlesungsreihen über Wissenschaft und NS an deutschen Universitäten*, 2nd edn, Frankfurt a.M., 1968.

Hein, C. *Der fremde Freund*, 6th edn, Berlin and Weimar, 1989.

Heißenbüttel, H. 'Schwierigkeiten beim Schreiben der Wahrheit 1964', in H.H., *Über Literatur. Aufsätze*, Munich, dtv 1970, 218–20.

Hillgruber, A. 'Die Zerschlagung des Deutschen Reiches und das Ende der europäischen Juden', in R. Kühnl (ed.), *Vergangenheit, die nicht vergeht. Die "Historiker-Debatte", Darstellung Dokumentation Kritik*, Cologne, 1987, 19–27.

Hölderlin, F. *Sämtliche Werke. Große Stutgarter Ausgabe*, ed. F. Beißner and A. Beck, 8 vols, Stuttgart, 1943–1985.

——. *Sämtliche Werke*, ed. D. Sattler, Frankfurt a.M., 1975–.

Holthusen, H.E. *Plädoyer für den Einzelnen. Kritische Beiträge zur literarischen Diskussion*, Munich, 1967.

Horkheimer, M. and Adorno, T.W. *Dialectic of the Enlightenment*, trans. J. Cumming, New York, 1972.

Houben, H.H. *Verbotene Literatur von der klassischen Zeit bis zur Gegenwart*, 2 vols, 2nd edn, Dessau, 1925, reprinted Hildesheim, 1965.

——. *Der gefesselte Biedermeier*, Leipzig, 1924, reprinted Hildesheim, 1973.

Huyssen, A. *Drama des Sturm und Drang*, Munich, 1980.

Iggers, W., (ed.) *Die Juden in Böhmen und Mähren. Ein historisches Lesebuch*, Munich, 1986.

Jackson, D.A. 'The Presentation of Political, Social, and Religious Issues in the Work of C.F. Meyer', D.Phil. Thesis, Oxford, 1969.

——. 'C.F. Meyer's *Die Richterin*. A tussle with Tolstoy?', *Trivium*, 9(1974): 39–49.

——. 'Storm at the foot of the cross', *The Germanic Review*, 59(1984): 82–89.

——. *Theodor Storm. The Life and Works of a Democratic Humanitarian*, New York and Oxford, 1992.

Janssen-Jurreit, M., (ed.) *Frauen und Sexualmoral*, Frankfurt a.M., 1986.

Jaspers, K. *Lebensfragen der deutschen Politik*, Munich, 1963.

——. *Wohin treibt die Bundesrepublik? Tatsachen. Gefahren. Chancen*, Munich, 1966.

Jens, W. 'Vorwort', in Nedelmann/Schäfer, *Politik ohne Vernunft*, 7–11.

Jeziorkowski, J. *Gottfried Keller. Dichter über ihre Dichtungen*, Munich, 1969.

Johnson, U. *Berliner Sachen. Aufsätze*, Frankfurt a.M., 1975.

Kafitz, D. *Grundzüge einer Geschichte des deutschen Dramas von Lessing bis zum Naturalismus*, Königstein, 1962.

Kafka, F. *Sämtliche Erzählungen*, ed. P. Raabe, Frankfurt a.M., 1994.

——. *Briefe an Milena*, ed. J. Born and M. Müller, Frankfurt a.M., 1986.

Kalbeck, M., (ed.) *Paul Heyse und Gottfried Keller im Briefwechsel*, Brunswick, 1919.

'Katechismus zur deutschen Frage', *Kursbuch*, 4(1966): 1–55.

Kienzle, M. and Mende, D., (eds) *Zensur in der Bundesrepublik. Fakten und Analysen*, Munich, 1980.

Klabeck, M., (ed.) *Paul Heyse und Gottfried Keller im Briefwechsel*, Brunswick, 1919.

Keller, G. *Sämtliche Werke und ausgewählte Briefe*, ed. C. Heselhaus, 2 vols, Munich, 1958.

Kersten, H. 'Nackedeis in "wilden Betten". Das Filmjahr 1981 in der DDR', *Deutschland Archiv*, 14(1981), 232–4.

Kieval, H.J. *The Making of Czech Jewry: National Conflict and Jewish Society in Bohemia*, 1870–1916, Oxford, 1988.

Kinder, H. *Poesie als Synthese. Ausbreitung eines deutschen Realismus-Verständnisses in der Mitte des 19. Jahrhunderts*, Frankfurt a.M., 1973.

Kipphardt, H. *Schreibt die Wahrheit. Essays, Briefe, Entwürfe*, vol. 1, *1949–1964*, Reinbek, 1989.

Kittel, M. *Die Legende von der "Zweiten Schuld". Vergangenheitsbewältigung in der Ära Adenauer*, Berlin and Frankfurt a.M., 1993.

Kleist, H.v. *Sämtliche Werke und Briefe* (Deutscher Klassiker Verlag), vol. 2, *Dramen 1808–1811*, ed. I.-M. Barth and H.C. Seeba, Frankfurt a.M., 1987, and vol. 3, *Erzählungen, Anekdoten, Gedichte, Schriften,* (ed.) K. Müller-Salget, Frankfurt a.M., 1990.

Klunker, H. *Zeitstücke und Zeitgenossen. Gegenwartstheater in der DDR*, 2nd edn, Munich, 1975.

Krämer-Badoni, R. *Vorsicht, gute Menschen von links. Aufsätze und Essays*, Gütersloh, 1962.

Kraus, K. *Schriften*, ed. C. Wagenbach, Frankfurt a.M., 1986.

Kremer, D. *Die Erotik des Schreibens*, Frankfurt a.M., 1989.

Kuhn, F. 'Tabus', *Sprache und Literatur*, 18(1987): 19–35.

Laage, K.-E. *Theodor Storm. Studien zur seinem Leben und Werk*, Berlin, 1985.

——. (ed.) *Theodor Storm – Gottfried Keller. Briefwechsel*, Berlin, 1992.

Lambrecht, C. *Männerbekanntschaften. Freimütige Protokolle*, Halle, 1986.

Lamport, F.J. *German Classical Drama*, Cambridge, 1990.

Langmesser, A., (ed.) *Louise von François und Conrad Ferdinand Meyer. Ein Briefwechsel*, Berlin, 1905.

Leavis, F.R. and Q.D. *Dickens the Novelist*, London, 1970.

Lehmann, C. *Das Modell Clarissa. Liebe, Verführung, Sexualität und Tod,* Stuttgart, 1991.

Lenz, J.M.R. *Werke und Briefe*, ed. B. Titel and H. Haug, Stuttgart, 1966.

Lessing, G.E. *Werke*, ed. J. Petersen and W.v. Olshausen, Berlin, 1925.

Levi, C. *Ich kam mit ein wenig Angst. Reisebilder aus Deutschland*, Frankfurt a.M., 1984.

Liebes, E. *Mütter-Töchter-Frauen. Weiblichkeitsbilder in der Literatur*, Stuttgart, 1993.

Lillo, G. *A London merchant*, ed. W. McBumey, Lincoln, Nebraska, 1965.

Lindemann, H. 'Die neuen Lehren und Lehrer. Deutsche Mentalität im Wandel', in Hammerschmidt, *Zwanzig Jahre danach*, 133–9.

Lorde, A. Sister Outsider. Essays and Speeches, Trumansburg and New York, 1984.

Lübbe, H. 'Es ist nichts vergessen, aber einiges ausgeheilt', Frankfurter Allgemeine Zeitung, 24.1.1983.

Ludwig, O. Werke in sechs Bänden (in 2), ed. A. Bartels, Leipzig, n.d.

Lütkehaus, L. '"O Wollust, o Hölle" – in der Onanie-Literatur', in Literatur und Sexualität, (ed.) J. Cremerius et al., Würzburg, 1991, 173–99.

McInnes, E. 'Lessing's Hamburgische Dramaturgie and the theory of the drama in the nineteenth century', Orbis Litterarum, 28(1973): 293ff.

——. 'Ein ungeheures Theater'. The drama of the Sturm und Drang, Frankfurt a.M., 1987.

Märthesheimer, P. and Frenzel, I., (eds) Im Kreuzfeuer: Der Fernsehfilm Holocaust. Eine Nation ist betroffen, Frankfurt a.M., 1979.

Mann, T. Briefe an Paul Amann, ed. H. Wegener, Lübeck, 1959.

——. Briefe 1889–1936, ed. E. Mann, Frankfurt a.M., 1961.

——. Der Tod in Venedig, ed. T.J. Reed, Oxford, 1971.

——. Der Tod in Venedig. (Text, Materialien, Kommentar), ed. T.J. Reed, Munich, 1983.

——. Gesammelte Werke in dreizehn Bänden, Frankfurt a.M., 1974.

Marcuse, L. Obszön: seit Jahrhunderten steckbrieflich verfolgt – und nicht gefaßt, Munich, 1962.

Marti, M. Hinterlegte Botschaften. Die Darstellung lesbischer Frauen in der deutschsprachigen Literatur seit 1945, Stuttgart, 1992.

Martini, F. Deutsche Literatur im bürgerlichen Realismus 1848–1898, Stuttgart, 1962.

Marx. K. and Engels, F. Ausgewählte Werke in sechs Bänden, 11th edn, vol. 1, East Berlin, 1985.

Mayer, H. Zur deutschen Literatur der Zeit. Zusammenhänge – Schriftsteller – Bücher, Reinbek, 1967.

——. Außenseiter. Frankfurt a.M., 1975.

Mattenklott, G. 'Kunst gegen das Künstliche', in H. Hoffmann and H. Klotz (eds), Die Sechziger. Die Kultur unseres Jahrhunderts (Ein Econ Epochenbuch), Vienna and New York, 1987, 75–93;

Mein Herz ist eine gelbe Blume. Christa Reinig im Gespräch mit Ekkehard Rudolph, Düsseldorf, 1978.

Meyer, C.F. Sämtliche Werke. Historisch-kritische Ausgabe, ed. H. Zeller and A. Zäch, Berne, 1958ff.

Michel, K.M. 'Die sprachlose Intelligenz II', Kursbuch, 4(1966): 161–212.

Mickel, K. Schriften I: Gedichte 1957–1974, Halle and Leipzig, 1990.

Mitscherlich, A. and M. Die Unfähigkeit zu trauern. Grundlagen kollektiven Verhaltens, Munich, 1967.

Mitscherlich, A. 'Humanismus heute in der Bundesrepublik', in Richter, Bestandsaufnahme, 135–56.

Mohler, A. Was die Deutschen fürchten. Angst vor der Politik. Angst vor der Geschichte. Angst vor der Macht, Frankfurt a.M. and West Berlin, 1966.

Morgner, I. *Leben und Abenteuer der Trobadora Beatriz nach Zeugnissen ihrer Spielfrau Laura. Roman in dreizehn Bänden und sieben Intermezzos*, 5th edn, East Berlin, 1980.

Müller, C. *Männerprotokolle*, East Berlin, 1985.

Nedelmann, C. and Schäfer, G., (eds) *Politik ohne Vernunft oder Die Folgen sind absehbar. Zehn streitbare Thesen. Mit einem Vorwort von Walter Jens*, Reinbek, 1965.

Neuhauser, P. 'Kehraus im Glashaus', in H.L.Gremliza (ed.), *30 Jahre KON-KRET*, Hamburg, 1987, 152, first published in *Konkret*, 21(1971).

Neutsch, E. *Spur der Steine. Roman*, Halle and Leipzig, 1964.

Nietzsche, F.W., *Werke*, ed. K. Schlechta, 5 vols, Frankfurt a.M., 1981.

Nils, M. Betsy Meyer. *Die Schwester Conrad Ferdinand Meyers*, Frauenfeld and Leipzig, 1943.

Noll, D. *Kippenberg. Roman*, East Berlin and Weimar, 1979.

Offenbach, J. (= L.F. Pusch) *Sonja. Eine Melancholie für Fortgeschrittene*, Frankfurt a.M., 1981.

Ogan, B., (ed.) *Literaturzensur in Deutschland*, Stuttgart, 1988.

Pappritz, A. *Herrenmoral*, Leipzig, 1903.

Paul, G. '"Über Verschwiegenes sprechen": Female Homosexuality and the Public Sphere in the GDR before and after the *Wende*', in Boa and Wharton, *Women and the Wende*, Amsterdam and Atlanta, 226–37.

Pascal, R. *From Naturalism to Expressionism. German Literature and Society 1880 to 1918*, London, 1973.

Pavel, E. *The Nightmare of Reason. A Life of Franz Kafka*, London, 1984.

Peitsch, H. 'Towards a History of "Vergangenheitsbewältigung": East and West German War Novels of the 1950s', *Monatshefte*, 87 (1995): 283–304.

——. 'Die Gruppe 47 und die Exilliteratur – ein Mißverständnis?', in J. Fetscher *et al.* (eds), *Die Gruppe 47 in der Geschichte der Bundesrepublik*, Würzburg, 1991, 108–34.

——. 'German Literature in 1945: Liberation for a New Beginning?', in N. Hewitt (ed.), *The Culture of Reconstruction. European Literature, Thought and Film, 1945–50*, London, 1989, 172–90.

——. 'Travellers' tales from Germany in the 1950s', in R.W. Williams *et al.* (eds), *German writers and the Cold War 1945–61*, Manchester and New York, 87–114.

Peters, W., (ed.) *Bibliographie deutschsprachiger Veröffentlichungen zur weiblichen Homosexualität 1968–1989*, Siegen, n.d.

Plumpe, G. *Theorie des bürgerlichen Realismus*, Stuttgart, 1985.

Postius, R. 'Die Bewältigung der Vergangenheit', in Nedelmann/Schäfer, *Politik ohne Vernunft*, 62–74.

Prang, H. and Kleinschmidt, H.H., (eds) *Durch Berlin zu Fuß. Wanderungen in Geschichte und Gegenwart*, 2nd edn, East Berlin and Leipzig, 1986.

Preisendanz, W. *Wege des Realismus. Zur Poetik und Erzählkunst im 19. Jahrhundert*, Munich, 1977.

Pross, H. *Vor und nach Hitler. Zur deutschen Sozialpathologie*, Olten and Freiburg, 1962.

Pusch, L.F., 'Ladies First – Ein Gespräch über Feminismus', Bamberg,1993, 79–82.

Prutz, R. 'Friedrich Hebbel', *Deutsches Museum*, 14(1864), no. 1: 6–10, 67–73.

Raddatz, F.J. 'Analyse, kaum Therapie', in Walser, *Die Alternative*, 81–84.

Reed, T.J. *Thomas Mann: The Uses of Tradition*, Oxford, 1974.

——. *Death in Venice: Making and Unmaking a Master*, New York, 1994.

*Regierung Adenauer 1949–1963*, ed. Presse- und Informationsamt der Bundesrepublik, Wiesbaden, 963.

Reich-Ranicki, M. *Literatur der kleinen Schritte. Deutsche Schriftsteller heute*, Frankfurt a.M., Berlin, and Vienna, 1971, first published in 1965.

Reid, J.H. *Writing Without Taboos. The New East German Literature*, New York, Oxford, Munich, 1990.

——. 'Erik Neutsch's *Spur der Steine*: The Book, the Play, the Film', in Goodbody, A. and Tate, D. (eds), *Geist und Macht: Writers and the State in the GDR*, Amsterdam and Atlanta, 1992, 58–67.

Reinig, C. *Drei Schiffe. Erzählungen, Dialoge, Berichte*, Frankfurt a.M., 1965.

——. *Entmannung. Die Geschichte Ottos und seiner vier Frauen*, Frankfurt a.M., 1977.

——. *Müßiggang ist aller Liebe Anfang. Gedichte*, Düsseldorf, 1979.

Reisner H.P. *Literatur unter der Zensur. Die politische Lyrik des Vormärz*, Stuttgart, 1975.

Reuter, G. *Aus guter Familie. Leidensgeschichte eines Mädchens*, Berlin, 1895.

Reventlow, F. Gräfin zu. *Von Paul zu Pedro. Amouresken*, Munich, 1912, reprinted Frankfurt a.M., 1987.

——. *Der Selbstmordverein*, Berlin, 1991.

Richter, H.W., (ed.) *Die Mauer oder Der 13. August*, Reinbek, 1961.

——. (ed.) *Bestandsaufnahme. Eine deutsche Bilanz 1962. Sechsunddreißig Beiträge deutscher Wissenschaftler, Schriftsteller und Publizisten*. Munich, Vienna and Basle, 1962.

Rimbaud, A. *Oeuvres*, Paris, 1962.

Rimmon-Kenan, S. *Narrative Fiction: Contemporary Poetics*, London, 1983.

Ritter, A., (ed.) *Günter Grass: Katz und Maus* (Erläuterungen und Dokumente), Stuttgart, 1977.

Robertson, R. *Kafka: Judaism, Politics, Literature*, Oxford, 1985.

Roßmann, A. 'Zwei problematische Klassiker – rehabilitiert? Wedekinds "Lulu" und Hebbels "Nibelungen" am Staatsschauspiel Dresden', *Deutschland Archiv*, 18(1965): 6–10.

Rüß, G. *Dokumente zur Kunst-, Literatur- und Kulturpolitik der SED 1971–1974*, Stuttgart, 1976.

Saeger, U. *Nöhr. Roman*, Rostock, 1980.

——. *Sinon oder die gefällige Lüge. Erzählung*, East Berlin, 1983.

——. *Warten auf Schnee*, Rostock, 1981.

Saße, G. *Die aufgeklärte Familie*, Tübingen, 1988.

Schallück, P. 'Vorurteile und Tabus', in Richter, *Bestandsaufnahme*, 432–43.

Scherrer, P. and Wysling, H., *Quellenkritische Studien zum Werk Thomas Manns*, Berne and Munich, 1967.

Scheuer, H. 'Väter und Töchter'. Konfliktmodelle im Familiendrama des 18. und 19. Jahrhunderts', *Der Deutschunterricht*, 46(1994), 18–31.

Schiller, F. *Werke in drei Bänden*, ed. G. Fricke and H. Göpfert, Munich, 1966.

———. *Sämtliche Werke* (Säkularausgabe), Stuttgart and Berlin, n.d.

Schlamm, W.S. *Die Grenzen des Wunders. Ein Bericht über Deutschland*, Zürich, 1959.

———. *Vom Elend der Literatur. Pornographie und Gesinnung*, Stuttgart, 1966.

Schmid, C. 'Litteratur des bürgerlichen Trauerspiels', *Deutsche Monatsschrift*, December 1798.

Schmidt, J. 'Der neueste englische Roman und das Prinzip des Realismus', *Die Grenzboten*, 2 Sem, 4(1856): 466–74.

Schmidt R. *Westdeutsche Frauenliteratur in den 70er Jahren*, Frankfurt a.M., 1982.

Schnurre, W.-D. 'Mit der Mauer leben', in R. Hartung (ed.), *Hier schreibt Berlin heute. Eine Anthologie*, Munich, 1963, 37–44.

———. *Schreibtisch unter freiem Himmel. Polemik und Bekenntnis*, Olten and Freiburg, 1964.

Schoenberner, G. *Der gelbe Stern. Die Judenverfolgung in Europa 1933–1945*, 5th edn, Hamburg, 1961.

———. 'Meinungslenkung contra Information', in P. Hübner (ed.), *Information oder Herrschen die Souffleure? 17 Untersuchungen*, Reinbek, 1964, 57–72.

Schonauer, F. 'Literaturkritik und Restauration', in Richter, *Bestandsaufnahme*, 477–93.

Schreiber, H. *Zwischenzeit. So leben wir*, Stuttgart, 1964.

Schrimpf, H.J., *Lessing und Brecht*, Pfullingen, 1965.

Schulz, G. 'Naturalismus und Zensur', in *Naturalismus. Bürgerliche Dichtung und soziales Engagement*, (ed.) H. Scheuer, Stuttgart, 1974.

Sengle, F. *Biedermeierzeit. Deutsche Literatur im Spannhungsfeld zwischen Restauration und Revolution 1815–1848*, vol. 1., Stuttgart, 1971.

Sharp, I. 'To the Victor the Spoils: Sleeping Beauty's Sexual Awakening', in Boa and Wharton, *Women and the Wende*, 177–88.

Sieburg, F. *Verloren ist kein Wort. Disputationen mit fortgeschrittenen Lesern*, Munich, 1969.

Siedler, W.J. 'Die Linke stirbt, doch sie ergibt sich nicht', in Richter, *Die Mauer*, 110–115.

Sørensen, B.A. *Herrschaft und Zärtlichkeit. Der Patriarchalismus und das Drama im 18. Jahrhundert*, Munich, 1984.

Sonnemann, U. *Das Land der unbegrenzten Zumutbarkeiten. Deutsche Reflexionen*, Reinbek, 1963.

Stefan, V. *Häutungen. Autobiographische Aufzeichnungen Gedichte Träume Analysen*, Munich, 1975.

Stifter, A. *Werke* (Winkler Ausgabe), *Studien*, ed. F. Krökel, Munich, 1966.

Stölzl, C. *Kafkas böses Böhmen: Zur Sozialgeschichte eines Prager Juden*, Frankfurt a.M., 1975.

Storm, T. *Sämtliche Werke in vier Bänden*, ed. K.-E. Laage and D. Lohmeier, Frankfurt a.M., 1987–88.

Strauss, D.F., *Der alte und der neue Glaube*, Leipzig, 1872.

Swales, E. *The Poetics of Scepticism. Gottfried Keller and "Die Leute von Seld-wyla*, Oxford and Providence, 1994.

——. 'Private mythologies and public unease: on Fontane's *Effi Briest'*, *Modern Language Review*, 75(1980): 114–23.

Tanner, T. *Adultery in the Novel*, Baltimore and London, 1979.

Thomas, D. *A Long Time Burning. The History of Literary Censorship in England*, London, 1969.

Uffhausen, D. *Friedrich Hölderlin, Bevestigter Gesang. Die neu zu entdeckende hymnische Spätdichtung bis 1806*, Stuttgart, 1989.

Ulbrich, B. *Abends im Park und nachts und morgens. Erzählungen*, Halle, 1983.

Vanovitch, K., *Female Roles in East German drama 1949–1977. A selective history of drama in the GDR*, Frankfurt a.M., 1982.

Wagenbach, K. *et al.* (eds), *Vaterland, Muttersprache. Deutsche Schriftsteller und ihr Staat seit 1945. Ein Nachlesebuch für die Oberstufe*, Berlin, 1979.

Walser, M., (ed.) *Die Alternative oder Brauchen wir eine neue Regierung?*, Reinbek, 1961.

——. *Heimatkunde. Aufsätze und Reden*, Frankfurt a.M., 1968.

Walsøe-Engel, I. *Fathers and Daughters. Patterns of seduction*, Columbia, 1993.

Walther, J. *Bewerbungen bei Hofe. Historischer Roman*, East Berlin, 1982.

Wangenheim, W.v. 'Man wird dabey zum Tantalus. Zum Erotischen in W. Heinses Schriften', in Härle *et al.*, *Erkenntniswunsch und Diskretion*, 293–305.

Wander, M.W. *Guten Morgen, du Schöne. Protokolle nach Tonband*, East Berlin, 1977.

Weber-Kellermann, I. *Die deutsche Familie. Versuch einer Sozialgeschichte der Familie*, Frankfurt a.M., 1974.

Wegener, H. *Wir jungen Männer! Das sexuelle Problem des gebildeten jungen Mannes vor der Ehe*, Königstein and Leipzig, n.d.

Weininger, O. *Geschlecht und Charakter. Eine prinzipielle Untersuchung*(1903), reprinted Munich, 1980.

Weiss, P. *Rapporte 2*, Frankfurt a.M., 1971.

Widhammer, H. *Realismus und klassizistische Tradition. Zur Theorie der Literatur in Deutschland 1848–1860*, Tübingen, 1971.

——. *Die Literaturtheorie des deutschen Realismus 1848–1860*, Munich, 1977.

Wierlacher, A. *Das bürgerliche Drama*, Munich, 1968.

Wilson, E. 'Erogenous tomes', *The Guardian*, 19.7.1994, G2, ii.

Winston, R. *Thomas Mann. The Making of an Artist*, London, 1982.

Wittig, M. *The Straight Mind and Other Essays*, Hemel Hempstead, 1992.

Wohlgemuth, J. *Egon und das achte Weltwunder*, 17th edn, East Berlin, 1977.

Wolf, C. *Der geteilte Himmel. Erzählung*, 15th edn, Halle, 1969.

——. *Kassandra. Vier Vorlesungen. Eine Erzählung*, East Berlin and Weimar, 1983.

——. in *Die Zeit*, 25.5.79, in Kienzle/Mende, *Zensur in der BRD*.

Woolf, V. *A Room of One's Own*, Panther Books, London, 1977.

Wurst, K., (ed.) *Lenz als Alternative?*, Cologne, 1992.

Wysling H., (ed.) *Thomas Mann – Heinrich Mann. Briefwechsel*, Franfkurt a.M., 1968.

———. (ed.) *Thomas Mann. Dichter über ihre Dichtungen*, vol. 1., Berne and Munich, 1967.

Zahn, E. *Facsimile durch die Jugend*, Berne and Munich, n.d.

Zimmermann, H., (ed.) *DDR Handbuch*, 3rd edn, Cologne, 1985.

Zweig, S. *Die Welt von gestern* (1944), Frankfurt a.M., 1962.

Zwerenz, G. *Wider die deutschen Tabus. Kritik der reinen Unvernunft*, Munich, 1962.